LEARNING THEORIES SIMPLIFIED

130+ THEORIES AND MODELS
FROM GREAT THINKERS

SECOND EDITION

LEARNING THEORIES SIMPLIFIED

BOB BATES

...and how
to apply
them to
teaching

SAGE

Los Angeles | London | New Delhi
Singapore | Washington DC | Melbourne

Los Angeles | London | New Delhi
Singapore | Washington DC | Melbourne

SAGE Publications Ltd
1 Oliver's Yard
55 City Road
London EC1Y 1SP

SAGE Publications Inc.
2455 Teller Road
Thousand Oaks, California 91320

SAGE Publications India Pvt Ltd
B 1/I 1 Mohan Cooperative Industrial Area
Mathura Road
New Delhi 110 044

SAGE Publications Asia-Pacific Pte Ltd
3 Church Street
#10-04 Samsung Hub
Singapore 049483

Publisher James Clark
Editorial assistant: Diana Alves
Production editor: Nicola Carrier
Copyeditor: Christine Bitten
Proofreader: Tom Bedford
Indexer: Cathy Heath
Marketing manager: Dilhara Attygalle
Cover design: Naomi Robinson
Typeset by: C&M Digitals (P) Ltd, Chennai, India

© Bob Bates 2019

First edition published 2015, reprinted four times in 2016, three times in 2017 & twice in 2018

Library of Congress Control Number: 2018947503

British Library Cataloguing in Publication data

A catalogue record for this book is available from the British Library

ISBN 978-1-5264-5937-4
ISBN 978-1-5264-5938-1 (pbk)

At SAGE we take sustainability seriously. Most of our products are printed in the UK using responsibly sourced papers and boards. When we print overseas we ensure sustainable papers are used as measured by the PREPS grading system. We undertake an annual audit to monitor our sustainability.

This book is dedicated to my wife, who has been a tower of strength and never moaned once when I disappeared at 5:00am to grab a McDonald's latte and four hours' worth of their electricity to work on a chapter in the book.

I would also like to thank the staff at New Cross Hospital in Wolverhampton and Heartlands Hospital in Birmingham for the excellent care and attention they have shown my wife.

PRAISE FOR BOB'S WORK

'*Learning Theories Simplified* is a wonderful book. It is an excellent example of sparking motivation to learn the subject. Even though I've always been interested in how people think and learn, reading his book makes me excited about continuing reading it.'
   Valeriy Kozmenko – Associate Professor: Department of Internal Medicine, University of South Dakota

'I have a bookshelf of management and coaching books. Bob's first book has pride of place. I look forward to the next one.'
                    Jo Morgan – Managing Director: Charlie's Training Academy

'I'm fascinated by how Bob is able to reduce complicated theory into so few words and make its understanding and application easy to follow.'
                         Gary Bird – CEO: Manor Farm Community College

'Bob's humour and fascinating insights into life and learning is what makes this book work so well.'
                      Trevor Cox – Managing Director: Phoenix Training

'Before I read the chapter in the book on Vygotsky, I never knew what the Zone of Proximal Development was. Bob makes it seem so simple to understand.'
              Summiah Habib – Student on the Diploma in Education & Training

'I wish that I'd had this book when I did my degree in Educational Studies.'
   Joy Cotterill – Higher Level Teaching Assistant & Community Cohesion Leader: Crockett's
                                               Community Primary School

'Both of the 'Special Needs and Disabilities' books and the original *Learning Theories Simplified* book are life savers throughout my studies and I'm excited to continue reading your work! I'd personally like to thank you for being such a big help during my first two years of university, and I know I will religiously rely on your books throughout my teaching career!'
           Kelsey Banks BA (Hons) – Primary Education Student at Wolverhampton University

CONTENTS

ABOUT THE AUTHOR

Bob Bates was a Senior Executive in the Civil Service for 20 years. During this time, he also worked as a staff trainer and coach and mentor to people with disabilities. He then set up his own management and training consultancy (The Arundel Group), which celebrates its 25th anniversary next year. His work as a management consultant covered a number of local and central government projects as well as working as a trainer with major UK private sector companies.

In the late 1990s Bob started a lecturing career, during which time he gained two masters degrees in management and education and a PhD in education. He has taught over 1000 teachers and trainers on graduate and post-graduate programmes at two universities. He currently manages and teaches on City & Guild Teaching Award, Certificate and Diploma courses in a community college.

The first edition of *Learning Theories Simplified* was Bob's third book. His first book, *The Little Book of BIG Management Theories*, written with Jim McGrath, was on WHSmiths' non-fiction bestsellers list for nearly a year, is being translated into 15 languages, including Japanese and Arabic, and was chosen by the Chartered Management Institute as the CMI's Practical Management Book of the Year for 2014. His second book, *The Little Book of BIG Coaching Theories*, published in February 2015, was also a bestseller and has been translated into German and Thai. His fourth book, *A Quick Guide to Special Needs and Disabilities*, was published by SAGE in 2016 and his fifth book, *Educational Leadership Simplified* co-written with Andy Bailey, was published by SAGE in 2018.

Bob shares his time these days between writing, working voluntarily for a charity that promotes health and education in the Gambia, researching into offender learning and homelessness and teaching Adult Education Teachers.

Bob can be contacted through his website **bobbates.co.uk** (here you get an option to pick *Research* or *Bad Bob Bates* – please choose the former) or email **saddlers9899@aol.com**.

Acknowledgements

There's just not enough room in this book to thank all of the people who have contributed to my understanding of learning theory. These include the many teachers and learners who it has been my privilege to work with. Some of these are used as case studies in the book. Special mention goes to Tara Dingle and Ruth Peach who helped me to choose the theories relating to Early Childhood Studies.

Jane Spindler also deserves special mention for the help with the diagrams and page layout and the encouragement she gave me when things were not going well. Jane is a rare talent both as a designer and teacher.

The team at Sage have been simply superb. From my first meeting with James Clark, who convinced me that this book would work, and subsequent meetings with him, Rachael Plant and Diana Alves to take the initial idea through to pre-production stage, they have been incredibly supportive (even laughing at my stories). Thanks to Naomi for the jazzy cover design and Christine for correcting my many grammatical errors. Nicola and Dilhara then took on the responsibilities for getting the book on the shelves. Without them, this just wouldn't have happened.

I am indebted to all of these people.

NEW TO THIS EDITION

This edition of *Learning Theories Simplified* offers an additional 30 theories, mostly related to early childhood theory and developmental strategies. There are also entries relating to working with learners with additional needs and examples of teaching and learning approaches from schools around the world and, by popular demand, more diagrams and some challenges, which Bob calls *Critical Perspectives*, where he invites you to critique: (a) what the theorist has to say about the subject, (b) his understanding of their work or (c) the appropriateness of any actions he may have taken in the case studies.

How to use this book

This book will:

- help you understand how people learn and your role in the process
- develop your skills as a teacher/trainer/coach/mentor
- enable you to apply learning theory to practice
- support you to manage key aspects of programme design, delivery and evaluation.

This book is easy to use but effective. It is written for busy people who are more interested in solutions to problems and the application of a theory rather than a critical analysis of the theory.

The book is divided into four parts:

- **Part 1** covers **classical learning theory** from the early educational philosophers through to the behaviourist, cognitivist, humanist and neuroscientists of the twentieth century.
- **Part 2** looks at more **contemporary thinking** on learning and teaching and covers the work of some of the most cited and respected current educational thinkers on issues related to the personal qualities of teachers and learners.
- **Part 3** looks at **early childhood and developmental strategies**. Although the emphasis here is on working with younger children, some of the ideas can be adapted and adopted for working with all ages. This part also looks at some approaches that you can undertake when working with learners with additional needs and examples of different teaching and learning approaches from schools around the world.
- **Part 4** looks at the theories and models underpinning **curriculum development, lesson planning, delivery, assessment and evaluation**. This part is for teacher/trainers who are involved in developing, delivering and evaluating programmes of study.

Each part is broken down into a number of theories and models from well-known thinkers in that field. Each model or theory will be explained in less than 500 words (many with accompanying diagrams) and then a *How to Use It* section, again in less than 500 words, where the theories are made practical for ease of application with key points for action in the classroom.

I've used a number of different approaches in the *How to Use It* entries:

- **Do it steps**: offering you a simple step-by-step approach, often using acronyms or mnemonics, which you can follow in order to apply the theory or model.
- **Reflection points and challenges**: encouraging reflection on real-life case studies or problems in order to develop your understanding of how to apply the theory or model. There's even the odd trip to the cinema.
- **Analogies and metaphors**: taking you out of the real world for just a moment and getting you to relate the theory to something which has no obvious bearing on the theory or model but from which understanding and meaning can be drawn.
- **Tips for the classroom**: three tips from each entry for you to try out in the classroom.
- **Critical perspectives**: this is where I encourage you to think about the entry. The challenge is for you to consolidate your learning by critiquing: (a) what the theorist has to say about the subject, (b) my understanding of their work or (c) the appropriateness of any actions I may have taken.
- **Further reading**: books or articles I've drawn the source material from.

With regard to your answers to any of the critical perspectives, please feel free to drop me an email if you want to give me feedback or if you want me to comment on your thoughts on the subject.

The one thing that I've learned over the years is that everyone has their own idiosyncratic preferences when it comes to learning. What I do hope is that there is something for everyone in the *How to Use It* entries.

INTRODUCTION

'People learn to hate but you can teach them to love'

Nelson Mandela

This book is written for teachers, trainers and managers of any individuals or groups who want to understand more about how people think and learn and more importantly how to use this understanding to get the best out of people. I've tried not to suggest that any one branch of theory is better than the rest or that any one theorist within a particular branch should be read to the exclusion of others. The decision on this is down to you and the context in which you are working with learners. I don't claim for one minute that, by reading Theory 32, you will know all you need to know about the work of Leon Festinger to be considered an expert on *cognitive dissonance*. What I do promise you is that you will know how *cognitive dissonance* works and how to apply it in practice.

This book doesn't attempt to trivialise great theory by its brevity but it does recognise that teachers, trainers and managers, and the people they are working with, are very busy and may not have the time to devote to reading Carl Rogers' *On Becoming a Person* or Robert Dilts' *Strategies of Genius*. Don't get me wrong, these are great books and if you want detailed academic perspectives on theories such as Cognitivism or Humanism go out and buy them. What I am offering is a basic insight into theories and models and, what's very often missing in academic works, how you can apply them in practice.

Throughout the book, I refer to:

- the organisation as being any work place, education or training institution
- learning as being any developmental process being undertaken by the individual (for example, teaching, training, coaching or mentoring)
- learners as being anyone benefiting from the developmental process
- the *teacher* as being anyone supporting the learner (this could be in their role as a teacher or as a trainer, mentor or coach)
- the classroom as being any environment where learning takes place
- a session as an event covering a learning experience.

If you see the term *teacher* and your role is as a *trainer, coach* or a *mentor*, then I don't think it's too great a leap of faith to recognise that the theories and models apply equally to you.

PART 1
CLASSICAL LEARNING THEORIES

INTRODUCTION TO PART 1

Theories relating to understanding how people learn date as far back as 500 BC and the Greek philosophers Plato and Aristotle. Plato argued that truth and knowledge were within (it was natural) and that people had an intrinsic desire to do what they did, whereas Aristotle's view was that it is something that is taught (it happened as a result of nurturing). The nature vs nurture debate is one of the oldest issues in human development that focuses on the relative contributions of genetic inheritance and environmental conditioning.

For many years this was a philosophical debate with well-known thinkers such as Rene Descartes suggesting that certain things are inherent in people, or that they simply occur naturally (the nativists' viewpoint), arguing the toss with others such as John Locke who believed in the principle of *tabula rasa*, which suggests the mind begins as a blank state and that everything we become is determined by our experiences (the empiricists' viewpoint). Towards the end of the nineteenth century the debate was taken up by a new breed of theorists who developed the discipline of psychology.

For most of the early part of the twentieth century behavioural psychologists suggested that humans were simply advanced mammals that reacted to stimuli. *Behaviourism* remained the basis of teaching and learning until it was challenged in the period between the two world wars by psychologists who argued that thinking and learning was a developmental cognitive process in which individuals create, rather than receive, knowledge. This gave rise to the movement known as *Cognitivism*. After the Second World War, a third branch of theory came into force with the belief that learners were individuals whose learning should not be separate from life itself and who should be given the opportunity to determine for themselves the nature of their own learning. This became known as *Humanism*.

The new millennium, and the growing interest in neuroscience, provided a fresh insight into how people process information. Although theories around what role the brain plays in the learning process are still mostly speculative, there does appear to be common consent that the mind was set up to process external stimuli, to draw connections with other stimuli and to make sense of what was happening.

Part 1 will give you an insight into some of the key theories that were developed from the early philosophers through to more modern-day philosophical viewpoints and variations within the psychological approaches of the twentieth century, culminating with the development of neuroscience and brain processing theory.

SECTION 1.1: EDUCATIONAL PHILOSOPHY

Knowing where to start and end in this section was probably the hardest part of writing this book. It seems almost sacrilegious not to include Confucius or Siddhartha Gautama (the Buddha) in any discourse on philosophy, or even to fail to acknowledge Thales of Miletus as the founding father of philosophy. The budget for this section was to be nine entries. I couldn't drop the contributions of any of the three great Greek philosophers (Socrates, Plato and Aristotle); wanted to continue the debate through the renaissance and age of reason (Descartes and Locke); into the age of revolution (Rousseau); and, finally, throw in writers with a more modern socio-philosophical perspective (Sartre, Nietzsche, Dewey and Freire).

So, with apologies to Pythagoras, Hobbes, Kant, Russell and dozens of others, I set about trying to condense the ideas of some of the truly great thinkers into less than 500 words. My first problem was with the theoretical contributions of the Greek philosophers. This was difficult on two fronts: Socrates, who is accredited as the founder of western philosophy and was the teacher of Plato, wrote very little about his ideas, established no school of learning and held no particular theories of his own. Much of what we know about Socrates came from the writings of Plato. Although Plato and Aristotle wrote more about their ideas, my second problem was that again, there was no discernible theoretical model to use as the basis for discussion. In each of the first three contributions therefore, I have tried to encapsulate the key message of each of the philosophers and show how they can be applied to teaching.

Things got a little bit easier some 2000 years down the road when clearer theoretical models began to emerge with the work of Descartes, Locke and, a bit later, Rousseau. Descartes and Locke continued the nature/nurture debate that Plato and Aristotle started about whether truth and knowledge are found within us (rationalism) or are something we acquire (empiricism). Rousseau's work is peppered with social commentary; a theme that Dewey, Sartre and Nietzsche picked up on and Freire so vigorously pursued in the latter part of the twentieth century.

Someone once claimed that philosophy is not just the preserve of brilliant but eccentric thinkers, it's what everyone does when they're not busy doing important things. The ideas that are used in this section are probably a bit more than that; they're less about finding answers to the issues you face in the classroom and more about the process of trying to find these answers. There are some great processes to follow in this section - give them a try and don't be confused if some processes contradict others; that's the fun of philosophy!

Socrates is often considered to be one of the founders of western philosophy. He developed the *Socratic* or *dialectical* method of philosophy which is based on persistent questioning and the belief that the life which is unexamined is not worth living.

Here is a summary of some of the key questions and answers that Socrates posed related to teaching and learning:

- **What is knowledge?** He categorised knowledge into the trivial and the important. Trivial knowledge doesn't provide the possessor with any useful expertise or wisdom. Important knowledge relates to ethics and morals and can be defined by how best to live one's life.
- **Why do we need to learn?** Although he believed that goodness and truth, and ethical and moral instincts were inherent in everyone, they could only be bought to the surface through learning.
- **How do we learn?** He described learning as the search for truth. Learning would only occur as the result of questioning and interpreting the wisdom of others and when one comes to recognise their own ignorance and faults.
- **Who do we learn from?** He didn't believe that any one person, or any one particular school of thought, had the wisdom or legitimate authority to teach things. He did however argue that individuals are not self-sufficient and that other people were necessary to share the experience and wisdom from which learning could flourish.
- **Where do we learn?** He questioned the established idea that learning could only take place in educational establishments and advocated that learning should take place wherever and whenever people met.
- **When do we learn?** He argued that this happened whenever two or more people engaged in meaningful dialogue and when one person was willing to see their own faults, weaknesses and negative tendencies.

The Socratic method of teaching is based on the teacher asking leading questions and guiding the learner to discovery. Its cornerstone was the dialogue between the teacher and the learner that used critical inquiry to challenge preconceived thoughts and established doctrines.

How to use it

If you follow the principle of the unexamined life being worthless, then you must be honest in how you examine what you've done. Admitting failure and learning from errors is as important as reflecting on your successes in making you a good teacher.

Michael Jordan, arguably one of the greatest basketball players of all time, admitted that, throughout a career spanning 15 years, he had missed more than 9000 shots at the basket; lost nearly 300 games; and missed important game-winning shots on 26 occasions. He admits to having failed time and time again; which is why he feels he was a success.

THE UNEXAMINED LIFE IS WORTHLESS

To be prepared to fully reflect on what you have done, look at the reflective practice models covered in theories 125-127. There's something there for everyone in terms of the scope and scale of reflection and some great models to use.

If you want to follow the doctrines of Socrates:

- Never be afraid of making mistakes. OK, giving out wrong information to learners will have to be corrected as soon as possible but mistakes are always forgivable if you learn from them.
- Be aware of the boundaries that you are working to. Although you may not have the licence to challenge your learners' ethics and morals, if they are preventing learning from taking place it may come into your jurisdiction and you may have to do something about it.
- Try to avoid giving out too many answers. Concentrate on guiding learners to discover more about the subject by asking them challenging questions. A good rule of thumb here is to ask four times as many questions as you give answers.
- Encourage members of the class to engage in meaningful dialogue, unhindered by your presence, whenever possible. Get them to summarise their discussions with the rest of the group. In this way the sharing of wisdom and experiences will be more wide-spread.

Socrates believed that unless people examined their lives and gained the wisdom that accrued from this, they would continue to make mistakes.

In the classroom

- Accept that mistakes will happen.
- Treat all mistakes as a learning opportunity.
- Encourage learners to constantly question what they, and you, are saying or doing.

Critical Perspective

Socrates coined the phrase that the unexamined life is not worth living. What do you think about his assertion that admitting failure and learning from errors is as important as reflecting on your successes in making you a good teacher?

For more on Socrates's ideas, read:

Navia, L.E. (2007) *Socrates: A Life Examined.* New York: Prometheus Books.
Plato (1997) *The Trial and Death of Socrates: Four Dialogues.* New York: Classic Books International.

Plato was a student of Socrates. His early writings were strongly influenced by those of his mentor and focused on the search for definitions of moral values such as virtue and justice. In *The Republic*, he described everything that our senses perceive in the material world as limited to mere shadows of reality and that the real truth lies within. He uses the *allegory of the cave* to explain this idea.

There are four phases to the allegory which can be summarised as follows:

- Imagine you are **imprisoned** in a cave. You are shackled to a wall and can only see the shadows of objects, illuminated by a fire, cast on the wall opposite. These shadows are the only things that you have ever seen and all that you have ever thought about. They represent your current reality.
- Suppose that you are **released from the shackles** and allowed to roam freely around the cave. You now begin to see things as they really are and begin to understand the origins of some of the shadows. You begin to question your beliefs about what is real.
- Eventually, you are **allowed out of the cave** where you start to see the fullness of reality. You realise the errors in your beliefs.
- You **re-enter the cave** and try to convince your former inmates that what they accept as the truth is only an illusion. Your arguments are only met with ridicule and rejection by others less enlightened than you. You either succumb to ridicule and go back to your original beliefs about reality or persevere with the truth.

The allegory highlights Plato's belief in the separation of two distinct worlds, one of appearance and one of reality, and his belief that truth and knowledge was to be found within someone. His disagreements with his student Aristotle sparked the *nature vs nurture* debate that still resonates with modern-day thinkers (see Theory 4).

How to use it

Stop me if you've heard this one before:

A forest fire is ranging on a deserted island, killing all of the animals in its wake. The only remaining survivors are a scorpion and a frog. The frog asks the scorpion if he knows the way to the sea. The scorpion tells the frog that he will show him the way there if he will give him a lift. The frog asks the scorpion why he should trust him not to sting him. The scorpion replies that if he did that they would both die and that if they worked as a team they would both be saved. The frog agrees and tells the scorpion to jump on his back. The scorpion does so and immediately stings the frog. When the frog asks the scorpion why he had condemned them both to certain death, the scorpion simply replied that, 'it was in his nature to do so'.

If you want to follow the doctrines of Plato:

- Start by believing that truth and knowledge is to be found within and that it is in a learner's nature to behave in the manner that they do.

- Accept that, if the territory represents reality, the map is merely a representation of that reality.
- Acknowledge that learners respond according to their individual maps and although they may act in ways that you find unhelpful or unacceptable, you must respect that it is their map.
- Appreciate that your learner's behaviour is created specifically with regard to the context and the reality currently being experienced. Change is necessary when the context and reality change.
- You may not be able to change a learner's ingrained behaviour, or even have the license to do this, but you can get them to reflect on the appropriateness of their actions.

In the classroom

- Accept that some behavioural traits are ingrained and will be difficult to modify.
- Recognise that you may not have license to change some aspects of a learner's behaviour.
- If it's questionable, get your learners to reflect on the appropriateness of their behaviour.

Critical Perspective

What do you think that Plato meant by his belief in the separation of two distinct worlds: one of appearance and one of reality?

For more on Plato's ideas, read:

Plato (1970) *The Republic: The Dialogues of Plato* (B. Jowett, trans./ed.). London: Sphere Books.

Plato (1997) *The Trial and Death of Socrates: Four Dialogues*. New York: Classic Books International.

Although Aristotle was a student of Plato's, he disagreed with Plato's assertion that truth and knowledge was to be found within someone. He argued that people needed to use the wisdom of others to look for truth and knowledge in the world outside.

Here is a summary of Aristotle's theories on learning and the belief that knowledge and skills are achieved by:

- examining the knowledge and expertise of those considered to be wise
- interpreting the statements of others
- undertaking self-examination based on this interpretation
- developing self-belief as a result of self-examination.

Aristotle's method of teaching is based on the teacher guiding the learner to reach their potential through the wisdom of others. Its cornerstone was the dialogue between the teacher and the learner that emphasised what the learner was capable of doing. This became the principle on which the concept of the *self-fulfilling prophecy* was based.

The self-fulfilling prophecy was a term introduced by Merton in the 1960s. It was based on Aristotle's belief that, if you have high expectations of a learner and they are aware of this, they will perform at a level that matches these expectations. Conversely, if you have low expectations of a learner and they are aware of this, their performance will suffer.

How to use it

How can you turn a coward into a hero, a dullard into a genius or an emotional vacuum into a great lover? That's exactly the challenge facing the Wizard in Frank Baum's immortal story of the *Wizard of Oz*. He gave the cowardly lion a medal for courage, the scatterbrain scarecrow a diploma and the tin man a ticking clock (well Christian Barnard hadn't perfected his techniques for heart transplants at this stage). You need to watch the movie to see what happens.

Never underestimate the effect that you have on others. You, like the wizard in the story, exert enormous power over their lives and, through your attitude towards them, can turn them into successes or failures. Tell them they are doomed to fail and they may begin to accept failure as an inevitable consequence. Tell them they have the potential for greatness and watch them grow. Here are some tips about how you can be the wizard.

- Give them a few tasks that are relatively easy to complete. Acknowledge their achievement of the task. A simple 'well done' or nod of approval will do, but celebrating the achievement with others will have a great impact on their self-belief.
- Reward effort as well as achievement. Make sure learners see the connection between effort and success.

- Get the learners in your class to share what they have learned with others. Develop a rapport within the class whereby learners acknowledge the efforts and successes of others. Simple nods of appreciation or a round of applause may be appropriate.
- Teach learners how to handle the failures that inevitably they will experience from time to time. Support them to learn from mistakes as well as successes.

Here's a little ditty that I once learned that sums up what this entry is all about. I promise you that in a year's time, you'll still be singing it:

I'm off to be the wizard, the wonderful Wizard of Oz.

I'm off to be the wizard, 'cos of all of the wonderful things I does.

In the classroom

- Don't keep spoon-feeding learners with information: get them to look for the answers themselves.
- Allow learners to have a few quick early successes as this will encourage them to want to know more.
- Make learners aware that you have high expectations of them.

Critical Perspective

Aristotle believed that if you have high or low expectations of a learner and make them aware of your feelings towards them they will act in accordance with your feelings. This became known as the self-fulfilling prophecy. What experiences do you have of the self-fulfilling prophecy in action?

For more on Aristotle and the self-fulfilling prophecy, read:

Merton, R.K. (1968) *Social Theory and Social Structure*. New York: Free Press.
Winch, C. and Gingell, J. (2005) *Key Concepts in the Philosophy of Education*. Abingdon: Routledge.

RENE DESCARTES (1596–1650) VS JOHN LOCKE (1632–1704)

This debate occurred as a result of Plato arguing that truth and knowledge were within (i.e. it was natural), whereas his student, Aristotle, claimed that they are something we are taught (i.e. it happened as a result of nurturing). The nature versus nurture debate is one of the oldest issues in human development, which discusses the relative merits of genetic inheritance and environmental conditioning.

Descartes revived Plato's rationalist concept of innate knowledge and argued that truth and knowledge existed within human beings prior to experience. He was sceptical of the philosophical ideas of many of his predecessors and his desire for some certainty in life led him towards his own powers of rationalisation for the answer. He developed a system of *Cartesian doubt* as a way of reaching his ultimate conclusion of 'I think, therefore I am' or in its Latin form *'cogito ergo sum'*.

Locke revived Aristotle's empiricist view with the concept that a child's mind is a blank tablet (*tabula rasa*) that can be filled with knowledge that comes directly or indirectly from experience of the world. He separated these experiences into two categories: ideas of sensation - seeing, hearing and feeling; and ideas of reflection - thinking, questioning and believing.

If Descartes and Locke can be accused of re-igniting the nature-nurture debate, then the impact this had on how education theorists viewed teaching and learning has been significant. This can be summarised as:

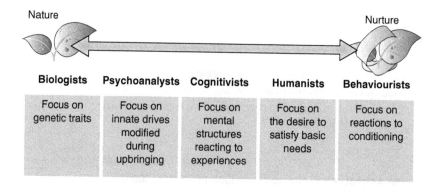

Biologists	Psychoanalysts	Cognitivists	Humanists	Behaviourists
Focus on genetic traits	Focus on innate drives modified during upbringing	Focus on mental structures reacting to experiences	Focus on the desire to satisfy basic needs	Focus on reactions to conditioning

Both sides in the debate have compelling arguments that make it difficult to decide whether a person's development is governed by their DNA or influenced by their upbringing.

How to use it

The stage musical *Blood Brothers* has been a great West End and Broadway hit. It is based on the classic story of twins, separated at birth, who meet in childhood and become friends oblivious of the fact that they are brothers. Their mother, unable to afford to bring up both sons, gave up one of the twins to her employer, a wealthy woman unable to have children of her own. The story explores the effects that the differences in lifestyles, values and morals of the two families have on the boys as they grow into young men. So, is the tragic end to the story a consequence of genetic traits or conditioning?

Few people these days would take such an extreme position in this debate as to argue for one side at the absolute exclusion of the other side. There are just too many facts on both sides of the argument which would deter an all-or-nothing view.

- If you are at the extreme end of the Nature scale, the likelihood is that you will believe in the virtue of neuroscience and the belief that the genetic structure of the brain is mostly responsible for an individual's ability or motivation to learn. You will be influenced here by the theorists in Section 1.5.
- As you start to move towards the centre of the scale, you begin to accept the cognitivist's view in Section 1.3 that the genetic structure of the brain is capable of being modified in response to reactions to experiences and the environment.
- Moving from the centre towards the end of the Nurture scale, you are likely to favour the ideas of the humanist theorists in Section 1.4 and the significance they attach to society's influence on an individual's capacity to think and learn.
- At the extreme end of the Nurture scale, the likelihood is that you will believe in the arguments of the behaviourists in Section 1.2 who suggest that all behaviour can be modified through conditioning.

There is no neat and simple way of resolving this debate. The more you read on the subject, the more confusing it gets. The best advice I can give is to go with what feels right for you.

In the classroom

- Accept what your default position is on this issue.
- Adapt and adopt this position to suit whatever circumstances you are teaching in.
- Reflect on what happened and revise your default position accordingly.

Critical Perspective

Where do you stand on the nature vs nurture debate?

For more on the nature-nurture debate, read:

Descartes, R. (1966) *Philosophical Writings* (G. Anscombe and P. Geach, trans./eds). London: Nelson.

Locke, J. (1961) *An Essay Concerning Human Understanding*. London: Dent.

Rousseau presented his theories on education in the story of his relationship, as tutor, with Emile. Rousseau's *Emile* was a landmark contribution to education theory but needs to be understood in the context in which it was written. This was during a time when society was built on people who enjoyed dominating others for personal gain and people who either passively accepted this domination and a life of servitude or resented those that wielded power over them and revolted. As Emile's tutor, Rousseau was faced with the dichotomy of not wanting to have an overt position of power over Emile but covertly exerting influence over his education.

Rousseau's theory of education was based on the belief in the inherent goodness of human beings and the effect of society in corrupting them. He argued that bringing up children in harmony with nature and its laws would facilitate learning and preserve their goodness.

His thinking is based on three key principles.

* People should be able to learn what they want to learn.
* They should be able to do this when they want to.
* Teaching should be based on discovery, enriched with the covert guidance of the teacher.

Rousseau's focus on nature, on the need to develop opportunities for new experiences and reflection and on the dynamic provided by each individual's development remains the cornerstone of modern pedagogical thinking.

How to use it

I'm not going to set out a series of steps here as I think you need to reflect on whether you feel the treatment of Emile was ethical or not. Your answer to this will help you decide how to use the theory. I am going to suggest that you watch Lewis Gilbert's film based on Willy Russell's play, *Educating Rita*, to give you some food for thought on this.

In the film, Rita, played by Julie Walters, wants to better herself by studying literature. Her tutor, Frank, played by Michael Caine, describes his teaching ability as 'appalling, but good enough for appalling students'. Issues of power and influence are common themes throughout the film as both Rita and Frank struggle to cope with personal and professional difficulties. The essence of the film is about Frank's attempts to teach Rita to value her own insights while still being able to pass the exams. Does he succeed? Watch the film to find out.

Here are some questions you might want to now ask yourself:

* Does Rita succeed or fail? You may need to reconcile your thoughts on what constitutes success and failure. Stepping out on to the Centre Court at Wimbledon (in my dreams) players see an inscribed saying from Kipling that equates success and failure as both being 'imposters'. What do you think he means by this?

- Does the end result justify the actions that Frank takes? You will certainly have to spend some time thinking this one through. Machiavelli claims that the 'ends always justify the means'. Do you agree?
- Have you ever played out the role of Rita as a learner? If so, how do you feel about it now?
- Have you ever played out the role of Frank as a teacher? If so, how do you feel about it now?

It's possible that, as a result of answering some of the above questions, you consider aspects of Rousseau's teaching to be unethical, but there are some compelling ideas in Rousseau's work around the freedom to learn (see Theory 91) and the use of discovery learning (see Theory 23) that are worth considering.

In the classroom

- Allow learners the opportunity to learn what they want to providing this doesn't conflict with the planned learning outcomes.
- Don't spoon-feed them the answers; make them think about them.
- Support them to learn through discovering key facts.

Critical Perspective

Work through the four questions listed above and then determine whether or not you agree with Rousseau's belief in the inherent goodness of people and that it is society that corrupts them.

For more on Rousseau's ideas, read:

Rousseau, J.J. (1911) *Emile or Education* (B. Foxley, trans.). London: Dent.
Rousseau, J.J. (1913) *The Social Contract* (B. Foxley, trans.). London: Dent.

Nietzsche was a nineteenth-century German philosopher, composer and student of the history of language. His work has exerted a profound influence on Western philosophy, primarily because of his attack on the concept of essential truth. Truth, according to Nietzsche, is a matter of perspective, not fundamental reality. This understanding of truth and morality has come to be known as *perspectivism*.

Nietzsche explains that the term 'perspective' comes from the language of vision and that we literally see things from and with a particular perspective. Our eyes are located at a particular point in the distance, from which some things are visible and others are not. A scene looks different from different perspectives. For example, from high up we can see further and things look smaller, from below things become obscured and we cannot see very far. Nietzsche describes this as 'foreground evaluations'; we take what is near to us (in the foreground) as the standard by which we learn from and interpret the world.

Perspectivism is therefore a theory that is based on:

- **Knowledge**: Learning about a subject is inevitably partial and limited by the individual perspective from which it is studied.
- **Judgements**: Assessments of truth and value depend on how someone sees it through their own individual viewpoint.
- **Interpretation**: It is left to the individual to interpret what they see, think and feel, in view of what they intuitively know is right and good.

Nietzsche believed that education should consist mainly of clearing away 'the weeds and rubbish and vermin' that he felt attacked and obscured the real groundwork for the development of the person. He argued that this kind of education cannot be formalised within institutions which are obsessed with progressing students through a system of tests, grades and qualifications.

Nietzsche produced a considerable amount of ideas dealing with subjects like morality, racism, atheism and consciousness. He was known for his erratic and controversial outbursts such as claiming that 'God is dead' and the emergence of 'over-man' (incorrectly translated as 'superman') which the Nazis hijacked to support the things that Nietzsche was most violently opposed to, notably anti-Semitism, racism and nationalism.

How to use it

Nietzsche believed that the focus in learning needed to shift from the teacher to the students, and that the classroom should no longer be a place where the teacher pours knowledge into passive students (who wait like empty vessels to be filled), but that the students are urged to be actively involved in their own process of learning (like fires waiting to be rekindled).

If you want to follow the philosophical ideas of Nietzsche, accept that:

- What the student currently believes, whether correct or incorrect, is important.
- Despite having the same learning experience, each student will base their learning on the understanding and meaning that is personal to them.
- Understanding or constructing a meaning is an active and continuous process.
- Learning may involve the student making some conceptual changes in how they think about a subject.
- When students construct a new meaning, they may not believe it but may give it provisional acceptance or even rejection.
- Learning is an active, not a passive, process and depends on the student taking responsibility to learn.
- Discovery is facilitated by providing the necessary resources.
- Learners construct their knowledge through a process of active enquiry.

The main activity in the classroom should therefore be around solving problems. Students should feel free to use inquiry methods to ask questions, investigate a topic, discuss their findings freely with others and use a variety of resources to find solutions and answers. As students explore the topic and view it from different perspectives, the teacher should encourage them to draw new conclusions, and, as their exploration continues, revisit those conclusions.

In the classroom

- Support collaboration in classwork, not competition.
- Create situations where the students feel safe questioning and reflecting on their own experiences.
- Encourage students to face up to the challenges they will encounter in life.

Critical Perspective

Nietzsche argued that achieving a true education is a process fraught with what he described as the 'three dangers': isolation, crippling doubt, and the pain of confronting one's limitations. He claimed that most people lack the fortitude and vigour to truly face and conquer these dangers. Do you agree with him?

For more on Nietzsche's ideas, read:

Cate, C. (2005) *Friedrich Nietzsche*. Woodstock, NY: The Overlook Press.
Deleuze, G. (2006) *Nietzsche and Philosophy*. London: Athlone Press.

Although Dewey was primarily a behavioural psychologist, his application of the philosophy of pragmatism, underpinned by his concern for interaction, experience and reflection, had a profound impact on educational thinking and practice. Dewey's basic belief was that traditional education was too concerned with the delivery of pre-ordained knowledge and not focused enough on the learner's actual learning experiences. He emphasised the importance of experience and education in his ground breaking book of that title, first published in 1938.

The main principles covered in the book can be summarised as:

- The task of teachers should not be to communicate knowledge and skills to learners but to use their learners' experiences as a teaching tool.
- The challenge for experienced-based education is to provide learners with quality experiences that will result in growth and creativity.
- Continuity and interaction are essential to discriminate between experiences that are worthwhile and those that can be discounted.
- Although control is necessary to establish order in the classroom, it should be based on what he describes as the moving spirit within the class and not on the desire or will of one individual.
- An education system that restricts learners' freedom of thought and movement will inhibit their intellectual and moral development.
- It is the teacher's responsibility to provide guidance to the learner in their use of observation and judgement and to select experiences that have the promise and potential to exercise the learner's intelligence.
- The danger of failure lies in the possible misunderstanding of what constitutes experience and experiential education.

Dewey began a movement that others, such as Kolb (see Theory 47), developed into the notion of experiential learning, which to this day remains the cornerstone of many educational approaches and learning programmes.

How to use it

Dewey's ideas on progressive education are still as progressive now as they were when he wrote them in the 20s and 30s. Sad to think, I was only 1 year old when Dewey died in 1952. As a senior citizen, I'm now able to get into the cinema at reduced rates. I'm not that old as to have seen the original version of *Goodbye Mr. Chips* at the cinema. It is however one of the most endearing films I've ever seen.

Goodbye Mr. Chips is the story of a history teacher in a traditional nineteenth-century English boarding school reflecting on his career as a teacher. He was looked on as a very private, stuffy disciplinarian who is constantly passed over for promotion. After 20 years in the job, and in his mid-40s, he marries Kathy who opens his eyes to the fun to be had in life and teaching, and makes him see the potential that he has, that he never recognised in himself. Chips goes on to experience many personal triumphs and tragedies over the years but the one constant is the love and admiration his pupils and colleagues have for him.

The significance of Dewey's ideas for modern-day teachers are:

- Having a passion for an education system that offers equality of opportunity for everyone is at the heart of what every teacher should be striving for.
- Learners should be provided with quality experiences that engage them and build on their existing experiences. The teacher's role is to help the learner assess the value of the experience.
- Each past or present experience should be viewed from the perspective of how it can shape future actions. This can be done through a cyclical process of action; reflection on what happened; having a theory about what might happen if things were done differently; experimenting with the new theory; and revising the course of action based on the experiments.
- Thinking and reflection should be the cornerstone of teaching practice. Encouraging learners to share these thoughts will allow the teacher to get to know the learner better and benefit the overall learning experience of the class.

Coincidently, *Goodbye Mr. Chips* was made the year after Dewey's *Experience and Education* was first published in 1938.

In the classroom

- Allow learners to share their experiences with others in the class.
- Encourage them to reflect on their experiences.
- Get them to think about what might happen if they did things differently.

Critical Perspective

What do you think of Dewey's basic belief that traditional education was too concerned with the delivery of pre-ordained knowledge and not focused enough on capitalising on the learner's actual learning experiences?

For more on Dewey's ideas, read:

Dewey, J. (1963) *Experience and Education*. New York: Collier Books.
Dewey, J. (1966) *Democracy and Education: An Introduction to the Philosophy of Education*. New York: Free Press.

Sartre was a twentieth-century French philosopher, novelist and political activist. He was one of the key figures in developing the concept of existentialism, a philosophy that emphasises individual existence, freedom and choice. In this respect he advocated the principle that *existence precedes essence*, which reversed the traditional philosophical view that the essence (the nature) of a thing is more fundamental and immutable than its existence (the mere fact of its being).

Here is a summary of some of the key questions and answers that Sartre posed related to education:

- **What are the goals of education?** He argues that the purpose of education is to help the learner to come to terms with their individuality in order to be able to emerge as the unique person they are.
- **What is knowledge?** He claims that knowledge comes from experience and reflection.
- **What knowledge and skills are worthwhile learning?** He stresses the importance of knowledge of the self as a unique individual combined with the skills to work through problems and conflict.
- **What are the limits of human potential?** He believes that limits are what we choose to create for ourselves and that in this respect we may be influenced by others. Given freedom of choice and action, therefore, human potential may be limitless.
- **What is a mistake?** He asserts that mistakes are made when an individual attributes blame to fate or determinism rather than individual will and the capacity to act on that will.
- **What is learning?** He describes learning as the state of being able to define oneself as having freedom of choice and will and the capacity to deal with others who limit this freedom.
- **What is the role of the teacher?** He claims that the teacher should support the learner to overcome resistance (self-imposed or by others) and provide them with the tools to attain personal freedom.
- **What is the purpose of the curriculum?** He argues that this should be designed to enable the learner to experience as much of the world as possible.

Sartre uses the analogy of cutting paper to explain the reverse of the existentialist principle and that in this instance *essence precedes existence*. In his analogy, scissors (or to be more precise, paper knives) were designed to address a problem of creating a convenient and accurate method of cutting paper. In this respect, their essence preceded their existence. Sartre explains that whereas the reverse of his principle relates to inanimate inventions like scissors it does not apply to people.

How to use it

If you follow the philosophy that all human beings possess the same capacity to learn and are guided by the same basic values then you risk missing what Sartre claims is the most fundamental aspect of existence, and that is the freedom to choose.

EXISTENTIALISM

If you want to follow the philosophical ideas of Sartre, help students to:

- Take responsibility for their own lives and their own decisions.
- Understand their role and responsibilities vis-à-vis themselves and others.
- Be able to engage in meaningful dialogue with their peers and deal effectively with any confrontation that occurs.
- Be able to deal with life's difficulties, tensions and ambiguities.
- Be able to unleash their own creativity and self-expression.
- Overcome difficulties in choosing what to study and how to study.
- Accept responsibility for making mistakes.

Sartre's philosophy of linking freedom with learning and responsibility has been labelled as pessimistic. He refutes this, claiming it to be the most optimistic philosophy possible, because within it we are able to choose how we learn and how we behave towards others as a result of that learning. The main activity in the classroom should therefore be around debate and discussion, where students should have the confidence to express themselves freely on a range of subjects.

In the classroom

- Encourage learners to interact with each other and be respectful of others' ideas.
- Foster an environment where creativity is allowed to flourish.
- Allow learners to have a say in what and how they are taught.

Critical Perspective

The very nature of philosophical debate is that there are often paradoxes that accompany even the soundest of arguments. Where do you think the paradoxes are in Sartre's theory?

For more on Sartre's ideas, read:

Sartre, J.P. (2001) *The Age of Reason*. London: Penguin Publishing Ltd.
Sartre, J.P. (2007) *Existentialism and Humanism*. London: Methuen Publishing Ltd.

Freire was a Brazilian educator who began a national literacy programme for peasants and slum dwellers in the 1950s and 1960s. Freire's basic belief was that the function of education was to build on the language, experience and skills of the learner rather than imposing on them the culture of the teacher. Throughout his writings he uses politically motivated phrases such as 'dialogue liberates – monologue oppresses'.

The concept of *critical consciousness*, the cornerstone of Freire's ideas, is that the richest learning begins with action, is then shaped by reflection, which gives rise to further action. His methodology is shown in the following five-step model:

Each step can be summarised as follows:

- **Identify the problem**: This is where teachers and learners engage in dialogue and research to establish the nature of the problem that needs to be answered.
- **Find an original way of representing the problem**: Get learners to use role playing, drawings, metaphors and analogies to do this and then compare what they have produced to see if there is a common theme to the problem.
- **See the problem through your learners' eyes**: Ask learners to describe the situation as seen in the representation and make the link between themselves and the problem.
- **Analyse the cause of the problem**: Get everyone concerned to discuss what is happening and what can be done to address the root cause of the problem.
- **Take action to solve the problem**: Produce a plan of action to identify what needs to be done in both the short term and long term to prevent the problem from reoccurring.

Throughout his work, Freire emphasises the importance of teaching based on dialogue rather than monologue. In this respect he argues that the teacher must allow the learners to talk freely and express themselves so that they feel they are an important part of the learning process.

How to use it

Jane Elliot taught a class of all white nine-year-olds. The day after Martin Luther King was shot she wanted to show them how it felt to be discriminated against. She divided her class into blue-eyed and non-blue-eyed children. She told them that the blue-eyed children were brighter and better than the others. The blue-eyed children started acting in an arrogant manner, deriding the others who became confused and withdrawn. She reversed the process the following day and found that the non-blue-eyed children became arrogant. By using role play to experience first-hand what effect prejudice had on people, she hoped to teach children the importance of tolerance. Many former pupils later confessed that this had a profound effect on their thoughts about segregation.

Here are some tips if you want to apply Freirian methodologies:

- Don't be afraid to get to know more about your learners and the issues they face on an ongoing basis.
- Use whatever approaches you can to get the learner to expand on these issues. Role playing, metaphors, analogies and drawings are tools you can use here. The important thing is to get a rich picture of the learner's current situation.
- As the picture becomes richer, and root causes of issues become clearer, start thinking about how to resolve these. Mind-maps or problem trees will help you and the learner come to terms with how to address the issues.
- You can now work with the learner to develop an appropriate plan of action to achieve the desired learning outcome. This may include quick wins and long-term planning.

In the classroom

- Take an interest in your learners' lives outside of the classroom.
- Don't be afraid to use different approaches to get learners to open up on issues that may be affecting their learning.
- Long-term learning plans are important but don't underestimate the value of a few quick wins in building up your learner's confidence.

Critical Perspective

What do you think of Jane Elliot's approach in how she taught her class about what it felt like to be discriminated against because of physical characteristics? Is it something that you would feel comfortable in doing?

For more on Freire's ideas, read:

Freire, P. (1972) *Pedagogy of the Oppressed*. London: Penguin.
For more on Elliott's research, visit her website at www.janeelliott.com.

SECTION 1.2: BEHAVIOURISM

Behaviourism is based on the principle of stimulus and response. It is a teacher-led activity which assumes the teacher is in control of what needs to be done, how it will be done and what evidence of behavioural change needs to be produced. The basic premise of behaviourism is that people need to be directed and that if the stimulus is something that the individual wants (a reward) or fears (a punishment) then the individual will respond accordingly and there will be a noticeable change in behaviour.

The theory is rooted in the late nineteenth-century studies into how people behave and the emergence of the discipline of psychology. Many of the principles that underpin behaviourism were developed from psychologists working with animals and then transferring their theories to human beings.

Although some of the theory was determined through research that may these days be considered unethical, behaviourism remained the basis of teaching approaches throughout the twentieth century and is still useful when working with learners who may need more direction, on subjects where precise adherence to procedures is essential or in environments where there are health hazards.

Behaviourism is not without its critics however who view it as an autocratic, transmission led approach which fails to recognise the independent and enquiring nature of people.

Here is the timeline for when the theories used in this section were introduced:

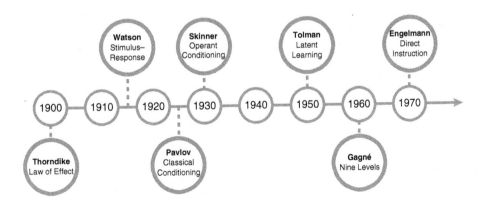

Thorndike is regarded as the first pure behavioural psychologist, although the term behaviourism was adopted long after his research had been completed. His most famous experiment was a study into how cats were able to escape from a locked box through the process of trial and error; what he referred to as the process of *connectionism*.

His research indicated that by trying different approaches to escape, the cats would either experience a *rewarding outcome* (escape) or a *profitless outcome* (trapped). Through these outcomes, the amount of trial and error would decrease as the cat learned which actions would lead to a reward and which were profitless. In this respect, Thorndike suggested that reward responses are *stamped in* and profitless responses are *stamped out*.

The principles underpinning Thorndike's work are:

- Learning requires the teacher to stimulate the learner by rewarding successful practices.
- A series of stimulus-reward connections can be linked together if they belong to the same action.
- Intelligence is a function of the number of connections learned.
- Connections become strengthened with practice and weakened when practice is discontinued.
- Transfer of learning occurs because of previously encountered situations.

Thorndike later refined his ideas to take into account other variables such as the effects of a lengthy delay between action and outcome and how quickly a task was forgotten when it wasn't repeated.

How to use it

Here's a great example of the use of trial and error:

The story goes that it took Thomas Edison 2000 tries to perfect the light bulb. Soon after his earth-shattering invention, he was asked what it felt like to fail 1999 times. His answer was that he hadn't failed that many times, he just found 1999 ways that didn't work.

If you are going to instruct people to use trial and error to solve a problem, you need to be aware that there are a number of different features to trial and error. For example, the desired outcome may be to find the best solution to a particular problem (specific) or to find a solution that can be used in other contexts (generalised).

Whichever approach you take, you need to:

- let the learner decide what outcome they are seeking to a problem
- investigate the root cause of the problem with them
- generate a list of possible solutions together addressing the cause, not just the symptoms
- help them to filter out the non-feasible solutions
- test each of the remaining solutions by trial and error
- support them to form conclusions as to which solutions work best.

Use the Edison story to demonstrate the value of perseverance and make sure that you use Edison's description of genius as being 1% *inspiration* and 99% *perspiration*.

In the classroom

- Discuss the nature of the problem you and the learners are looking to solve.
- Work with your learners to analyse the cause of the problem.
- Generate a list of possible solutions to the problem and use trial and error to test each solution to see if it works.

Critical Perspective

Thorndike developed many of his ideas on learning by studying the behaviour of animals in what he called a 'problem-box' where they would either experience a *rewarding outcome* (escape) or a *profitless outcome* (trapped). What do you think of Thorndike's argument that learning requires the teacher to stimulate the learner by rewarding successful practices?

For more on Thorndike's ideas, read:

Thorndike, E.L. (1913 [1999]) *Education Psychology: Briefer Course*. New York: Routledge.
Thorndike, E.L. and Gates, A.I. (1929) *Elementary Principles of Education*. New York: Macmillan.

Watson is largely credited as the founding father of the behaviourist movement. Although he was not the first of his generation to look at how behaviour could be modified through neutral stimuli, his work is generally considered to be the most conspicuous and arguably the most controversial amongst the behaviourists.

Some of the images (recorded on film) of his work with Albert, a 9-month-old baby, are quite disturbing. In his experiments he introduced the baby to a range of different animals (a neutral stimulus). The baby showed no fear of any of the animals. In separate tests Watson made a series of loud noises (an unconditional stimulus) which distressed the baby. By pairing the two tests (the animal and the loud noise) the child's natural responses to the noise (fear and distress) had become associated with the animal and when the loud noise was removed the baby had now been conditioned to show fear and distress at the animal. The conditioning process can be displayed as:

Pre-conditioning	Conditioning	Post-conditioning
Baby Albert enjoys petting a rat. He displays no fear towards it	Every time Albert pets the rat, Watson makes a loud noise that frightens Albert	When Albert sees the rat (with no accompanying noise) he becomes frightened and distressed

In further experiments, Watson replaced the animals with a series of inanimate objects, producing the same effect on the baby. In this way Watson was able to demonstrate that people can be conditioned to produce emotional responses to objects and to postulate that anyone, regardless of their nature, can be trained to be anything, and that learning is a direct consequence of the conditioning.

How to use it

I first wrote this entry on the afternoon of Monday 7 April 2014.

The fourth season of the wonderful TV series *Game of Thrones* was about to start (in 5 hours 35 minutes to be precise). The series is based on George R.R. Martin's brilliant books, *A Song of Ice & Fire*. The TV series is about three books behind what Martin has written. I've read all of the books and am a great fan of the TV series. Unfortunately, I have to bite my lip when something dramatic occurs in the series because I know from the books what happens. A teacher in Denmark who has also read the books and, knowing his students do nothing but talk about the TV series, threatened to tell them what happens if they misbehave. It worked! Students not wanting to have their enjoyment of the TV series spoiled started to behave.

If you want people to respond in a particular way, you simply spell out the rules and regulations relating to these and the penalties for infringing them.

Do this by:

- explaining at the outset what it is that people will know, or be able to do, by the end of their session with you
- telling them what they can expect in terms of rewards (e.g. 'you will be able to answer test questions' or 'I won't spoil your enjoyment of the film')
- warning them what they can expect in terms of punishments (e.g. 'you will not be able to answer test questions' or 'I will spoil your enjoyment of the film').

Be aware of the point that critics of Watson's theory make that the results from *stimulus-response* methods may be short-lived if the stimulus is not repeated. By the way, if you haven't read the books and are waiting for the next series of *Game of Thrones*, and you don't recommend this book to your friends and colleagues, I will tell you what happens to Tyrion Lannister.

In the classroom

- Tell your learners what the expected outcomes from the lesson are.
- Explain the rewards for succeeding and the penalties for failure.
- Place more emphasis on the rewards.

Critical Perspective

Watson famously once declared, 'give me a dozen healthy infants, and my own specified world to bring them up in and I'll guarantee to train them to become any type of specialist I might select – doctor, lawyer, artist, merchant-chief and, yes, even beggar-man and thief'. What do you think of this claim?

For more on Watson's ideas, read:

Watson, J.B. (1919) *Psychology from the Standpoint of a Behaviourist*. Philadelphia: Lippincott.
Watson, J.B. (1928) *The Ways of Behaviourism*. New York: Harper & Brothers.

Pavlov was a physiologist whose research into the digestive secretions of dogs gained him a Nobel Prize in 1904. His research indicated that presenting a dog with an unconditioned stimulus (food) would provoke an unconditioned response or reflex action in the form of the dog salivating. Adding an accompaniment to the stimulus (ringing a bell) and, after a period of time of food + bell, remove the original stimulus (the food) and the dog will salivate just at the sound of the bell. He referred to this phenomenon as *classical conditioning* because the dog had been conditioned to associate food with the sound of the bell ringing.

1st Pre-conditioning Act

The dog is offered food and starts to salivate.

2nd Pre-conditioning Act

A bell sounds provoking no reaction from the dog.

Conditioning

The food is offered and the bell is rung simultaneously. This is repeated time and time again.

Post-conditioning

When the bell is rung the dog salivates even when no food is offered.

The principle of *classical conditioning* marked a groundbreaking step in establishing psychology as a scientific discipline and influenced the work of other behaviourist psychologists.

How to use it

Karen was a trainee teaching assistant. Part of the entry requirements for the course is that trainees demonstrate a level of competence in literacy and numeracy. This is assessed through a short multiple-choice test. When Karen sat down to do the numeracy test, she started to panic and fled the room in tears. When I asked her what had happened she explained that her mind had gone a complete blank and she was unable to focus on the questions. When I went through the questions with Karen face-to-face, it was clear she knew the answers, and her excellent results in the literacy test demonstrated she was not afraid of exams, but she did clearly have a real phobia of numeracy tests.

Deal with someone's fear or phobia of a subject by removing their negative responses to the subject. Do this by:

- getting the individual to examine the root cause of their negative feelings towards the subject
- making them aware of the relevance of the subject to them
- taking out some of the menace about failing tests in the subject by giving some easy tasks where the individual can achieve a few successes
- building up the intensity of the tasks gradually
- making sure that you are generous in your praise when they complete a task.

CLASSICAL CONDITIONING

By doing this, you will condition people to look forward to the subject. Let's be clear here, you are unlikely to turn someone with a dread of maths into a Stephen Hawkins or even a Carol Vorderman overnight but you can at least work with them to help them to overcome their fear of the subject.

In the classroom

- Ask learners to discuss what problems they have with the subject matter.
- Get them to appreciate the relevance of the subject to them.
- Give them some easy tasks to complete and build up the intensity of the subject gradually until the learner feels able to master it.

Critical Perspective

Think of an example where you have experienced classical conditioning (either as a teacher or as a learner). What worked well about it and what didn't work so well?

For more on Pavlov's ideas, read:

Malone, J.C. (1990) *Theories of Learning: A Historical Approach*. California: Wadsworth.
Pavlov, I.P. (1927) *Conditioned Reflexes: An Investigation of the Physiological Activity of the Vertebral Cortex*. London: Oxford University Press.

Skinner developed the ideas of a number of his predecessors (notably Pavlov and Watson) by subjecting animals and humans to a series of rigorous experiments to arrive at the concept of what he termed *radical behaviourism*.

Skinner designed a number of ingenious devises which he used for his experiments. The most famous of these was the Skinner Boxes. The inside of these boxes were fitted with a lever, which if pressed would produce either water or a food pellet. Rats were placed in the box. At first by accident, then by design, the rats discovered that water or food would appear when they pressed against the lever. He referred to this phenomenon as *positive reinforcement*. In later experiments he added grids that produced electric shocks when activated. Through this he studied the impact of what he called *negative reinforcement* on behaviour.

Skinner argued that not only did positive reinforcement have a longer lasting effect on behaviour than negative reinforcement but that negative reinforcement could actually be counter-productive.

At first glance it would appear that Skinner is merely confirming Pavlov's notion of a conditioned response. Skinner argued however that whereas the response made by Pavlov's dogs was a reflex action (a reaction to the environment), the rats in his experiments operated not out of reflex but acted *on* the environment (rather than reacting *to* it). This was what became known as *operant conditioning*.

How to use it

Ofsted-type inspections are a stressful time for staff. During the run up to an inspection at a university where I worked, a colleague took a day's unauthorised leave of absence. On his return, he was summoned by the Dean and told that he would not be allowed to take part in the inspection. Imagine how popular he was with colleagues when he came into the staff room with a big grin on his face.

An important principle to bear in mind with any aspect of behaviourism is that it is the behaviour that needs to be addressed, not the individual displaying the behaviour. If you are going to work with people whose behaviour needs modifying then you will have to understand that there are two types of behaviour modification approaches referred to as positive and negative reinforcement.

- Positive reinforcement is where good behaviour can be encouraged by offering rewards.
- Negative reinforcement is where the likelihood of poor behaviour can be discouraged through pairing it with an unpleasant consequence.

If you are going to use reinforcement as a behaviour modification tool then the following points are important:

- Rewards and punishments will only act as reinforcements if the reward is something an individual desires or the punishment is something they fear.
- You can shape behaviour in a series of gradual steps by offering rewards for simple behaviour modifications and then increasing the complexity.

Remember to check out with your organisation what their policies and practices are in relation to learners misbehaving. Rewards and punishments should only be used when there is compliance with these policies and practices.

In the classroom

- Only offer rewards for good behaviour if the rewards are things the learner cherishes.
- Only threaten punishments for bad behaviour if the punishments are things the learner fears.
- Remember that positive reinforcement will have a longer lasting effect than negative reinforcement.

Critical Perspective

What do you think about Skinner's argument that not only did positive reinforcement have a longer lasting effect on behaviour than negative reinforcement, but that negative reinforcement could actually be counter-productive?

For more on Skinner's ideas, read:

Skinner, B.F. (1953) *Science and Human Behaviour*. New York: The Free Press.
Skinner, B.F. (1958) Reinforcement today. *American Psychologist, 13*, 94–99.

Although he was regarded as one of the leading figures in the behaviourist movement, Tolman took a different viewpoint from his contemporaries and his theories arguably straddled the behaviourist/cognitivist divide.

Like Skinner (see Theory 13) he used rats as the basis for his studies but questioned Skinner's notion of *operant conditioning* by arguing that rats could learn about the environment without the need for constant reward. He did this by observing the differences in behaviour of three separate groups of rats who were rewarded with food for successfully negotiating a maze at intervals of one day, two days and six days. He was able to demonstrate that the rewards on offer produced no significant difference in the ability of each of the groups of rats to escape the maze.

From these experiments he rejected the notion of focusing on one-off stimulus–response relationships and outlined his theory of *latent learning* in which people build up cognitive maps of their environment from past experiences. The key principles of this are:

- Learning is the potential to perform, whereas the actual performance is the manifestation of that potential.
- Learning is always purposeful and goal directed; people therefore don't apply their learning unless they have a reason to do so.
- Latent learning is what people have learned from previous experience but which lies dormant. The decision to keep it dormant may be subconscious and the individual may need some prompting to apply it.

Tolman's reinforcement of early behaviourism inspired a raft of research into the subject and was attractive to many teachers who were repelled by the dry, mechanistic theories of learning of earlier behaviourist theorists.

How to use it

I always regret not putting a massive effort into learning a second language at school. On a trip to Ephesus in Turkey a few years ago, I encountered a young French lady in a state of distress. She had lost her son and didn't speak any English. Without thinking I asked her '*quel âge a votre fils?*' and '*de quelle couleur sont les vêtements de votre fils?*' This may not be perfect French but was enough to determine his age and the colour of his clothing. I still don't know where it came from. Unfortunately, I also remember travelling through France with my family during the school holidays and, displaying my excellence in the French language, phoning through a booking with a travel lodge for two rooms that evening only to find out when we turned up that I'd booked ten rooms for October!

Think about latent learning in terms of frequent journeys that you make as a passenger in a vehicle travelling from A to B. You may not be aware of certain landmarks on the journey until you have to find one. In this respect your recollection of the landmark is said to be in the subconscious or lying latent.

LATENT LEARNING

The same principle applies to your learners who may have experiences that are lying latent. Explore these further by following these simple steps:

- Ask the individual(s) what experience they have of the subject matter.
- If you don't get an immediate response, don't panic – give them time to think.
- After a reasonable period of time has elapsed without any response, try to find out if they have had experiences on subjects closely related to the matter in hand.
- If you are still not getting any responses, share with them some prepared experiences of your own. This may prompt some response.

You may have to fish around or play detective to get the type of responses that are going to be valuable in enhancing learning. Persevere, as drawing out someone's experiences can be a very powerful developmental tool for the class as well as the individual.

In the classroom

- Test learners' prior knowledge or skills level at the start of the lesson.
- Adapt your lesson plan to cater for prior learning levels.
- Make use of learners with existing knowledge or skills by pairing them off in group activities with less-knowledgeable or less-skilled learners.

Critical Perspective

What do you think that Tolman meant by his belief that people built up cognitive maps of their environment from past experiences?

For more on Tolman's ideas, read:

Malone, J.C. (1990) *Theories of Learning: A Historical Approach*. California: Wadsworth.
Tolman, E.C. (1951) *Behavior and Psychological Man: Essays in Motivation and Learning*. Berkeley: University of California Press.

Gagné was one of a wave of neo-behaviourists who pioneered the science of instruction and identified what mental conditions were necessary for effective learning.

Gagné suggests that instruction can be represented as beginning with a phase of *expectancy* (motivation to learn), proceeding to *apprehension* and *acquisition*, through *retention*, *recall* and *generalisation* to *performance* and *feedback*. In this respect he considers the instructor to be the designer and manager of the learning process and the evaluator of outcomes.

He argues that learning has a hierarchical nature where the teacher has to ensure that the individual has mastered the relevant lower-order parts of the process before learning at the next level can be undertaken. The process can be represented as:

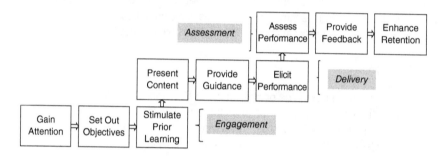

Although some critics of Gagné's work argue that his theories are little more than an eclectic, mechanistic mix of instructional techniques, his supporters welcome his account of the levels of learning as a major contribution to understanding learning behaviour.

How to use it

Nothing could be more simple, nine easy steps to help you through the learning process. Here are a few practical tips to help you apply the tool:

- Step 1: Grab your group's attention by doing something novel. When I taught mathematics (a million years ago), I had to demonstrate how to factorise an equation (yawn!). I started by telling the students that I was going to use algebra to prove the existence of God (you can see this proof by emailing me). Well that got 'em.
- Step 2: Don't tell them what you are going to do but what they will be able to do by the end of the session.
- Step 3: Test prior knowledge or understanding. You don't want to *teach your granny to suck eggs* and you may want to use individuals with prior experience of the subject in group work.
- Step 4: Organise the information in a logical and easy-to-understand manner.
- Step 5: Support individuals to remember the information by using examples, anecdotes, acronyms or metaphors.

- Step 6: Get them to demonstrate that they have understood what is being covered. Don't wait till the end of the session to assess this, do it as a matter of course throughout the session.
- Step 7: Give them feedback throughout the session. Don't just tell them they're doing something right or wrong; explain why it's right or wrong. Try and do this in a constructive manner.
- Step 8: If you've been using assessment throughout and giving regular feedback, the final assessment of skills or knowledge should be a formality. Hopefully they responded correctly. If not, work with them till they do.
- Step 9: This is what I refer to as 'use it or lose it'. Getting them to understand what they have learned is great but getting them to apply the learning in a different context is fantastic.

Didn't I tell you it was simple? Now go out and apply it!

In the classroom

- Explain lesson objectives in terms of what the learner will know or be able to do by the end of the lesson.
- Look for novel ways of grabbing learners' attention at the start of the lesson.
- Give your learners feedback on their performance throughout the lesson.

Critical Perspective

Think about a subject that you are going to teach. Use Gagné's nine levels for your lesson plan. Do you think that this is a lesson that will work better by using this structure?

For more on Gagné's ideas, read:

Gagné, R.M. (1985) *The Conditions of Learning and Theory of Instruction* (4th edn). New York: Holt, Rinehart & Winston.

Gagné, R.M. and Briggs, L.J. (1974) *The Principles of Instructional Design* (1st edn). New York: Holt, Rinehart & Winston.

Engelmann's Direct Instruction model for teaching emphasises the need for well-developed and carefully planned lessons designed around small learning increments and clearly defined and prescribed teaching tasks. It is a behaviourist model, based on Engelmann's belief that clear instruction which eliminates misinterpretations can greatly improve academic performance as well as certain affective behaviours.

Direct Instruction operates on five key philosophical principles:

- All children can be taught.
- All children can improve academically and in terms of self-image.
- All teachers can succeed if provided with adequate training and materials.
- Low performers and disadvantaged learners must be taught at a faster rate than typically occurs if they are to catch up to their higher-performing peers.
- All details of instruction must be controlled to minimise the chance of students misinterpreting the information being taught and to maximise the reinforcing effect of instruction.

Engelmann argues that in order for Direct Instruction to work effectively:

- Each student needs to be tested to find out which skills they have already mastered and which ones they need to work on. From this, students are grouped together with other students needing to work on the same skills.
- The programme must be structured so that skills are introduced gradually, giving students a chance to learn those skills and apply them before being required to learn another new set of skills.
- Instruction should be modified to accommodate each student's rate of learning. If some students need more practice with a specific skill, teachers must provide the additional instruction within the programme to ensure students master the skill. Conversely, if a student is easily acquiring the new skills and needs to advance to the next level, they can be moved to a higher level so that they may continue adding to the skills they already possess.

Engelmann argues that the implementation of Direct Instruction and the five key philosophical principles requires teachers to behave differently to before. The popular valuing of teacher creativity and autonomy as high priorities must, according to Engelmann, give way to a willingness to follow certain carefully prescribed instructional practices.

How to use it

One of Engelmann's favourite sayings is, 'if the students haven't learned, the teacher hasn't taught'. Here are some tips as to how you can use Direct Instruction:

- Organise your learners into small groups which are constituted by ability and rate of progress.
- Focus your attention on lesson planning which is designed to bring students to mastery as quickly as possible.
- Accept that delivery should be high pace explicit instruction based on well-scripted lesson plans.
- Make sure that there is frequent assessment of progress to help place students in ability groups and identify students who require additional intervention.
- Provide feedback after each lesson or part of a lesson.
- Organise your lesson plans into small steps arranged in what is assumed to be the prerequisite order.
- Make sure that learning objectives are stated clearly and in terms of learner outcomes or performance.
- Provide learners with opportunities to connect their new knowledge with what they already know.
- Give learners every opportunity to apply their learning to practice.

In the school

- Differentiate learners by ability.
- Have well-scripted lesson plans with clearly stated learning outcomes.
- Give plenty of feedback to your learners on what progress they are making.

Critical Perspective

What do you think of Engelmann's assertion that, 'if the students haven't learned, the teacher hasn't taught'?

For more on Engelmann's ideas, read:

Barbash, S. (2012) *Clear Teaching: With Direct Instruction, Siegfried Engelmann Discovered a Better Way of Teaching*. Tennessee: Education Consumers Foundation.
Engelmann, S.E. and Carnine, D. (1982) *Theory of Instruction: Principles and Applications*. New York: Irvington Publishers.

Section 1.3: Cognitivism

Cognitivism is based on the principle that information is actively processed inside the mind of the person and that behaviour modification takes place by searching for the relationships that exist between the various bits of information.

The basic premise is that learning is a process of gathering all of the relevant pieces of information together until they begin to form a complete picture. The analogy with a jigsaw can be drawn in which each individual piece has little meaning until connected with other pieces and a picture begins to emerge.

Cognitivist theory grew out of dissatisfaction with the behaviourist approach, which its staunchest critics felt was too focused on achieving a specific outcome and not on developing the individual's potential. There are many branches within cognitivism such as constructivism and connectivism which some would argue are separate theories in their own right. My stance in this section is to treat these as variations on the main theme of cognitivism.

As the need grew within practice to promote people who were capable of deeper understanding and reasoned thinking, cognitivism became a new trend in thinking. Critics of the cognitive approach argue that it is too focused on personal developmental encounters rather than learning outcomes and that not all people have either the capacity, or the desire, to want to spend a vast amount of time processing information.

Here is the timeline for when these theories were introduced:

Cognitivism

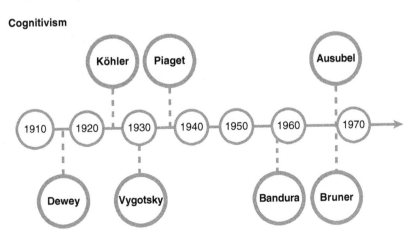

Dewey believed that education should not be separate from life itself and that behaviour modification occurs when the individual is able to relate the behaviour to their experiences. In this respect he argued that modification has to be viewed in the context of the individual and their environment and not set apart from it.

He coined the phrase *intelligent action* as the foundation for education that gives people a personal interest in social relationships and control, and the capacity to change behaviour. He described three attitudes that link together to form intelligent action. This can be represented as:

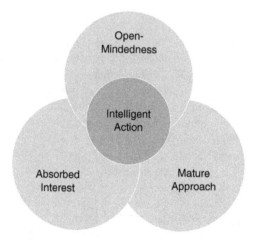

The key aspects of each of these attitudes are:

- **Open-mindedness**: freedom from prejudice or pre-conceived notions on the subject.
- **Absorbed interest**: wholehearted approach to learning about the subject.
- **Mature approach**: accepting responsibility for the consequences of action in the application of learning.

Dewey further advocated that behaviour modification should be learner-centred and set out the following principles for intelligent action:

- Encourage people to have a personal interest in the subject matter.
- Design experiences that lead to independent learning.
- Respect the viewpoint of each individual.
- Create opportunities for social involvement.

How to use it

I have been privileged over a number of years to sit in on some really good teaching sessions. Observing new teachers teach and watching their development is a great learning experience for me. This is certainly the case with Sumiah. She teaches English as a Foreign Language to students mostly from Eastern European backgrounds. The thing that really impresses me about her teaching is her use of recent events to stimulate discussion. Her material is always up-to-date and eye catching. What's also impressive is that she researches the interests of her group beforehand so that the material is of relevance to them. She always listens to her learners' views on the subject and never tries to impose her own views. I've never yet seen Sumiah fail to engage her learners.

Here are some tips to bear in mind if you want to be like Sumiah:

- Boost someone's motivation to want to learn the subject by highlighting the relevance that the subject has in the real world. Try and show how ideas can be connected to issues in the news.
- Never be afraid to interact directly and actively with learners by supporting them to discover new information for themselves. Never be afraid to admit that you've learned something new from them.
- Never pressure someone to conform to your viewpoint. Accept the diversity in cultures, religious beliefs and values that others have. Allow everyone that you work with to have the freedom to express their views and be treated with respect.
- Encourage people to participate in learning about current issues through discussion and active participation.

Remember to make the subject being discussed related to your learners' interests, not just yours. Also remember that the learning outcome may not just be related to demonstrating an understanding of the subject (in Sumiah's case, it was to get them to talk in English).

In the classroom

- Let learners know the relevance of what they are going to learn.
- Be prepared to be a learner in your own lessons and acknowledge what you've learned from your learners.
- Encourage your learners to discuss their feelings on a subject with their peers.

Critical Perspective

What do you think of Dewey's belief that education should not be separate from life itself and that real learning occurs when the individual is able to relate the learning to their experiences?

For more on Dewey's ideas, read:

Dewey, J. (1958) *Experience and Nature*. New York: Dover.
Dewey, J. (1963) *Experience and Education*. New York: Collier Books.

Wolfgang Köhler, alongside Kurt Koffka and Max Wortheimer, was one of the founders of the gestalt movement in Germany in the 1920s. The word gestalt means both 'pattern' and 'organised whole'. The basic principle behind gestalt theory is that concepts such as *perception, learning, understanding* and *thinking* should be considered as interacting relationships and not as separate entities. It is through this interaction that Köhler claims that people have a flash of inspiration (a *ping* moment) when trying to formulate solutions to a problem.

Köhler studied apes solving task-related problems. He observed that they would try out a number of possible solutions before finding the answer through a moment of insight. He argues that people are capable of mentally organising the components of a problem and developing insightful solutions. He describes the process of doing this as including:

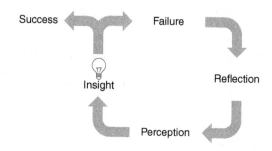

1. Failure: Not getting the right result.
2. Reflection: Pause for thought on why the result wasn't right.
3. Perception: Thinking about approaches that might produce the right result.
4. Insight: Having a flash of inspiration.
5. Success: Getting the right result.

If your first flash of insight doesn't produce the right result then keep repeating the process until it does, but remember the adage that madness is doing the same thing over and over again and expecting a different result. So don't be afraid of trying something different. Who would have thought that putting bits of coloured glass in the middle of roads would have made its inventor millions and prevented lots of night-time accidents?

How to use it

It's incredible how certain things learned at school stick in your mind. The name Archimedes cropped up in one of the articles I was reading and immediately the following flashed into my mind: *When a body is totally or partially immersed in liquid it experiences an upthrust, hence an apparent loss in weight. This loss in weight is equal to the weight of fluid displaced.* This was something that I had learned 50 years ago and not used till now.

INSIGHT THEORY

The story goes that Archimedes was summoned by his king to determine whether he was being conned by the goldsmith who had made his crown. The king suspected the goldsmith was adding silver to the gold in the crown. As Archimedes was pondering how to set about this task without damaging the crown, he jumped into a bath and when the water overflowed, he realised that he could check the mass of the crown with the mass of the gold the goldsmith claimed to have used by immersing both into water and comparing the subsequent overflows. It's said that he was so excited at finding this solution, he ran naked through the streets shouting *Eureka* ('I've found it').

You cannot teach insight to people so trying to tell you how to use this theory would be defeating the object. As a teacher your objective should be to create the conditions in which insight is allowed to flourish. Do this by having a EUREKA moment and:

- **E**ncouraging learners to try out new ideas.
- **U**sing techniques such as Petty's ICEDIP (see Theory 38) to promote creative thinking.
- **R**eassuring learners that failing a task doesn't make them a failure, providing they...
- **E**valuate what went wrong and...
- **K**eep on trying to find the solution.
- **A**llowing them not to be bound by too much emphasis on covering content.

If any of your learners ever doubt their ability to be insightful or have a Eureka moment, just tell them it was professionals who built the *Titanic* based on research and development, and amateurs who built the *Ark* based on instinct and insight.

In the classroom

- Encourage learners to take risks and try out new ideas.
- Let learners know that there is nothing wrong with making mistakes if they learn from them.
- Get them to reflect on what they have learned and make a note of their thoughts.

Critical Perspective

What do you think of critics of gestaltism who argue that the solution to a problem may be as a result of past experience of dealing with the problem rather than a flash of inspiration?

For more on insight, read:

Barber, P. (2002) *Researching Personally & Transpersonally*. Guildford: University of Surrey.

Vygotsky believed that knowledge and thought are constructed through social interaction with family, friends, teachers and peers. He referred to the people that we learn from as **Most Knowledgeable Others (MKOs)** and the process of learning through social interaction as being in the **Zone of Proximal Development (ZPD)**. He suggested that when learners were in the ZPD, they developed an understanding of a subject that may have been beyond their previous level of comprehension. He also developed the concept of *scaffolding* to describe the teacher's role in engaging with people and supporting their development while they were in the ZPD.

The three concepts can be linked in the following:

The principles underpinning **scaffolding** are:

- Build interest in the subject and engage with people.
- Break the given task into smaller sub-tasks.
- Keep the individual or group focused on completing the sub-tasks but don't allow them to lose sight of the main task.
- Use MKOs to support people.
- Model possible ways of completing the task which individuals can imitate then eventually internalise.

Vygotsky maintained that scaffolding could be used by a practitioner to help people safely take risks and reach a higher level of understanding than would be possible by the individual's efforts alone.

How to use it

The analogy of constructing a building is useful here. Scaffolding is essential in the early stages to support the structure as building work progresses but can be withdrawn as the shell of the building is complete. In the same way learners will need support at appropriate

SCAFFOLDING – THE ZONE OF PROXIMAL DEVELOPMENT

times, at an appropriate level and by appropriate people, thus emphasising the importance of social interaction in the learning process.

Don't be put off by the phrase *zone of proximal development*; it just means that if a person has no direct experience of a particular subject then using the experiences of others will help them overcome this. ZPD is one aspect of scaffolding that can best be achieved by:

- Testing prior knowledge or understanding of the subject is a great way of engaging with learners. Making a note of each contribution on a flip chart will demonstrate that you value their contribution.
- Getting members of the group to share their experiences with the rest of the group. Alternatively you could split the main group into smaller groups (useful if you feel some individuals may be intimidated by discussing experiences in front of a large group). Make sure that you have at least one MKO in each of the groups.
- Breaking the main task down into smaller sub-tasks will take the menace out of daunting tasks. Allowing people some early successes by completing sub-tasks will keep them motivated but don't allow them to become complacent and keep them focused on the main task.
- Challenging the individual to move beyond their comfort zone by listening attentively to the experiences of others, examining what may be of relevance to them and adapting and adopting this information to build on their understanding of the subject.
- Emphasising to people that, although they have benefited by listening to the experiences of others, they may also have something to contribute to the learning of others.

The emphasis in this process is on you as a facilitator (see Theory 25) who provides the individual with the scaffold to establish a sound foundation for further learning. Don't hesitate to suggest possible approaches to solve the problem but avoid wherever possible spoon-feeding them the answer.

In the classroom

- Test learners' prior knowledge of the subject.
- Use more knowledgeable learners to work alongside less knowledgeable colleagues.
- Prepare learners to come out of their comfort zones.

Critical Perspective

Vygotsky placed a lot of importance on the roles of community and culture in the learning process. What do you think about his critics who argue that the theory does not recognise that individuals can rise above social norms based on their ability to bring about personal understanding?

For more on Vygotsky's ideas, read:

Vygotsky, L.S. (1962) *Thought and Language*. Cambridge, MA: MIT Press.
Vygotsky, L.S. (1978) *Mind in Society*. Cambridge, MA: Harvard University Press.

Piaget is arguably the most influential of the cognitive theorists. His belief that people construct knowledge (as opposed to receiving it) is at the heart of most cognitive theories. He suggests that the construction of knowledge is based on the individual's experiences which in turn are influenced by their emotional, biological and mental stage of development.

Piaget argued that there are four stages of development:

- The **sensorimotor** stage, where learning takes place through touch and feel.
- The **pre-operational** stage, where the ability to arrange objects logically starts to develop.
- The **concrete operational** stage, where the ability to think logically about objects and events starts to become more structured.
- The **formal operational** stage where abstract thinking and verbal reasoning starts to develop.

Although Piaget's theories were developed from his studies of children, I would expand them to include people of all ages and summarise them as:

- People react differently to learning according to their stage of cognitive development.
- Teachers should take an active, mentoring role towards their learners.
- Learners should be encouraged to learn from their peers.
- Learners should be allowed to learn from their mistakes.
- The focus should be on the process of learning as well as the outcome.
- Teachers should respect each learner's interests, abilities and limits.

Although not without his critics (notably on his assertion that children are autonomous in their construction of knowledge and understanding), Piaget's theories have been seminal in the work around human cognitive development.

How to use it

I was using football as a way of getting young people with behavioural issues to engage in the learning process. One of the exercises we do on this programme is to have a six-a-side competition in which the winning team have a penalty shoot-out against each other, with a prize for the individual winner. We then explore issues related to cooperation and competition. Danny was one of the players. He suffered with Asperger's Syndrome. His cognitive development was below that of his peers and he had difficulty socialising with other young people. He was also very passionate about football. I put him in a team with some real hard knocks. His team won the six-a-side competition and, as they lined up for the penalty shoot-out, the hardest of the hard knocks whispered to me that they'd rigged it for Danny to win. The sheer joy on Danny's face when he scored the winning penalty and the emotion of his mother telling me he'd never had friends who did that for him before is something I'll never forget.

Here are some tips as to how to apply Piaget's theory:

- People reacting differently to learning may not be as a result of their age, but at what stage they are at in their cognitive development.
- Some learners will flourish in group-working whereas others may need more one-to-one support. Try to balance your time so that you can cater for all of your learners' needs.
- Encourage your learners to learn from each other and emphasise that everyone will have something to offer in this respect.
- Convince them that failing at something doesn't mean they are a failure; simply that they have failed a task. The important thing is to get them to learn from their mistakes.
- Congratulate your learners on their efforts as well as their achievements.

I do admit to a moment of panic when Danny missed his first penalty, only for the goal-keeper to put his hand up and admit that he'd moved before the penalty was taken and the referee (the hard lad) ordered the penalty to be re-taken. Some so-called professional footballers could have learned a lot from this.

In the classroom

- Try to get an understanding of what stage in their cognitive development your learners are at.
- Adapt your teaching strategies to deal with this.
- Acknowledge effort as well as achievement.

Critical Perspective

Piaget argued that people react differently to learning, not as a result of their age, but according to the stage they are at in their cognitive development. Can you think of examples that prove or disprove this argument?

For more on Piaget's ideas, read:

Piaget, J. (1957) *Construction of Reality in the Child*. London: Routledge & Kegan Paul.
Piaget, J. (1970) *Genetic Epistemology*. New York: Columbia University Press.

Bandura based his theory on controlled experiments conducted with two groups of children. One group of children witnessed scenes of adults physically and verbally attacking an inflatable doll. The other group witnessed scenes of adults caressing and talking affectionately to the doll. When the children were left alone with the doll, they imitated the behaviour of the adults that they had observed.

Bandura suggests that the observational process is underpinned by the notion that behaviour modification is achieved by: observing the actions of other, mentally rehearsing whether these actions are appropriate and then initiating behaviour that was considered appropriate.

Role Modelling

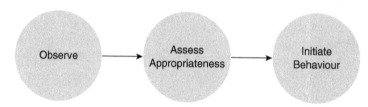

In order for someone to successfully imitate the behaviour of a role model, Bandura suggested the individual must be encouraged to:

- Pay attention to the behaviour.
- Remember what was seen or heard.
- Have the capacity to reproduce the behaviour.
- Have the motivation to want to reproduce it.

He argued that people would be more receptive to modelling good behaviours if they believed that they were capable of executing the behaviour. He used the term *self-efficacy* to describe this.

How to use it

Malcolm was a graphic designer on a post-graduate teacher training course. I was his tutor. I was aware that just prior to starting the course, Malcolm's sister had died. Malcolm was always first in the class and eager to discuss things that we had covered in the previous session. He was also last out, often accompanying me to my car and discussing things that we covered in that session. His enthusiasm was infectious but his written work was a disaster.

The day before Malcolm's mid-term tutorial, I received an email from the head of department telling me that Malcolm's brother had been stabbed and killed in a gang fight. Imagine my surprise when Malcolm turned up for his tutorial. He told me that training to be a teacher was more than just a career move for him; it was his way to stay out of the gang culture.

I observed Malcolm teach on three occasions over the next term. He wasn't a bad teacher, relying more on enthusiasm than a precise appreciation of the subject. The problem was that his written work was dreadful and without me rewriting large chunks of his assignments he was going to fail the course.

If you are working with someone like Malcolm, what would you do? Here's the dilemma that I faced: if I chose to rewrite his assignments was I being a good role model and setting a good example for him as a teacher? Ethically, I had a responsibility to the other trainees that I was teaching and the standards of the profession. If I chose to rewrite his assignments was I allowing the emotions of the situation to influence my actions? What impact was this likely to have on the way that Malcolm works with his learners? These are questions that I've been asking myself for the past 15 years. You will have to email me to find out what I did but I doubt whether Malcolm will forget me, but maybe not for the right reasons. Being a good role model is a massive responsibility!

In the classroom

- The way that you behave in the class will have a positive or negative effect on your learners.
- Don't choose stereotypes to reinforce good behaviour. Remember there were some excellent white activists and some awful black activists who fought to end apartheid.
- If you choose role models, make sure your learners are capable of replicating their behaviour.

Critical Perspective

I use the example of working with Malcolm in this entry. What do you think about my actions?

For more on Bandura's ideas, read:

Bandura, A. (1977) *Social Learning Theory*. New York: General Learning Press.
Malone, J.C. (1990) *Theories of Learning: A Historical Approach*. California: Wadsworth.

Ausubel's notion of reception learning argued that behaviour modification was achieved through the process of deduction: linking new concepts with existing understanding and knowledge, thus subsuming previously held knowledge.

In order to be able to comprehend complex concepts, Ausubel suggested that the individual must be presented with a series of less-complex and more generalised information on the subject. This can gradually be extended but any extensions have to be related to what was presented previously. This can be represented as:

Increase the intensity of the subject

Link to previous experience

Increase intensity of the subject

Link subject to previous experiences

Introduce the subject at a basic level

Ausubel maintains that new material should not be introduced unless it can be integrated into what is already known.

How to use it

There are no points for telling me that you have read something like this before. Ausubel and Bruner (see Theory 23) are both from the cognitivist school and believe in the same basic principles that underpin cognitivism, notably that understanding and meaning are vital for learning to take place. Both also agree that this must be organised and structured. Where they disagree is on the degree of structure and who assumes responsibility for organising it.

If you subscribe to Ausubel's teacher-centred approach, then your mantra is: *Tell them what you are going to teach them; teach them the subject; then tell them what you have taught them.* There's nothing wrong with this approach, providing you do it correctly:

- Start the session by *recapping* on what was covered in the previous session.
- *Explain* how you are going to expand on what has already been covered.
- Organise and *deliver* the new material to be covered so that the links with existing knowledge can be established.
- *Test* whether the new knowledge has been understood.
- *Recap* on what has been covered.
- Describe what you will cover in the next session.

Now go through each step and work out what the italicised verbs in each step have in common. Compare your answers with those in Theory 23.

In the classroom

- Recap on learning from the previous lesson.
- Explain how you intend to build on this.
- Assess whether new knowledge has been understood.

Critical Perspective

What do you think of Ausubel's approach to teaching: Tell them what you are going to teach them, teach them the subject and then tell them what you have taught them?

For more on reception learning, read:

Ausubel, D. (1963) *The Psychology of Meaningful Verbal Learning.* New York: Grune & Stratton.

Ausubel, D. (1978) *Educational Psychology: A Cognitive View.* New York: Holt, Rinehart & Winston.

Bruner's notion of *discovery learning* argued that behaviour modification was achieved through the person participating actively in the process rather than being spoon-fed information, thus discovering important aspects of knowledge.

In order to develop their problem-solving skills, Bruner suggested that the practitioner's role is not to impart information by rote-learning but instead to facilitate the learning process by designing sessions that help the individual to discover the relationship between bits of information. This can be represented as:

Bruner maintained that giving the individual the essential information they need to solve the problem but not organising it for them is a critical aspect of discovery learning.

How to use it

There are no points for telling me that you have read something like this before. Bruner and Ausubel (see Theory 22) are both from the cognitivist school and believe in the same basic principles that underpin cognitivism; notably that understanding and meaning are vital for learning to take place. Both also agree that this must be organised and structured. Where they disagree is on the degree of structure and who assumes responsibility for organising it.

If you subscribe to Bruner's learner-centred approach, then your mantra is: *Find out what they know about the subject; support them to discover more about the subject; then ask them what they've learned*. There's nothing wrong with this approach, providing you do it correctly:

- Start the session by *assessing* what prior knowledge individuals have of the subject.
- *Ask* what people's expectations of the session are.
- Organise and allow people to *discover* the new material to be covered so that they can make the links with their own understanding of the subject.
- *Determine* what they now understand about the subject.
- *Find out* what they want to cover in the next session.

Now go through each step and work out what the italicised verbs in each step have in common. Compare your answers with those in Theory 22.

In the classroom

- Test learners' prior knowledge of the subject.
- Ask them how they would like to expand on this.
- Assess whether they have absorbed new knowledge.

Critical Perspective

What do you think of Bruner's approach to teaching: find out what they know about the subject; support them to discover more about the subject; then ask them what they've learned?

For more on discovery learning, read:

Bruner, J.S. (1966) *Towards a Theory of Instruction*. New York: W.W. Norton
Bruner, J.S. (1971) *The Relevance of Education*. New York: W.W. Norton

Section 1.4: Humanism

Humanism is based on the belief that the individual is self-determining; free to make their own choices. It is a person-centred activity in which the individual plays an active role in deciding what they should be allowed to learn.

The basic premise of humanism is that people have a natural potential for learning and that significant learning takes place when the individual can see that the subject matter is relevant to them. In this situation, the practitioner acts as a facilitator; encouraging learning rather than identifying specific methods or techniques of instruction.

Although the catalysts for the humanist movement, the Montessori and Summerhill schools, were launched at the beginning of the twentieth century, the theory wasn't developed until the early 1940s. It was popularised throughout the 1960s and 1970s as a result of a group of psychologists questioning the virtue of the behaviourist approach (which they felt portrayed a negative view of the person's capacity for self-determination) and the cognitivist approach (which they argued was too obsessed with meaning and understanding).

As the movement grew to empower more people in making decisions about issues that affect their lives, so the emphasis switched from teacher-centred to learner-centred learning. Supporters of the humanistic approach argue that students appreciate not being evaluated or judged and relish the opportunity for their thoughts to be understood. Critics claim that not everyone seeks empowerment or feels comfortable when empowered, arguing that some people clearly want to be instructed in what to do.

In this section I have tried to cover what I feel are the two key phases (pre- and post-Second World War) of the humanist movement during the twentieth century. Here is the timeline for when these theories were introduced (for Montessori and Neill see Section 3.5):

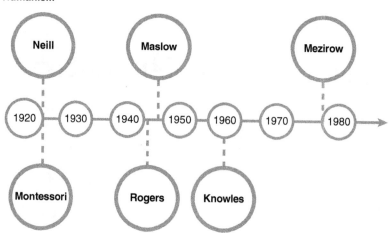

Humanism

Neill

Maslow

Mezirow

1920 — 1930 — 1940 — 1950 — 1960 — 1970 — 1980 →

Montessori

Rogers

Knowles

Knowles argued that most adult learners want to be in control of their learning. He suggested that adult learners:

- Have their own particular views of themselves and their needs and are goal-oriented in terms of meeting those needs.
- Bring a vast array of life experiences and knowledge which can be a valuable resource for learning.
- Are more concerned with learning in order to complete tasks or solve problems than just learning subjects.
- Have a need to be valued and respected.

Knowles maintained that, as an individual matures, the motivation to learn is driven more by internal motivators (an inner desire) rather than extrinsic motivators (external stimuli). Knowles also emphasised the value of learning that is problem-based and collaborative rather than didactic and imposed. In this respect, he argued for the need for more equality between the teacher and learner in terms of choosing the content and style of delivery.

How to use it

Although Knowles acknowledged that not all people may be at the adult learner's stage, he argued that it is important that they be encouraged to take on more characteristics of adult learners.

I first met David nearly 40 years ago when he was 17 and I was giving him careers advice. He suffered from hydrocephalus and had been categorised throughout his school life as *educationally sub-normal* (a dreadful term used in the 70s to describe someone with an IQ below 40). David wanted to train as a gardener. Much to my shame I felt unskilled labouring was more appropriate. I asked David what experience he had as a gardener. I still remember his words 'I'm confident with transplantation of seedlings but I need more training in propagation techniques'. I met David a few years ago and he had defied both the medical assessment of a short-life prognosis and my assessment of his unrealistic training aspirations by working as an assistant gardener in a garden centre for over 30 years.

Don't make the same mistake as I did when underestimating people's learning potential and failing to give them the support to achieve this:

- Involve learners in setting the goals for the learning experience but accept that not all of them will jump at the opportunity to be involved in this way.
- Find out about their interests and past experiences and support them to draw on these when working individually or in a group; most people thrive on the opportunity to share their knowledge and experiences.
- Recognise that they are motivated to learn when they can see the need to acquire knowledge or skills to address a real-life problem or situation.
- Use real-life case studies as a basis from which to learn about theory.
- Demonstrate your respect for them by taking an interest in them, acknowledging their contributions and encouraging them to express their ideas at every opportunity, even if you disagree with them.

I had met David as he was going into a betting shop to pursue his second passion in life. He gave me a tip on a horse to back. The horse lost. I guess I had that one coming.

In the classroom

- Involve your learners in setting the learning goals.
- Make the subject matter relevant to them.
- Get them to express their ideas at every opportunity.

Critical Perspective

Do you agree with Knowles that most adult learners want to be in control of their learning, whereas most children prefer others to be in control?

For more on andragogy, read:

Knowles, M. (1988) *The Modern Practice of Adult Education*. Cambridge: Cambridge Book Company.
Knowles, M. (1988) *The Adult Learner*. Houston, TX: Gulf Publishing.

Rogers was a driving force in the humanist movement which advocated a shift in emphasis in the learning process away from the teacher towards the learner. In the humanist approach, the teacher's role changes from one of authority or expertise, providing solutions, to one of facilitating the process of individuals arriving at their own solutions.

Rogers identified three elements which he felt were an important part of effective facilitation:

These can be summarised as:

- **Congruence**: being true to yourself and not being afraid to express your feelings in an effort to establish a rapport with others.
- **Empathy**: being willing to consider issues from the other person's standpoint.
- **Respect**: accepting others for what they are in a non-critical and non-judgemental manner.

Rogers argued that his belief in 'his inability to teach anyone anything, merely to provide an environment conducive to effective learning' is the guiding principle behind his theory.

How to use it

Facilitation is more about how you practise, than what you practise. It's about making the process of learning easier for people. In order to use this approach you must have a firm belief in your role as the class facilitator, not the class controller or director. Do this half-heartedly and you will not be adopting a humanistic approach. It's important therefore to look at the actions necessary for good facilitation:

- Start by setting the mood and climate for the session. How you come over to others in the opening stanza of the session will have a significant impact on how they perform during the session.
- Find out what others are expecting from the session. Get full agreement on what the learning outcomes will be. Write it on a flip chart (this will be useful to refer to during the session).
- Have a range of learning resources available (exercises, tasks, etc.).
- Act as a flexible resource to be utilised by learners.
- Become a learning participant. You will be surprised how much you can learn from your learners.
- Find out what your learners gained from the session. Go round each learner and ask one thing they have learned from the session.
- Don't be afraid to share your own feelings about the learning experience.
- Be receptive to criticism and never be afraid to recognise and accept your own limitations.

The behaviours and actions you display during a session will often stimulate other people's desire to want to learn more about the subject rather than the actual content of the session.

In the classroom

- Always be genuine and honest with your learners.
- Try to understand how they are feeling about the subject.
- Think positively about your learners' potential to achieve.

Critical Perspective

Rogers argues that the teacher's role should be facilitating the process of individuals arriving at their own solutions rather than providing answers to problems. Do you agree with this?

For more on Rogers' ideas, read:

Rogers, C. (2004) *On Becoming a Person*. London: Constable.
Rogers, C. (1994) *Freedom to Learn*. New York: Prentice Hall.

Maslow's most famous work was the 'Hierarchy of Needs' in which he suggested that an individual's response to learning is dominated at any given moment by whichever need has priority.

The hierarchy of needs is divided into two phases. The lower order needs relate to the physiological and safety aspects of learning (physical and psychological). Maslow argued that progression to the higher levels is not possible unless lower level needs have been met. The steps can be summarised as:

Self-fulfilment
Reaching full potential

Esteem
Self-belief and satisfaction (reputation, respect)

Affiliation
Sense of belonging (affection and love)

Psychological
Freedom from fear (certainty, stability, organisation)

Physical
Basic survival needs (food, warmth, rest)

Maslow claimed that the motivation to progress through each level can be driven through either extrinsic or intrinsic forces. It is the inner desire to want to achieve (intrinsic motivation) however that is the cornerstone of the humanistic approach.

How to use it

Not everyone will experience self-actualisation in its full sense but many will enjoy periods of *peak experience* when they derive a sense of achievement at mastering a skill. Don't feel that it is down to you to ensure that everyone's needs must be fully met. People can, and do, function in various states of contentedness. They also have expectations from you that, although conditions may not always be perfect, they should at the very minimum be tolerable. The following is an attempt to demonstrate how a learner's needs can be met, partially if not fully.

- Learners will want to feel comfortable in the session so make sure heating and ventilating systems are functioning properly. Build in drinks and toilet breaks. Arrange seating according to needs.

HIERARCHY OF NEEDS

- Learners will want to feel safe from physical and psychological harm so make sure that you have well-planned lessons and good classroom control. Deal with threatening behaviour in an appropriate manner.
- Learners will want to feel respected by you so show them that you care for them by taking time out to find out about their interests.
- Learners will also want to feel accepted by their peers so encourage interaction by mixing members of the group up in practical activities.
- Learners will want to feel a sense of pride in their achievements. Praise from you when they come up with new ideas and original solutions to problems is good but praise from their peers is even better, so get them to share their ideas with the rest of the group.
- Learners will want to feel that they have realised their full potential. You may have to be realistic about what you can achieve here but always be positive about what they can achieve next.

In the classroom

- Make sure your learners are comfortable in the class.
- Get your learners working together.
- Give your learners every opportunity to achieve their learning ambitions.

Critical Perspective

Maslow claimed that people can't be motivated to learn unless they have an inner desire to do so. Do you agree with this?

For more on Maslow's ideas, read:

Maslow, A.H. (1987) *Motivation and Personality* (3rd edn). New York: Harper Collins.
Maslow, A.H. (1993) *The Further Reaches of Human Nature*. London: Penguin.

Mezirow introduced the concepts of *meaning perspectives* (an individual's overall view of the world) and *meaning schemes* (smaller bits of knowledge and values relating to the individual's experiences). He argued that meaning perspectives change as a result of responses to life experiences, and provide the raw material of the changes that occur in transformational learning. Mezirow's theory on transformational learning in the classroom is based on three main themes:

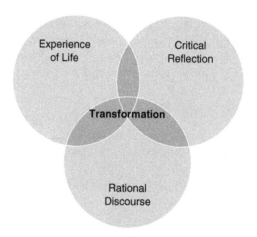

These can be summarised as:

- **Experience of life** provides the essential starting point in any learning event.
- **Critical reflection** is the distinguishing feature of adult learning and the mechanism by which the learner questions the validity of their beliefs and values.
- **Rational discourse** induces the learner to explore the depth and meaning of their beliefs and values and to share these with their teachers and peers.

Mezirow suggested that transformational learning would induce more far-reaching behavioural change in the person and produce a more significant impact, or paradigm shift, than other kinds of learning. He argued that the combination of reflection and discourse encouraged the learner to transform their views on life to be more inclusive which in turn would lead to greater interdependency and compassion for others.

How to use it

Not all teachers are predisposed to engage in transformative learning, not all learning situations lend themselves to this kind of experience and not all learners will feel comfortable being challenged over their values and beliefs. There will however be circumstances in the classroom when you may feel it is your responsibility to challenge unacceptable behaviour.

Dealing with learners behaving in a racist or sexist manner may be a good example of this. Here are some important points to help you deal with this situation:

- Never impose your views on others. If you feel it is your responsibility to challenge someone's unacceptable behaviour, encourage them to critically reflect on and discuss their beliefs openly.
- Try to get a commitment from the learner to be receptive to different points of view.
- Look for different ways to stimulate transformational learning such as metaphors, role plays, case studies and sharing experiences.
- Once the learner realises that their old patterns of thinking are giving way to new patterns, support them to embed these patterns into their values and beliefs.

Always question yourself 'what rights do I have to engage in transformational learning?' If you are satisfied that you have the right to do this then be prepared for a significant change in your learners' attitudes and behaviour. The story of Jane Elliot in Theory 9 is worth reading in this context.

In the classroom

- Never try to impose your beliefs on a learner.
- If their behaviour is unacceptable, get them to reflect on this.
- If they realise that they have to change their ways of thinking, support them to do this.

Critical Perspective

How much do you believe that it is your responsibility as a teacher to challenge behaviour that you consider unacceptable based on your own views and values?

For more on Mezirow's ideas, read:

Mezirow, J. (1991) *Transformative Dimensions of Adult Learning*. San Francisco, CA: Jossey-Bass.

Mezirow, J. (1997) Transformative learning: Theory to practice. *New Directions for Adult and Continuing Education, 74,* 5–12.

SECTION 1.5: NEUROLISM

The theories in this section come under the heading of *neurolism*. Don't go rushing to the dictionary or try googling this term. It doesn't exist. It's a term that I have adopted from the neuroscience of learning to cover the phenomena known as *Brain-based Learning* or *Information Processing Theory*. The basis of *neurolism* therefore is the anatomy of the brain and its capacity to cope with complex human reactions such as intelligence, thinking and learning.

In order to make sense of the entries that follow, think of the brain in terms of a computer and the way that it receives, processes and stores information. If you can relate to this metaphor, you can appreciate that incoming information is acted upon by a series of processing systems. Each of these systems accepts, rejects or transforms the information in some way, resulting in some form of a response.

Where there is a difference between the computer and the brain is in the type of processing of which each is capable. Computers are only capable of processing one bit of information at a time before moving on to the next bit, whereas the brain often engages in a multitude of bits of information simultaneously. There is also an issue about predictability with the computer always reacting to the same input in exactly the same manner, whereas the brain may be subjected to emotional or environmental pressures that cause differences in reactions. Differences apart, there are similarities in terms of how information is received and stored that I want to explore in this section. Here is the timeline for when these theories were introduced:

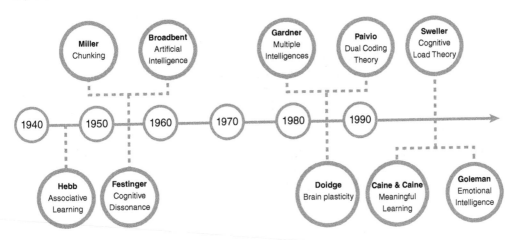

Hebb was a student of Karl Lashley who was at the forefront of research into neural connections. It was Hebb however who formulated a theory to explain what actually happens when nerve cells in the brain are simultaneously and repeatedly active. He claimed that this created the synapses (or links) that lead to cell assemblies through which connections are made.

Hebb uses the example of a baby hearing footsteps to describe how the process works. After the footsteps, an assembly is excited and the baby will either have a positive or a negative reaction to the footsteps, depending on whether the person is someone they have grown to love or fear. Here's how this can be depicted:

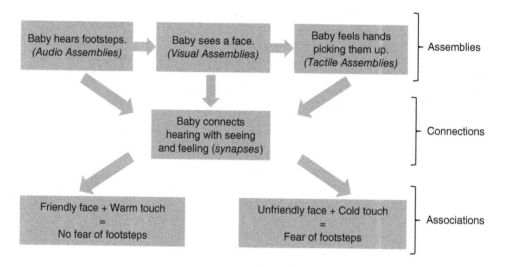

Hebb's theory is the cornerstone of modern neuroscience and his explanation of associative learning, commonly referred to as Hebbian learning, remains the accepted model.

How to use it

Understanding how to apply Hebb's theory is based on the principle that learning affects the brain in two different ways: it creates brand new synapses or links (most common in younger people) or rearranges existing ones (more common in adults). Either way, the brain is remoulded to take in new data and, if it is useful, retains it.

To use Hebb's theory effectively, you need to:

- Accept that people learn differently. Some will have a greater capacity to organise the input of knowledge and therefore be able to make the associations easier than others.
- Develop a strategy for dealing with the different levels of learners in a class. Someone with well-formed neural connections can attach new data to existing networks and

learning will take place when you encourage them to connect with what they already know. Someone with less-developed connections will struggle to assimilate new data because of the energy it takes the brain to create new synapses. In this instance break learning down into chunks (see Theory 29).

- Appreciate that there is no proven link between the capacity to make neural connections and intelligence. Use the computer analogy to make sense of this. Something with a higher operational specification will function quicker and more effectively than something with a lower operational specification. That doesn't mean that the lower specification machine is incapable of making connections, just that you have to spend more time and effort getting it to a stage where it can do it.
- Use powerful tools such as metaphors, stories and analogies to help people to develop meaningful connections, see patterns develop and make sense of the new data. The phrase 'cells that wire together, fire together' is often used as a metaphor to describe Hebb's theory.

In the classroom

- Accept that your learners may have different learning styles.
- Have a lesson plan that differentiates between learning abilities.
- Use learning materials that will stimulate a range of senses.

Critical Perspective

What do you think that Hebb meant when he claimed that, 'cells that fire together, wire together'? How will this influence the way that you teach?

For more on Hebb's ideas, read:

Hebb, D.O. (1949) *The Organization of Behavior: A Neuropsychological Theory*. New York: Wiley and Sons.

Hebb, D.O. (1959) A neuropsychological theory. In S. Koch (ed.), *Psychology: A Study of a Science*, vol. 1. New York: McGraw-Hill.

Miller focused on the study of mental processes such as memory and span of attention. He suggested that there were limits on our capacity for processing information. He admitted that he became obsessed by how often the number 7 (plus or minus 2) recurred in his studies in terms of how accurately people can distinguish a number of different stimuli.

Miller's idea can be explained by the following process:

- Before information is stored in long-term memory it is processed by a filter known as Working Memory.
- Working Memory can only retain about 7 (plus or minus 2) bits of information at a given moment in time.
- Organising these bits of information into meaningful patterns of information make them easier to store.

Although later studies argued that the figure for the capacity of working memory was probably less than 7, depending on the length and complexity of the data, the debate that Miller provoked over the process of memorising made a significant contribution to our understanding of the brain as an information processor.

How to use it

The longest town name in the UK is a little Welsh village called:

Llanfairpwllgwyngyllgogerychwyrndrobwllllantysiliogogogoch.

I suspect that even the residents of the village have difficulty in remembering the name of the place where they live. If we apply Miller's theory of 7 (plus or minus 2) we can break the village's name into bite-sizable chunks and then into further chunks.

- Llanfairpwll   *(clan-fair-pwill)*
- Gwyngyll   *(gwyn-gill)*

- Gogery (*go-gery*)
- Cwyyrn (*kwern*)
- Drobwyillanti (*drob-will-aunty*)
- Silio (*silly-o*)
- Gogogoch (*go-go-gock*)

I apologise for my pronunciation to all my Welsh mates, particularly those that play rugby (a little known game invented by the English). I guess that it might have been easier using *that* word from the Mary Poppins film.

Now try it out on a more complicated exercise. Look at the following statement and, by breaking it down into six smaller statements (*chunking*) work out what it means:

As the derivative referred to as the implied subject, having a predisposition for eternal abstinence from the impartation of knowledge to one's maternal predecessor is essential, relative to the vacuum induction of avian induced ovum.

I apologise if I haven't taught you anything new here but you can find the answer to this by emailing me (or you could read Theory 31 for a clue).

In the classroom

- Don't overload learners with complicated material.
- Break this down into bite-sizable chunks of 5-9 bits.
- Accept that learners' spans of attention will vary considerably.

Critical Perspective

Do you agree with Miller's belief that working memory can only retain 7 (plus or minus 2) bits of information at a given moment in time? Think of something that you are going to teach and see if you can break it down into bite-sizable chunks.

For more on Miller's ideas, read:

Miller, G.A. (1956) The magical number seven, plus or minus two: Some limits on our capacity for processing information. *Psychological Review, 63*, 81-97.

Miller, G.A., Galanter, E., and Pribram, K.H. (1960) *Plans and the Structure of Behavior*. New York: Holt, Rinehart & Winston.

Sweller describes the cognitive process as having three main parts: sensory memory, working memory and long-term memory.

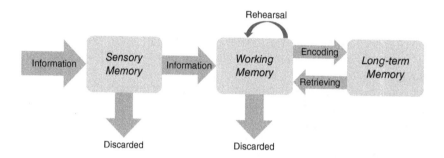

The model is based on the notion that every day you are bombarded with sensory information. Sensory memory filters out most of this information, but keeps an impression of the most important items long enough for them to pass into working memory. When the filtered out information reaches working memory it is either processed or discarded.

Central to cognitive load theory is Miller's claim (see Theory 29) that working memory can only hold between five and nine items (or chunks) of information at any one time. When the working memory processes information, it categorises that information and moves it into long-term memory, where it is stored in knowledge structures called *schemas*. Schemas, rather than consisting of rote-learned facts, are actually made up of a set of sophisticated structures that give us the capacity to perceive, think and solve problems.

Sweller argues that cognitive load theory differentiates cognitive load into three types:

- **Intrinsic** cognitive load is the effort associated with a specific topic.
- **Extraneous** cognitive load refers to the way information or tasks are presented to a learner.
- **Germane** cognitive load refers to the work put into creating a permanent store of knowledge.

Sweller acknowledges that individuals differ in their processing capacity. This may be determined by an individual's age, skills or knowledge levels or socioeconomic status. He claims that identifying the processing capacity of individuals could be extremely useful for teachers in further adapting instruction for individuals.

How to use it

During teaching, any information you pass on will be held in a learner's working memory until it has been processed sufficiently to pass into their long-term memory. A learner's working memory's capacity is very limited, so when too much information is presented at once, it becomes overwhelmed and much of that information is lost. Here are some tips to help you prevent overloading your learners:

- Identify the processing capacity of your learners and adapt your teaching accordingly.
- Change problem solving methods by breaking problems down into parts, and by using partially completed problems and worked examples.
- Merge together multiple sources of visual information whenever possible.
- Eliminate the working memory load associated with having to mentally integrate several sources of information by using both visual and auditory channels.
- Eliminate the working memory load associated with unnecessarily processing repetitive information.
- Only use technology when it enhances the learning experiences.
- Use group working wherever possible in problem-solving activities.

It is important to remember that when applying any of these tips that individuals will differ in their ability to process information and master learning. The stories of Ayan Quereshi and Peggy Gwilt in Theory 114 are worth reading to see how, despite significant differences in their ages and backgrounds, both flourished because of the expertise and support given by teaching staff at the organisations where they were learning.

In the classroom

- Arrange desks so that learners are not distracted by external influences.
- Make sure that learners only use technology devices if it adds to their understanding or assists them with the prescribed assignment.
- Encourage learners to find a distraction-free environment for doing homework.

Critical Perspective

While there seems to be some agreement that a heavy cognitive load can have a negative effect on task completion, it is important to note that the experience of cognitive load is not the same in everyone. For example the age and socioeconomic status of the learners may have implications. How is this likely to impact on your teaching approaches?

For more on cognitive load theory, read:

Sweller, J. (1988) Cognitive load during problem solving: Effects on learning. *Cognitive Science*, 12, 257-285.

Sweller, J. (1999) *Instructional Design in Technical Areas*. Camberwell, Victoria, Australia: Australian Council for Educational Research.

Paivio asserts that cognition involves the activity of two independent mental codes: a verbal code (logogens) specifically for dealing with language in all its forms and a non-verbal code (imagens) for dealing with mental images. These coding systems are separate but interconnected so that they can operate independently, in parallel, or through their interconnections.

Paivio suggests that there are three types of processing:

- **Representational**: the direct activation of verbal or non-verbal representations.
- **Referential**: the activation of the verbal system by the non-verbal system or vice-versa.
- **Associative**: the activation of representations within the same verbal or non-verbal system.

Paivio claims that a given task may require any or all of the three kinds of processing. He also claims that if teachers design lessons that involve the two different types of coding, they will increase the likelihood of learners retaining the information on the premise that their mind will store it as a representation of both a verbal and non-verbal mental image that can be accessed at a later time.

How to use it

Dual coding theory (DCT) suggests that combining verbal and visual material in learning should increase the probability that words will activate corresponding images and vice-versa. I apologise if you have seen something like this somewhere else in the book but look at the following to see how DCT works in practice.

> *Teach not thy parent's mother to extract the embryonic juices of the bird by suction. The graceful lady can that feat enact, quite irrespective of your kind instruction.*

=

Just take a minute or two to consider the above. How difficult was it to process the written clue without the associated image and vice-versa. When you are preparing your class materials, find visuals that go along with the information you want to pass onto your learners but be careful.

- Be creative while drawing the visuals but accept that certain types of visuals work very well with certain subjects. For example, a timeline may work well for remembering history, and a diagram may work very well with geography.
- Don't get what I call *desktoppublishingitus* and go overboard with the visuals. You don't want to cause cognitive overload (see Theory 30).
- Learning material will be easier for learners to relate to if it is less abstract.
- Because the imagen system has superior memory capacity, students recall more pictures than words.

Please email me if you can't work this one out.

In the classroom

- Make sure that any visuals you use enhance the learning experience.
- Don't have too many elaborate visuals.
- Don't be too abstract in your terminology.

Critical Perspective

What do you think about Paivio's critics who argue that dual coding theory does not take into account the possibility of cognition being mediated by something other than words and images?

For more on dual coding theory, read:

Paivio, A. (1971) *Imagery and Verbal Processes*. New York: Holt, Rinehart, and Winston.
Paivio, A. (1990) *Mental Representations: A Dual Coding Approach*. Oxford: Oxford University Press.

Festinger was a student of Kurt Lewin, who spearheaded the social psychology movement in the USA. Festinger suggested that people continually seek to bring order or meaning to their learning by developing routines and opinions that may give rise to irrational and sometimes maladaptive behaviour. He claimed that when these routines are disrupted, or opinions are contradicted, the individual starts to feel uncomfortable: a state that Festinger referred to as *cognitive dissonance* (discord in reasoning).

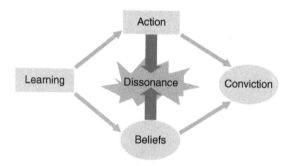

Festinger's theory of cognitive dissonance is based on three fundamental assumptions:

- People are sensitive to inconsistencies between action and belief.
- Recognition of these inconsistencies will cause dissonance or discord which the individual will be motivated to resolve.
- Dissonance can be resolved by either (a) changing their beliefs, (b) changing their actions or (c) changing their perception of action.

Festinger argued that cognitive dissonance makes someone of strong conviction unlikely to change their opinion even if they are presented with a rational argument to the contrary.

Festinger was inspired to study people's unshakeable conviction in their beliefs when he read an article about a cult whose members believed the earth was going to be destroyed by floods. When the anticipated apocalypse didn't materialise, committed cult members, who had given up their homes and jobs, convinced themselves that it was due to their dedication that the world was spared.

How to use it

I heard on the news recently that local authorities in the UK generate a total of £820m each year from parking fines. If you are training traffic wardens, telling someone of a sensitive disposition that their role as a traffic warden is to punish illegal parking, they may experience some dissonance when giving a fine to someone (especially if the person has a disability). Explaining that their role is to make sure that all vehicles, including emergency vehicles, will not be deprived access to dealing with fires or accidents by the actions of illegal parking, and dissonance is less likely.

You are unlikely to be faced with individuals whose beliefs are as radical as the cult that Festinger studied, but you need to be wary that:

- There will be some whose convictions are so strong that they will be resistant to your teaching. Trying to get them to act in a way that is inconsistent with their beliefs or convictions is likely to cause cognitive dissonance.
- Forcing someone to change their beliefs may not be feasible or even acceptable. Making them feel bad or guilty about their actions is not a great way of teaching someone and may cause even greater cognitive dissonance.
- Trying to get an individual to think about their actions in a different manner or context so that it no longer appears to be inconsistent with their beliefs is an approach worth considering. Do this and dissonance is less likely.

You should never try to get individuals to learn by questioning their firmly held beliefs on a subject, even if you consider that belief to be inappropriate.

In the classroom

- Accept that there are some learners who will never change their ideas or ways of doing things.
- Question whether it is your right to try to change their ways.
- If change is necessary get the learners to reflect on their beliefs and reconcile what's right or wrong.

Critical Perspective

Think of an instance when your convictions on a subject were so strong that you refused to back down and accept a well-presented argument to the contrary. How did you feel? What impact will this have on the way that you teach?

For more on Festinger's ideas, read:

Festinger, L. (1957) *A Theory of Cognitive Dissonance*. New York: Harper & Row.
Festinger, L. (1962) Cognitive dissonance. *Scientific American, 207*(4), 93-107.

Broadbent served in the RAF and was interested in applying psychology to reach a better understanding of the causes of pilot error. He observed that pilots had to cope with large amounts of incoming information and had to select what was relevant to enable them to make the right decisions. He argued that errors happened when there were too many sources of incoming information. From his observations, Broadbent deduced that when a number of stimuli are presented simultaneously, the brain has a limited capacity to deal with all of them. The majority of stimuli are therefore filtered out, leaving only a select few to progress through to the brain's memory banks. The process can be represented as:

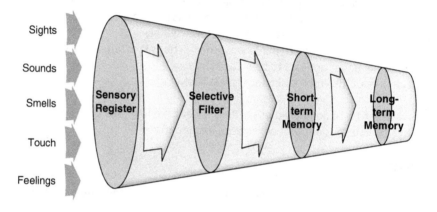

The stages in this process can be summarised as:

- The **sensory register**: this is where the visual, audio or tactile stimulus is stored just long enough to decide if it should be allowed to progress to the next stage.
- The **selective filter**: this will process which one of the sensory stimuli should be allowed into the short-term memory banks.
- The **short-term memory banks**: the stimulus remains here until it is allowed into the long-term memory bank or despatched from the memory altogether.

Broadbent's theory suggests that it is the intensity of the physical characteristics of the stimulus that will allow it to progress to short-term memory and that not everything progressing there will go through to long-term memory storage.

How to use it

Ever been in a group where a flurry of ideas was being thrown around and you didn't know which conversations to tune into? Ever wondered why some people's ideas are listened to more than others? Ever wished you could have more control over the attention seekers in the group?

It may surprise you to know that the selection of what you and others choose to tune into is less about the content of the information (what's being said) and more about volume, clarity or tone (the way it's being said). What may also be surprising is that, although this registers in the short-term memory data banks it is only after the filtering process that what goes in is actually processed for meaning and understanding.

I used to have a colleague called Bill whose physical presence (he was an ex-Coldstream Guardsman) and loud voice would often sway opinion in most meetings. Another colleague was Jim. He was the exact opposite to Bill in terms of physical presence and spoke in a quiet, deliberate but incredibly menacing tone that made everyone afraid to challenge him. It was only sometime after being in meetings with Bill or Jim that you would say 'what the h*** was that all about?' and begin to realise they were both talking nonsense. Unfortunately, I met both of these characters at different times in my career so they were never in the same meeting. That would have been an interesting contest!

Be aware of the Bills and the Jims in your group. Their nature may be deemed by some to be attention-seeking or at worst bullying. Don't allow them to satisfy their cravings for attention and remember the old adage *Garbage In – Garbage Out*. Not everyone in the group however will filter the garbage from Bill or Jim quickly and some maybe not at all. Support them to question what they are saying by getting Bill or Jim to explain or rationalise what they have said. Do this in a non-threatening manner however as being seen to pick on them may have an adverse effect on what you are trying to achieve and turn the rest of the group against you.

In the classroom

- Don't be afraid of challenging overbearing learners.
- Ask them to allow others to have a say.
- If they are in full flow, get them to pause and explain what they are saying.

Critical Perspective

Do you agree with Broadbent's claim that what you choose to tune into in a noisy room is less about what's being said and more about the way it's being said? If you do, how will this influence the way that you teach?

For more on Broadbent's ideas, read:

Broadbent, D.E. (1987) *Perception and Communication*. Oxford: Oxford University Press.
Moray, N. (1995) Donald E. Broadbent: 1926-1993. *The American Journal of Psychology*, 108(1), 117-121.

Gardner proposed that human beings have several types of intelligence that form the potential to process information in a range of different contexts. Gardner made two fundamental claims about his ideas: first, that they accounted for the full range of human cognition; and second, that each individual had a unique blend of the various intelligences that made them into who they are. He suggested that there are nine intelligences which can be summarised as:

- *Linguistic*: the capacity to understand and use spoken and written language.
- *Logical-Mathematical*: the capacity to analyse problems logically.
- *Musical*: the capacity to compose, perform and appreciate musical patterns.
- *Bodily-Kinaesthetic*: the capacity to use and interpret expressive movement.
- *Visual-Spatial*: the capacity to recognise patterns and dimensions.
- *Interpersonal*: the capacity to understand the intentions and desires of others.
- *Intrapersonal*: the capacity to understand one's own feelings, fears and needs.
- *Naturalistic*: the capacity to recognise and categorise objects in nature.
- *Existential*: the capacity to tackle deep questions about the meaning of life.

Gardner argued that an individual's capacity in a particular intelligence will have a direct bearing on the way they learn.

How to use it

If you take the ideas set out by Gardner seriously, identifying individual differences amongst a group of learners will help you to be better at understanding the learning process and more prepared to work with learners. Here's an interesting scenario:

Imagine that you are appearing as a survival expert on one of those *I'm a legend, get me out of here* programmes. Your legendary guests on the show are. Emily Bronte (Writer), Albert Einstein (Physicist), Margot Fontaine (Ballerina), Salvador Dali (Painter), Mozart (Composer), Alexander the Great (Military Genius), Alexander Graham Bell (Inventor), Anita Roddick (Founder of Body Shop), The Dalai Lama (Spiritual Leader of Tibet) and Socrates (Philosopher). You have been asked to teach your legends how to make the best out of their predicament. Here's how you might handle the teaching:

- Emily Bronte: Get her to keep a diary of events on the island to help others who may get stranded there.
- Albert Einstein: Get him working on logical problems and complex operations to construct means of escape.
- Margot Fontaine: Get her participating in activities involving movement and touch to help keep everyone in shape.
- Salvador Dali: Get him to experiment with shapes and colours to construct maps of the island.
- Mozart: Get him to compose an inspirational piece of music to keep people's spirits up.

- Alexander the Great: Get him working in groups and directing others.
- Alexander Graham Bell: Get him working independently on challenging tasks to create lighting, energy and warmth.
- Anita Roddick: Get her working with natural products for food and medicine.
- The Dalai Lama: Get him reflecting on important issues facing the survivors.
- Socrates: Get him to search for a deeper meaning of why the survivors are there.

Simply googling 'Test your Multiple Intelligence' will give you dozens of sites for questionnaires that you can use to get some idea of your legends' intelligences. These might be a useful indicator but should be treated with a degree of caution as none of them are infallible.

In the classroom

- Be aware that individuals have different strengths and will react differently according to the nature of the tasks set.
- Allow learners the opportunity to tackle assignments in different ways.
- Consider taking learners out of their comfort zones and approach problems in ways that might not be compatible with their preferred intelligences.

Critical Perspective

What do you think about Gardner's assertion that measuring intelligence on the basis of scholastic performance and psychometric tests is too constrictive?

For more on Gardner's ideas, read:

Gardner, H. (1993) *Multiple Intelligences: The Theory in Practice*. New York: Basic Books.
Gardner, H. (2009) Reflections on my works and those of my commentators. In B. Shearer (ed.), *MI at 25* (pp. 113–120) New York: Teachers College Press.

Goleman suggested that intelligence is not just about developing a high IQ or being technically skilled, but that people also need to develop their emotional intelligence. He argued that there were five key elements of emotional intelligence which can be interpreted for teachers. These are summarised as:

- **Self-awareness**: Teachers must be aware of the relationship between their thoughts, feelings and actions. They must be able to recognise what thoughts about a situation sparked off which emotions and the impact these emotions can have on themselves and those around them.
- **Managing emotions**: Teachers must analyse what is behind these emotions and be able to deal with them in a positive manner.
- **Empathy**: Teachers must also be able to deal with the emotions of those around them in a positive manner. This requires them to be able to understand more about the nature of any concerns being expressed about their teaching.
- **Social skills**: Teachers need to develop quality relationships. This will have a positive effect on all involved. Knowing how and when to take the lead and when to follow is an essential social skill.
- **Motivation**: Teachers can't always rely on external rewards to motivate others. They must support their learners to develop their own source of intrinsic motivators by encouraging them to appreciate what they can do and not to focus on the things they can't do.

Goleman argued that having a high level of self-awareness and an understanding of others makes you a better person as well as a better teacher. He also argued that rather than losing brain cells through the aging process, the brain continuously reshapes itself in line with the experiences we have. Goleman suggests that by persisting with positive thoughts and actions your newly reformed brain will ensure you will have a positive outlook in how you work as a teacher and will result in you naturally doing the right thing for your learners, in the right way. Of course Goleman's theories are speculation. But don't they sound good and worth trying out!

How to use it

John was having a bad day. He'd just found out that his school was being visited by Ofsted that week. The plans for the teacher training day on *Team Teaching* had been changed to an Ofsted briefing session. In their infinite wisdom, the Local Authority had decided to do some roadworks near to his house causing him to turn up 30 minutes late and stressed for the session. Like other teachers there, he'd gone along in the hope that it wouldn't be boring, that he might just learn something valuable and that he might not be asked to participate in anything 'embarrassing' such as role play. He found out early on in the session that he was going to be observed by Ofsted and couldn't think about anything else other than the lesson that he'd planned for that day. 'Yes', he kept telling himself. 'I've got a good plan for the lesson, I know that I can deliver it well but is anybody going to learn anything from it?'

EMOTIONAL INTELLIGENCE

If you have ever been in the situation that John was in, here are some tips from Goleman's theory of emotional intelligence that might help you out:

- Be aware that whatever the cause of your stress, the emotional state that you enter the school with is likely to be your default emotional state for the rest of the day. Learn to relax. Try finding a spot on the way into the school (e.g. a tree or a picture) where you can park the things that are triggering your stress.
- In terms of your fears about your lesson planning, try putting yourself in the shoes of your learners by asking yourself questions about how you can bring your lesson to life with questions, individual and group activities, peer discussions and quizzes.
- Try pre-framing lessons with a little excitement and lots of interest. I once told my maths class that in the next lesson, I was going to use algebra to prove the existence of God. Better than telling them we were going to learn how to factorise equations.
- Don't rely on extrinsic rewards or threats to motivate your students.

In the classroom, keep reflecting on how well your day is going by asking yourself

- What two things are going really well for me today?
- What two things can I do to really enjoy the next lesson with my students, and maximise their learning?
- If the rest of today was going to be exciting, enjoyable and worthwhile for my students and me too, what two things would I need to do to make this happen?

Critical Perspective

What do you think of Goleman's suggestion that persisting with positive thoughts and actions will ensure that you will have a positive outlook in how you work as a teacher and will result in you naturally doing the right thing for your learners, in the right way?

For more on Goleman's ideas, read:

Goleman, D. (1996) *Emotional Intelligence: Why it can Matter more than IQ*. London: Bloomsbury.

Goleman, D. (1998) *Working with Emotional Intelligence*. London: Bloomsbury.

Although I have attributed this entry to Doidge, the origins of *brain plasticity* can be traced back to the late nineteenth century and the work of William James who noted that the nervous system was endowed with an extraordinary degree of plasticity. This theory was neglected for over 60 years until people, like Hebb and Merzenich, began to fashion a more persuasive proof of brain plasticity and, more importantly, its application in supporting people with brain disorders. I have used Doidge because he has taken their ideas a step forward to produce a fascinating insight into how a number of people have managed with illness or injury to the brain.

According to Doidge, brain plasticity can be defined as the property the brain possesses that allows it to change its function and its structure through its perception of the world, life experiences and imagination. Doidge suggests that there are three principles that underpin neuroplasticity:

- **Age variability**: Although plasticity is a lifetime occurrence, some types of changes are more predominant in the early stages in someone's life. As people age therefore and plasticity declines, learning becomes increasingly more difficult for them.
- **Process variety**: Although plasticity is an ongoing process, it involves brain cells other than neurons, such as optical and vascular cells, connecting with each other. The failure to do this is what Doidge refers to as 'cells out of sync, fail to link'.
- **Nature and nurture**: Although it can happen as a result of damage to the brain, loss of learning or memory functioning, genetics can also have an influence.

Despite the fact that the concept of *brain plasticity* is broad, vague and hardly new, Doidge claims that it is one of the most important discoveries about the brain.

How to use it

Adam suffered with a type of autism. He had very limited social skills and his ability to communicate with others was very limited. What he did have was exceptional IT skills. If anything went wrong with any of the PCs in class, he was the one the staff turned to for help. Computers were his life; he spent most of his time at school and home working on them. The downside of this was that, when he did talk, his speech was in Americanised computer-speak. There are ethical considerations about whether Adam's transfer of functions from one part of his brain (the damaged parts that caused his autism) to the undamaged parts (the parts that contain the logic and reasoning that underpin his talent in IT) should have been discouraged and his social skills encouraged.

I don't have the answer to this dilemma. Neglecting Adam's social development was wrong, but taking Adam away from his computer would have been like chopping his right arm off.

Here are some tips for how to apply the theory when working with learners like Adam who may have a disability affecting their development.

- Make sure that your teaching has the right balance of challenge and support. Don't make the challenge too difficult or else you run the risk of damaging the learner's confidence. Don't make the challenge too easy or else you run the risk of making them complacent.
- Encourage the individual to be actively involved in the learning process. Support this process by encouraging learners to reflect on what's been learned and to challenge their understanding of the subject matter.
- Use different teaching approaches to engage the individual with the subject matter in a way that is meaningful to them. Discuss the subject matter in such a way as to allow the individual to develop their own interpretation of its meaning.

In the classroom

- Make sure you challenge your learners but with concern for their feelings.
- Make learning relevant to the learner's needs.
- Get learners to reflect on what they've done.

Critical Perspective

How would you have resolved the dilemma facing Adam's teachers?

For more on brain plasticity, read:

Doidge, N. (2007) *The Brain that Changes Itself*. London: Penguin.

Caine and Caine suggested a set of principles as a theoretical foundation for brain-based learning. They argued that the principles would lead to a paradigm shift in approaches to teaching and assessment away from memorising information towards meaningful learning.

Caine and Caine's principles are:

- The brain is a living system where thoughts, emotions and imagination interact with other systems such as health and well-being and socialisation.
- Learning engages the entire physiology and is as natural a function as breathing.
- The search for meaning is innate and cannot be halted, only channelled and focused.
- The search for meaning occurs through patterning in which the brain accepts patterns that are relevant and rejects patterns that are meaningless.
- Emotions are critical to patterning, crucial to memory retention and evoke long-term recall.
- Every brain simultaneously perceives and creates parts and wholes.
- Learning involves both focused attention and peripheral perception thus responding to the entire sensory context in which learning occurs.
- Learning involves both conscious and unconscious processes.
- We have at least two ways of organising memory.
- Experiences change the physiological structure and operation in the brain.
- Learning is enhanced by challenge and inhibited by threat.
- Each brain is uniquely organised.

Caine and Caine claimed that understanding how the brain learns would have significant implications for curriculum design, teaching methodologies and a host of other issues critical to educational reform.

How to use it

The beauty of this theory is that the principles are simple, straightforward and neurologically sound. The difficulty, I suppose, is in the application. Further reading of Caine and Caine would indicate that three interactive elements are necessary for the application of the principles. I'm going to use these elements as the basis for how to apply the theory.

- Create a state of **relaxed alertness** by providing an atmosphere that has the right balance of significant challenge and understanding of the learner's feelings and attitudes. Don't make the challenge too difficult or threatening or else you run the risk of damaging your learner's confidence or self-esteem.
- **Orchestrate the immersion** of your learners in the subject matter at hand by use of different teaching approaches and by making it relevant to their learning needs. Although you may have the responsibility for choosing most of what learners have to learn, you should present the learning in such a way as to allow your learner to develop their own meaningful patterns of interpretation of the subject matter.

- Allow your learners to take charge of the learning process in a way that is meaningful to them, but support this process by asking challenging questions and encouraging reflection. **Active processing** of information in this way will help your learners to recognise and deal with their own biases and attitudes.

In the classroom

- Make sure that your lesson has the right level of challenge.
- Vary your teaching approaches and make the content relevant to your learners' needs.
- Give your learners a say in the learning process.

Critical Perspective

Meaningful learning is based on the ways our brain learns best. Do you think that we know enough about the way the brain works to be able to base our teaching on this principle?

For more on meaningful learning, read:

Caine, R. and Caine, G. (1994) *Making Connections: Teaching and the Human Brain.* Somerset, NJ: Addison Wesley.
Caine, R. and Caine, G. (1997) *Unleashing the Power of Perceptual Change.* Virginia: ASCD.

Summary of Part 1

In Part 1, I have tried to demonstrate the many different ways in which people of all ages, levels and outlooks think and learn. Each theory reflects different degrees of human activeness in learning:

- Education philosophy concentrates on the debate between rationalism and empiricism.
- Behaviourist theory relates to *reactive* learning and is underpinned by conditioning and reinforcement.
- Cognitivist theory relates to *responsive* learning where mental acts are the primary aim.
- Humanist theory is about *reflective* learning dependent on experience and self-efficacy.
- Neurolism [*sic*] emphasises the importance of *receptive* learning, where information processing and memory are the focus.

The key points to emerge from this part of the book are:

- The unexamined life is worthless.
- Tell learners they are doomed to fail and they may begin to accept failure as inevitable as a consequence.
- Tell learners they have the potential for greatness and watch them grow.
- People learn best when they relate the learning to their own learning goals, knowledge or experiences.
- Accept that mistakes will happen so treat them as a learning opportunity.
- Don't allow yourself to be a perpetrator or victim of the blame culture.
- Don't spoon-feed learners with the answers.
- Allow learners to have a say in what or how they want to learn.
- Explain what the rewards for success and the punishment for failure are.
- Test learners' prior knowledge or skills at the start of every lesson.
- Use learners with experience of the subject being taught to work alongside less-experienced learners.

- Express lesson objectives in terms of what the learner will know or be able to do at the end of the lesson.
- Give constant feedback on performance throughout the lesson.
- If you fail at something try again but this time fail better till you get the right result.
- Using an individual's prior experiences can be a very powerful learning tool.
- An individual will learn best when they feel connected to the subject.
- People should never be afraid of trying out something new.
- If you are supporting someone, consider their feelings and beliefs, avoid being judgemental and don't try to force your values and beliefs on someone.
- Help someone to understand complicated instructions by getting them to break it down into bite-sizable chunks.
- Someone with deep convictions on an issue will be a hard person to change.
- The majority of stimuli are filtered out, leaving only a select few to progress through to the brain's memory banks.
- A learner's working memory's capacity is very limited, so when too much information is presented at once, it becomes overwhelmed and much of that information is lost.
- Combining verbal and visual material in learning should increase the probability that words will activate corresponding images and vice-versa.
- Human beings have several types of intelligence that formed the potential to process information in a range of different contexts.
- Persisting with positive thoughts and actions will ensure that you will have a positive outlook in how you work as a teacher.
- The brain possesses powers that allow it to change its function and its structure through its perception of the world, life experiences and imagination.
- Creating the right environment and level of challenge will help stimulate the brain to be more receptive to learning.

PART 2

CONTEMPORARY THINKING ON TEACHING AND LEARNING

INTRODUCTION TO PART 2

Part 1 was a potted history of how our understanding of the way people think and learn has developed over the last 2500 years. It traced the subject from the early philosophical debates through the ages of reason and revolution and into the psychological and scientific perspectives of the twentieth century.

In Part 2, I want to take a look at more contemporary thinking and learning and the writers who are influencing our perspectives on this. There is a mass of material on this subject and whenever I mention to colleagues and learners the writers who I intended to include in this book, I get the inevitable 'but what about...?' Don't get me wrong, I quite like it when people say that because it encourages me to read up on the writer and in some instances I went on to include them in this second edition. There is a limit however and if I have missed your particular favourite, email me and, if there is to be a further edition, then I'll see if I can squeeze them in.

I've taken a cross-section of ideas from a number of writers and tried to balance them out, without showing preference or favour to any particular line of thought. It is important to stress that the interpretation and application of other people's ideas are my own idiosyncratic representations of their thoughts. Unlike the writers in Part 1, most of the contemporary writers are still alive and kicking and if I'm honoured enough to have my work read by them, and I haven't done their work justice, I'll invite them to contact me and I'll see if I can put it right.

I've broken Part 2 into sections that cover what I feel are the key aspects of attitude, skills and knowledge that underpin good teaching. These include: professionalism, learning styles, motivation, behaviour management, coaching and mentoring, and teamwork.

SECTION 2.1: PROFESSIONALISM

It's important to draw the distinction between being *a* professional and being professional. The former suggests someone who abides by the standards to operate required by licensing bodies (*they do things right*). The latter relates to someone who makes the learning experience the most valuable one possible for the individual (*they do the right thing*). Inevitably, there has to be a balance between efficiency and effectiveness which may be tipped in one way or the other by the financial demands placed on an organisation. This creates a dilemma.

- Failure to satisfy the requirements of the licensing bodies may result in the organisation being forced to close or put into special measures.
- Failure to satisfy the needs and expectations of its customers may result in learners voting with their feet or the organisation becoming bankrupt.

Either way, the organisation becomes vulnerable and may not survive.

Rather than write this section from an institutional perspective, the entries draw on the knowledge and experience of a group of trainee teachers. The group were set an exercise to come up with what they considered to be the values and capabilities of a professional teacher. They came up with seven qualities that they wanted to call *The 7 Habits of Highly Effective Teachers* or *The Magnificent Seven* but were worried about infringing copyright laws.

According to the group, the seven qualities that the teacher needs to be considered professional are:

- creative in their use of materials
- competent in their knowledge of the subject
- caring towards their learners
- communicative in the way they support learners to believe in themselves

- confident and having a high sense of value of self and others
- considerate in the way they approach learners
- calm in being able to understand and manage difficult situations.

Each of the entries that follow covers each of the above qualities in turn. There was a lot of soul searching to decide which theories to choose here and which ones to leave out but the theories and models chosen will give you an interesting and powerful perspective on the qualities required to be a good teacher.

Petty argues that creative work is important in the teaching of any subject in order to: develop learners' ability to think creatively and to solve problems; enable them to use knowledge productively and meaningfully; increase their desire to want to learn; and provide an opportunity for them to explore feelings and develop skills in self-expression.

He uses the acronym *ICEDIP* as an aid to remembering the constituent terms. These can be summarised as:

- **Inspiration**: this involves an uninhibited exploration for new ideas. It is characterised by spontaneity, intuition, imagination and improvisation.
- **Clarification**: this is to have a clear understanding of the purpose or objective of the learning intentions.
- **Distillation**: this is where the ideas are evaluated and either chosen for further development or rejected.
- **Incubation**: this may involve taking a backward step and taking a fresh look at the idea to gauge whether or not it is viable.
- **Perspiration**: this is the effort required to take the ideas forward.
- **Evaluation**: this involves examining the strength and weaknesses of the idea and looking for areas for further development.

Petty explains that the key words in the sequence actually need reorganising to spell *ICEDIP* (although he explains that e*valuation* is a thread that runs throughout the process) and that there could be many variations on the actual sequence depending on the mindset of the individual and the task being undertaken.

How to use it

Callum is teaching a session on capacity and measurement to 12-year-old pupils with learning difficulties. He reads them an extract from one of the *Harry Potter* books where Harry and his friends are mixing potions. He then brings in some bottles of coloured water and a set of plastic beakers. He gives each of his learners a magic wand (a large straw) and a formula for a magic potion. Using the right measures (for example; one third blue, one third green, one third red) he gets them to make their potions, whilst shouting out a magic word. Just for fun he then asks them what they would use the potion for. Amongst making one learner a great footballer and another a great singer, we had 'to turn teacher into a frog'.

Here's how you can use the *ICEDIP* approach when your learners have to complete a task:

- Give your learners a blank sheet of paper and get them to brainstorm for ideas. Make it clear that they shouldn't reject any ideas at this stage and that their first idea won't necessarily be their best one.

- Get them to work through each idea systematically and reject the ones that aren't compatible with what they want to achieve.
- Get them to go through the remaining ideas and select the ones that are worthy of further development. Warn them that they need to think with their heads and not with their hearts and not go with something because it looks nice or easy to achieve.
- Give them the opportunity to distance themselves from the idea so that they can have a clear head before undertaking the effort required to bring the idea to fruition.
- Stress to them the importance of evaluating the piece of work. Get them to look for strengths as well as weaknesses in the idea. Many great ideas are rejected because of the individual's failure to see the good points in the idea.

How long do you think Callum has been a teacher? He's not; he still has 6 months to go to complete his teacher training. I hope he never becomes a frog and never loses the spark he displayed in the observation. Nothing against frogs; I love them.

In the classroom

- Encourage your learners to think about a wide range of ideas.
- Get them to choose the ideas that best fit with achieving the learning outcomes.
- Impress on them the hard work they need to do to turn the idea into a reality.

Critical Perspective

What do you think of Callum's approach? Can you see ways in which you can be more creative in your lesson planning?

For more on Petty's ideas, read:

Petty, G. (1997) *How to Be Better at Creativity*. London: Kogan Page.

n his article 'The four stages for learning any new skill', Noel Burch suggested that individuals go through the following stages when learning something new:

These can be summarised as:

- Stage 1: *Unconscious incompetence* (doing things wrong, oblivious to the fact that they are wrong).
- Stage 2: *Conscious incompetence* (still doing things wrong but now aware they are doing it wrong).
- Stage 3: *Conscious competence* (doing things right but having to keep thinking about how to do it).
- Stage 4: *Unconscious competence* (doing things right without having to think about it).

Burch argues that Stage 4 is a dangerous stage where individuals may become complacent about their newly acquired skills and run the risk of slipping back into unconscious incompetence.

Being aware of the four stages that you need to go through when learning a new skill is important for you to appreciate, both from the perspective of you as a teacher learning a new skill and as a teacher teaching learners a new skill. From both perspectives, it's necessary to accept that learning can sometimes be a slow and often uncomfortable process.

There's an Arabic saying that seems to embody what this theory is about:

He that knows not, and knows not that he knows not is a fool; shun him.

He that knows not, and knows that he knows not is a learner; teach him.

He that knows, and knows not that he knows is asleep; wake him.

He that knows, and knows that he knows is a teacher; learn from him.

COMPETENCY AND THE CONSCIOUS-UNCONSCIOUS MODEL

How to use it

Here are some of the critical points in each stage using my latest hobby, *Walking Football*:

- **Unconscious incompetence:** The first time I tried this, I inadvertently broke into a run when chasing the ball. Years of playing sport had conditioned me in this way and I felt very awkward doing something that didn't come natural to me. As a teacher, there may be aspects of your teaching that you will feel less comfortable with than other aspects. Listen to what others may have to say about this.
- **Conscious incompetence:** After the third session I had learned not to run but, in trying to remember this, I was less effective in other areas of the game (ball control, passing and shooting) than I had been when playing a normal game. As a teacher, reflect on every lesson and be willing to accept that you can improve on your teaching.
- **Conscious competence**: By the fifth session, I was able to master the basics of walking fast to the ball, controlling it and passing or shooting with confidence. It was still tough and I needed to think and work hard to get it right. If you have reached this stage as a teacher, you are now performing well, but still need to work hard for teaching to come more naturally to you.
- **Unconscious competence**: I've now completed ten sessions and things have become easier for me. I can do many more moves with the same natural grace that I had when I was playing regularly at a good level (some may not agree with this!). As a teacher don't allow yourself to become complacent if you reach this stage and find yourself slipping back into the *unconscious incompetence* stage.

Always remember just how difficult it was for you as a teacher to reach the stage of unconscious competence so that you can empathise with any learners who are struggling to get there.

In the classroom

- Don't be afraid to recognise that you have faults that need to be addressed.
- Ask others to give you feedback on your performance.
- Never get complacent. Thinking there's no room for improvement is a recipe for disaster.

Critical Perspective

In this entry I used my experiences of struggling with playing walking football. Can you relate the competency model to any learning situation that you have encountered?

For more on conscious competence, read:

www.businessballs.com/consciouscompetenecelearningmodel.htm

Bryk and Schneider's notion of *relational trust* describes the social exchanges that take place in a school community. This refers not just to what takes place in the classroom and staffroom but to the relationships that develop with all stakeholders and their mutual dependency on each other to achieve desired outcomes.

Bryk and Schneider claim that this dependency is based on the obligations and expectations that people have of each other and can be categorised under the following headings:

- **Respect**: this is marked by a willingness to listen to what others are saying and a genuine commitment to take others' views into account.
- **Regard**: this grows as a result of someone willing to extend themselves beyond the basic requirements of their job.
- **Competence**: this can be measured by the confidence that everyone has in the person's ability to perform.
- **Integrity**: this is recognised through people behaving ethically and keeping promises.

Bryk and Schneider argue that relational trust cannot be taught, occurs as a result of day-to-day exchanges and that even the most simple interactions can have a significant impact on building trust in the organisation. They suggest that educational leaders and teachers have a key role to play in developing and sustaining relational trust. How they behave and the vision they have for their organisation sets the standards for respect and integrity.

How to use it

Like many parents whose child is starting secondary school, I was concerned over whether we had made the right choice of school for our daughter, Amy. By the end of the first term all doubts had disappeared. Not only was my daughter doing well academically but she was a member of her school netball and rounders teams and was participating in the school orchestra. The icing on the cake was when the school staff performed a pantomime at Christmas, with the Head Teacher playing the arch villain. I met the Head some three years after he had retired and when I opened by saying 'you won't remember me but...' He cut me short and said, 'of course I do, you're Amy's dad; how's she doing at university?'

Here are some lessons that can be learned from my daughter's school:

- Through their actions in running after-school clubs, the staff at the school demonstrated their obligations to their pupils and their parents and each other. Through the pantomime, staff were interacting socially with each other, parents were acknowledging the extra effort staff were putting into rehearsals and pupils were seeing a different side to their teachers.
- The head teacher embodied everything that is critical in relational trust. I've seen many Heads who *talked the talk* (their words were more impressive than their actions). My daughter's Head Teacher was loved and respected by everyone in the school because he *walked the walk* (he believed actions spoke louder than words).
- In the same way that pupils and parents have an expectation that your professional ethics and teaching skills should be of a good standard, so you should be willing to recognise they have a part to play in contributing to achieving learning outcomes.
- Accept that you may make promises that are just impossible to keep. If you do this then take action to explain what's gone wrong and look at how you can rectify the situation.

Of course, I accept that not all staff want to devote three months of their own time rehearsing for a one-off performance and have head teachers with the vision and commitment that my daughter's Head had. I guess that's the difference between an outstanding school and an adequate one.

In the classroom

- Earn the respect of your learners by showing an interest in them as individuals.
- Don't be afraid to go the extra mile when it comes to extra curricula activities.
- Always keep the promises that you make to learners.

Critical Perspective

The head teacher that I refer to in this entry was exceptional. Can you think of teachers whose care and integrity have left a lasting impression on you?

For more on relational trust, read:

Bryk, A.S. and Schneider, B.L. (2002) *Trust in Schools*. New York: Russell Sage Foundation.

Purkey argues that a major precursor to learning is engagement and that teachers need to communicate effectively and *invite* students to participate in learning. He claims that this invitation conveys respect, care, trust, optimism and intentionality by the teacher. He suggests that there are four major dimensions in which a teacher's actions can be categorised, and the consequences of this. This can be depicted as:

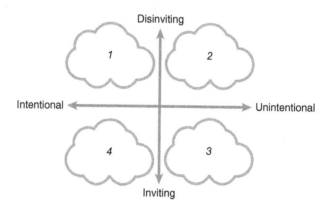

Each of the sections can be summarised as:

1. **Intentionally disinviting**: this is the most negative level of human interaction where teachers deliberately demean, dissuade and discourage their learners.
2. **Unintentionally disinviting**: at this level, although they don't intend to be harmful, teachers can be uncaring, condescending and thoughtless.
3. **Unintentionally inviting**: this is where teachers have stumbled serendipitously into ways of functioning that may prove to be effective.
4. **Intentionally inviting**: this is the most positive level of human interaction where teachers exhibit positive qualities and encourage the same positivity in their learners.

Writing later with Novak, Purkey claimed that *invitational education* offered a comprehensive approach to education in which learners are 'cordially, creatively and consistently summoned to realise their full potential'.

How to use it

In order to *invite* young learners who have become disillusioned with mainstream education to re-engage with education, simply recreating the same model which has been rejected won't work. What is essential is that an environment is created in which the young person feels safe, supported and where their creativity is nurtured.

This is the ethos of an independent school based in London called The Complete Works (TCW). TCW work with young people who have become disillusioned and are refusing to engage with mainstream schooling. Their goal is to reach every young person who is referred to them and to 'find the creative spark which will ignite their interest in learning'. They consider each learner on an individual basis and develop a tailor-made programme of learning that may involve one-to-one tuition, group work or a combination of both. Since their formation in 1999, TCW have supported thousands of young people to re-engage with education.

Here are some tips on how to emulate the work of TWC:

- Get rid of policies that create anxieties and mindless conformity and replace them with policies that encourage learner responsibility and participation.
- Treat all learners as individuals and have programmes in place that cater for their individual needs.
- Do away with the 'us and them' attitude and encourage all staff and learners to work together as teams.
- Foster a mutual sense of trust and respect amongst everyone involved in the learning process.

In the classroom

- Always treat learners as able, valuable and responsible individuals.
- Make sure that all lessons lead to cooperative and collaborative engagement in the learning process.
- Get the message over to learners that they possess untapped potential in learning what you are teaching.

Critical Perspective

Do you agree with the ethos of The Complete Works to replace school policies that demand conformity and compliance with rules with policies that encourage learner responsibility and participation?

For more on invitational trust, read:

Purkey, W.W. (1978) *Inviting School Success*. Belmont, CA: Wadsworth.
Purkey, W.W. (1992) An introduction to invitational theory. *Journal of Invitational Theory and Practice* 1(1), 5-15.
For more on The Complete Works, go to their website at www.tcw.org.uk.

Berne's model is based on the principle that the level of confidence and regard we have for ourselves and others will influence the way we interact with them. His model is usually depicted as a 2 x 2 matrix with one axis showing low to high self-confidence and the other showing low to high confidence in others.

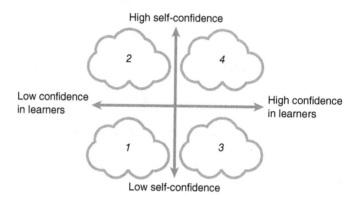

The characteristics and interactional modes of each quadrant in respect of teaching are:

1. **Low self-confidence** and **low confidence in learners**: results in a desperate classroom situation which can descend into depression and loathing (both with yourself and for your learners).
2. **High self-confidence** but **low confidence in learners**: results in frustration and anger with your learners and a feeling that they will never live up to your expectations of them.
3. **Low self-confidence** but **high confidence in learners**: results in a lack of personal self-worth and a tendency to let the learners get away with what they want to.
4. **High self-confidence** and **high confidence in learners**: results in a harmonious situation in the classroom which will be characterised by constructive and cooperative relationships.

Berne argued that this model can be used to challenge your existing beliefs and values, and replace them with more constructive thoughts about yourself and others.

How to use it

Time for a confession:

I have to be honest and admit that working as a teacher/trainer in prisons and bail hostels wasn't exactly my cup of tea. A number of offenders that I was teaching there had committed crimes of a violent or sexual nature. I was put in my place by one of my tutor team who said that we were there, 'not to judge the person; others had already done that, but to educate them'. It was at this point that I began to challenge my beliefs and values. As a result, I quickly developed an 'OK with me – OK with my learners' philosophy. From this point, instead of going through the motions, my sessions with the learners became more productive both for myself and for my learners.

Use Berne's model by acting as follows:

- Identify how you feel about yourself and your learners.
- If you are not okay with yourself, get real and accept that you are an imperfect person; you have flaws so give yourself a break and stop setting unachievable standards for yourself.
- If you are not okay with your learners, find out why. Decide if you are being fair towards them. If not, then take action to change your feelings towards them.
- Try to replace negative thinking about yourself and your learners with some positive thoughts. You will find that the more positively you think about yourself, the more positive you will think about your learners, and the more positive you think about your learners, the more positive you will feel about yourself.
- Think of a scenario where you were in a desperate situation in your teaching because of a low sense of self-confidence or regard for your learners. See what you could have done to get it to the 'OK with me – OK with them' position.

This is one of the really powerful theories in this book because it calls on you to be totally honest with yourself and be willing to share any frailties with other people. There are a number of theories on the different types of reflective practices that might help you out here (see Theories 125–127). If all else fails turn to the Bard himself who, in *Hamlet*, urges that, 'To thine own self be true'.

In the classroom

- Accept that neither you, nor your learners, are perfect and have flaws.
- Never allow your personal feelings for a learner to affect the way you teach them.
- If you lack confidence in your teaching ability, talk to people who can help you to improve this.

Critical Perspective

How easy do you find it not to let your personal feelings for a learner affect the way that you teach them?

For more on Berne's ideas, read:

Berne, E. (2010) *The Games People Play*. London: Penguin.
Harris, T. (1989) *I'm OK – You're OK*. London: Pan Books.

Covey used the analogy of making deposits and withdrawals in a bank account to demonstrate the interactions that we have with other people; deposits being when we do something good for the other person and withdrawals when we do something bad. He argued however that, unlike a bank where we may only have one or two accounts, we have an **emotional bank account** (EBA) with each person that we come into contact with.

He highlighted five major deposits that build up the EBA:

- Understanding the individual.
- Attending to the little things.
- Keeping commitments.
- Clarifying expectations.
- Showing personal integrity.

Failing to act in accordance with any of the above may constitute a withdrawal. It is inevitable however, that there will be occasions when you have to make a withdrawal. If this happens then Covey suggested a sixth deposit may be possible if you explain why you did what you did and, if necessary, apologise sincerely.

How to use it

Here's a true story, only the names are fictitious to protect the innocent:

Walt, Molly and George became teachers and friends together at the same university at the same time. The person responsible for their appointment and subsequent mentor, Les, was a bit of a hero to all three. His approachability, wisdom and humour were something all three treasured. Over a period of time however, Les started to undermine individuals and tried to turn what had been a close friendship between the three of them into one of suspicion and mistrust with each other. From making many emotional deposits with all three, Les had started to make some big withdrawals; so much so that his emotional bank account with all three became bankrupt and they reported his actions to the faculty Dean.

I heard the expression *hero to zero* the other day which sums up what Les had become. If you want to avoid reaching this point with your learners refer to Covey and simply ask, am I:

- understanding what my learners have to say by listening to them, not just going through the motions and hearing them?
- attending to the little things by being thoughtful and meeting their learning needs?
- keeping commitments by following through on what I said I would do for them?
- clarifying expectations by agreeing that we both know what we expect of each other?
- showing personal integrity by treating everyone by the same set of principles?

CONSIDERATION AND THE EMOTIONAL BANK ACCOUNT

As a teacher, working with others, you will inevitably have to make some withdrawals. Sadly, even with your support, people that you are working with fail to achieve set assignments or have to be warned about aspects of their behaviour. If your *emotional bank account* is sufficiently high with them, and you explain why the action was necessary, you can even turn a withdrawal into a deposit. Don't try doing this with the bank though.

In the classroom

- Always listen to what your learners have to say.
- Follow Covey's advice and make sure that what you have to say is understood, not just heard.
- Act with integrity and never try to play one learner or colleague off against another.

Critical Perspective

Covey's *emotional bank account* is based on people making emotional deposits and withdrawals. Think of a situation where this has happened to you. How did you feel?

For more on Covey's ideas, read:

Covey, S. (2004) *The 7 Habits of Highly Effective People*. London: Simon & Schuster.

Thomas and Kilmann suggested five approaches that can be used to resolve conflict between parties (A & B). In their model they categorised each approach in accordance with levels of *assertiveness* and *cooperation*. In terms of the likely win-lose outcome, this can be represented as:

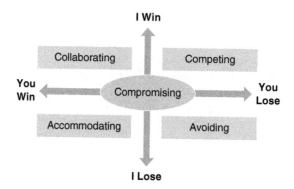

They described the consequences of each approach as:

- **Avoiding**: neither party being satisfied (both lose).
- **Accommodating**: one party sacrificing their own needs to satisfy the needs of the other party (B wins-A loses).
- **Compromising**: both parties being partially satisfied (both partially winning/losing)
- **Competing**: one party winning at the expense of the other (A wins-B loses).
- **Collaborating**: both parties being fully satisfied (both win).

Thomas and Kilmann argued that understanding the possible consequences of each approach will enable you to select which one to use.

How to use it

I have news for you! Conflict in the classroom is inevitable. You can deal with this in a *fight or flight* manner. If you fight, be wary of the victims. If you flee, then be aware that you may only be putting things off.

    I've taught all ages in schools, colleges, universities, training organisations, even prisons and bail hostels. It's very rare that conflict has resulted in violence, but on one occasion (two elderly women on a teacher training course) that it did happen, I had to act decisively and exclude the perpetrator from future classes. It was the only fair thing to do! Or was it?

THE CONFLICT RESOLUTION MODEL

I realised some 20 years after the event that I acted instinctively. My default position was that violence was unacceptable, a risk to the health and safety of others and exclusion was the only solution. The individual was a third of the way through her teacher training programme and my decision almost certainly meant the end of her teaching career. I admit I didn't like the woman: she was a bit odd and not popular with other learners. Excluding her went down well with the rest of the group and I was pleased with myself as I had a tendency to avoid confrontation. Now what do you think – was I being fair?

To be fair, you need to:

- identify what your default position is – fight or flight
- gather as much information as you can about the circumstances that have led to the conflict
- approach the situation in a calm and assertive manner
- listen to what all concerned in the conflict (observers as well as contributors) have to say
- make an assessment as to which approach you need to adopt
- set out the facts and explain why you have adopted the approach you have
- try to remain non-confrontational and focus on the issue not the person.

No need to send me a postcard with your answer to whether or not I was being fair. I'm not sure the end result would have been any different but, had I acted in line with the above, I may not have been questioning myself some 20 years later.

In the classroom

- Always treat everyone equally.
- If conflict does arise, act in a calm manner and gather as much information as you can about the incident.
- Focus on the issue, not the person.

Critical Perspective

How do you feel about the way that I dealt with the violent behaviour of the student in my class?

For more on conflict resolution, read:

Thomas, K.W. and Kilmann, R.H. (1974) *Thomas-Kilmann Conflict Mode Instrument*. New York: Xicom.

Thomas, K.W. (1977) Toward multi-dimensional values in teaching: The example of conflict behaviors. *Academy of Management Review, 2*, 484–490.

SECTION 2.2:
LEARNING STYLES

Do you ever get that sinking feeling when your partner wakes up and says 'let's go to IKEA'? OK they do a good Swedish Meatballs but, inevitably, it means having to bring home one of their infernal self-build furniture packs. If you've ever been in this predicament, how do you start? Are you the sort who: (a) likes to see a demonstration of how to assemble the item before starting; (b) gets stuck into it and starts putting bits together; (c) likes to ponder ages over the plans before starting; (d) thinks there may be a better way of doing it than it says in the plans; or (e) makes a model of what the finished article should look like.

It's unnerving how accurate the IKEA test can be in indicating what your preferred learning style is, and possibly an argument for not reading the rest of this section. It would be a shame if you didn't read the entries because there are some interesting theories about how thinking and learning styles can be related to characteristics such as attitude and personality.

A learning style can be described as the idiosyncratic way in which an individual acquires, processes, comprehends and retains information. It's now widely accepted that each individual has a different learning style preference and that this preference can either be a dominant feature apparent in all learning situations, one that may vary according to circumstances or one that blends in with other learning styles. What is certain is that there is no single blueprint for learning styles that fits every individual in every situation.

It's worth examining your own thinking on this issue. In order to help you do this, I've chosen seven different learning style theories that vary from the established, pragmatic approach to a more speculative, metaphorical approach. Most of the learning style theories have a questionnaire that you can use to determine your own preferred style of learning. Some of these are available free online, others you will have to pay for. The good news is that most of the ones you have to pay for contain a license that allows you to copy and use with other people. I would suggest that by trying them out first you will get an idea of any problems or pitfalls that may occur when you use them with others. The important thing is not to be fazed if you turn out to be an *extroverted monarchic pragmatist* (although I'd hate to bump into you in a dark alley). I would be interested to know however if you found major conflicts in what different theories were telling you about your learning styles.

There is a debate worth getting involved in around the value of using learning styles as a means of differentiating between learners in the classroom. I'm not going to spell out where I stand in this debate but suggest that you read Coffield et al.'s (2004) *Should We Be Using Learning Styles* (London: Learning and Skills Research Centre) and Honey and Mumford's (1986) *Manual of Learning Styles* (London: P. Honey) for a balanced view on the debate.

Herrmann developed Roger Sperry's concept of left and right brain thinking by suggesting that the basic principles of left brain thinkers seeing things in sequential and logical parts and right brain thinkers seeing things as a whole can be further divided into four different learning styles. This can be depicted as:

The four quadrants formed what is referred to as the Herrmann Brain Dominance Instrument (HBDI) and can be summarised as:

*   ***Theorists***: upper left brain thinkers who prefer logical and rational learning activities.
*   ***Organisers***: lower left brain thinkers who prefer organised and well-ordered learning activities.
*   ***Innovators***: upper right brain thinkers who prefer creative and imaginative learning activities.
*   ***Humanitarians***: lower right brain thinkers who prefer interpersonal and people-oriented learning activities.

Herrmann argued that although learners will have a preference for no more than two of the four styles they will need to be able to work in all four styles and should therefore be encouraged to develop the full range of styles.

How to use it

I suspect that most of the teaching strategies you use are structured, rational and language-based. They would fall into the left hand side of Herrmann's model. If you want to develop the imaginative and interpersonal abilities of your learners, you need to take note of activities that will stimulate the right side of the brain.

Katie was one of the best trainee teachers I've had the pleasure to teach. She worked as a staff trainer in a major high street retailer. Her school education had been, in Katie's words, a 'disaster'. She was not diagnosed as having dyslexia until late in her school life, which had resulted in mediocre exam results. I had observed her train staff on three occasions and although she performed adequately, she never really seemed at home with the organisation and the detail required of her. After a mid-term review of her progress, Katie made a major decision to leave retail and concentrate on teaching jewellery making. Using her artistic and imaginative abilities to the full, she became an outstanding teacher.

If you have learners like Katie who may have struggled with the more conventional left brain teaching approaches, here are some ideas worth considering that will involve right brain approaches:

- Get them to use mind-mapping to organise their work and summarise a topic.
- Use analogies and metaphors to stimulate their thinking on a subject.
- Encourage them to present their ideas in the form of pictures, music or dance.
- Involve them in simulations or role plays.
- Use case studies, anecdotes and role models as a means of stimulating discussion.
- Get them to make linkages between the past and the present and encourage them to visualise what might happen in the future.

Although Katie was utilising the creative and emotional aspects of her brain, she still needed to be organised and evaluative to be a good teacher. A similar scenario could have been presented for Jim, a teacher who I observed who was structured and systematic in his teaching but lacked originality and interpersonal skills. It's important therefore that you focus on whole-brain learning and, whatever side of the brain is dominant, don't neglect essential aspects of the other side.

In the classroom

- Use one of the online tests for left brain/right brain thinkers to get a feel for the balance between which preferences your learners have.
- Use a range of teaching activities to stimulate their dominant side.
- Don't lose sight of the need to include exercises that stimulate their less dominant side.

Critical Perspective

In this entry, I have suggested six teaching ideas that involve the right side of the brain. Which ones have worked/could work for you?

For more on Herrmann's ideas, read:

Herrmann, N. (1996) *The Whole Brain Business Book*. New York: McGraw-Hill.
Petty, G. (2014) *Teaching Today: A Practical Guide* (5th edn). Oxford: Oxford University Press.

Fleming's *Visual, Auditory, Reading, Kinaesthetic* (VARK) model of learning styles has become one of the most widely used assessments of learning styles. The descriptions for these can be summarised as:

- *Visual* learners tend to learn through seeing, think in pictures and create mental images to retain information.
- *Auditory* learners tend to learn through listening, think in words rather than pictures and learn best through lectures and group discussions.
- *Reading* learners have a preference for working from written material in hand-outs and book references.
- *Kinaesthetic* learners tend to learn through doing, express themselves through movement and learn best through interacting with others and the space around them.

Fleming argued that, although demonstrating a preference for one style, some people have a mixed and balanced blend of all four styles. He warned that an over-reliance on any one style and an unwillingness to adopt another style when it might be more appropriate might hinder learning.

How to use it

There are numerous online tests for VARK. The most common one is made up of a number of statements (usually around a dozen) with a number of responses which indicate a preference for one of the four styles. Here are a few tips to help you out with planning approaches that cater for people with each preference.

- *Visual* learners will have a preference for seen or observed things, for example pictures, diagrams, demonstrations, displays, hand-outs or films. They will prefer to perform a new task after observing someone else do it first.
- *Auditory* learners will have a preference for listening to the spoken word or sounds and noises. They will be best able to perform a new task after listening to instructions from the teacher.
- *Reading* learners will be disappointed when you fail to give them a pile of hand-outs. Their retention of verbal information given out during the lesson will be limited and their real learning takes place when they later go through the hand-outs. They will likely be the ones who want a list of books to read about the subject.
- *Kinaesthetic* learners have a preference for physical experiences including touching, feeling, holding, doing. They will be best able to perform a new task by going ahead and trying it out, learning as they go. These are the people who like practical hands-on experiences.

THE VARK MODEL

Don't fall into the trap of thinking that, with someone who has a particular preference, your approach should only cater for their preferred style. Work with someone with a pronounced preference to develop other learning styles as not all information they are ever presented with will be in their preferred style.

In the classroom

- Get a feel for your learners' learning style preferences.
- Don't think that you should only have materials that cater for learners who display a particular learning style preference.
- Look at how you can develop learners' weaker learning style preferences.

Critical Perspective

Do you agree that you should always concentrate on catering for your learner's preferred style of learning?

For more on VARK, read:

Fleming, N.D. (2001) *Teaching and Learning Styles: VARK Strategies.* Honolulu: VARK-Learn.
Petty, G. (2014) *Teaching Today: A Practical Guide* (5th edn). Oxford: Oxford University Press.

K

Kolb's *Learning Style Model* is based on two continuous dimensions concerning:

a. How people take in information: through *concrete experience* (doing) or *abstract conceptualisation* (thinking).

b. How people internalise information: through *active experimentation* (testing) or *reflective observation* (watching).

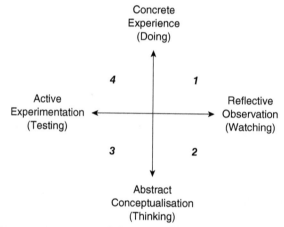

Source: KOLB, DAVID A., EXPERIENTIAL LEARNING: EXPERIENCE AS A SOURCE OF LEARNING & DEVELOPMENT, 1st Ed., ©2018. Reprinted by permission of Pearson Education, Inc., New York, New York

Kolb developed his Learning Style Inventory (LSI), in which he suggested that there were four dominant learning styles that could be located in any one of four quadrants.

Kolb described the characteristics of these in respect of learners as:

1. **Divergers** are located in the doing-watching quadrant. They are imaginative and sensitive learners, capable of grasping the big picture.

2. **Assimilators** are located in the watching-thinking quadrant. They focus more on developing theories than on practical application.

3. **Convergers** are located in the thinking-testing quadrant. They remain emotionally detached and organise information through deduction and experimentation.

4. **Accommodators** are located in the testing-doing quadrant. They rely on their intuition and solve problems through trial and error.

Kolb explains that the LSI does not relate to fixed personality traits; it is a snapshot of an individual's learning style preferences at a given moment. Although these are relatively stable patterns of behaviour, he also warned that they can change.

LEARNING STYLE INVENTORY

How to use it

This is one of the most used of all learning style assessments, particularly for adults. There are numerous online tests for this.

To plan teaching approaches that cater for people with each preference, consider the following:

Learning style	How they learn
Divergers	By being encouraged to look at things from different perspectives. They learn best by observation and brainstorming.
Assimilators	By working on ideas and abstract concepts. They excel at learning wide-ranging information and organising it a clear logical format.
Convergers	By working on technical tasks and experimenting with new ideas. They learn best by working with practical applications.
Accommodators	By being faced with new challenges and experiences. They prefer to learn by working in teams to complete tasks.

Learning style	What's difficult for them
Divergers	Focusing attention on one specific point and not getting feedback on their work.
Assimilators	Dealing with concrete ideas and not being given sufficient time to think things through in the class.
Convergers	Dealing with abstract concepts and not being allowed to experiment with new ideas in the class.
Accommodators	Handling the logical flow of an argument and not being given new challenges to work on.

In the classroom

- Get a feel for the learning style preferences in your group.
- Don't use materials that only cater for one particular preference.
- Work with learners who may have a strong preference for any one learning style to develop other styles.

Critical Perspective

What do you think about the critics of Kolb's LSI who argue that because people's preferred learning style will change depending on different circumstances, the inventory has little value when it comes to lesson planning?

For more on experiential learning, read:

Kolb, D. (1984) *Experiential Learning: Experience as the Source of Learning and Development*. New Jersey: Prentice Hall.

Honey and Mumford suggest that we need to adopt one of four different learning styles in order to complete a given task. They used Kolb's Learning Style Inventory as the basis for their diagnostic tool, the Learning Styles Questionnaire (LSQ). As with the LSI, there are two dimensions for the learning styles.

a. How the person takes in information – through *doing* (Activists) or *thinking* (Theorists)
b. How the person internalises information – through *experimenting* (Pragmatists) or *watching* (Reflectors)

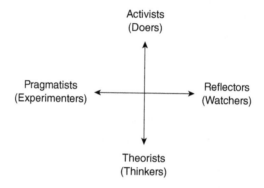

The characteristics of each preference are:

*   **Activists** prefer to learn by doing. They are often open-minded learners who are enthusiastic and not afraid to try out new ideas.
*   **Reflectors** like to stand back and observe. They are meticulous in their approach to problem solving and like to consider why things happen in the way that they do.
*   **Theorists** like to think of original ways of doing things. They can come up with fresh insights into problem solving.
*   **Pragmatists** are most at home in problem-solving exercises and keen to make use of new ideas.

Honey and Mumford make the point that no single style has an overwhelming advantage over any other. Each has strengths and weaknesses which may be important in one situation but not another. Preferences can also be modified if strengthening an underdeveloped style is necessary.

How to use it

The LSQ consists of 80 statements (there are some shorter versions). People are asked to indicate whether or not they agree with each statement. Positive responses are then transferred onto a four column grid headed: 'Activist', 'Reflector', 'Theorist' and 'Pragmatist'. The positive responses in each column are then added to give an indication of which of the four areas is most prominent.

Here are a few tips to help you out with planning approaches that cater for people with each preference.

Learning style	How they learn
Activists	They like to work in groups, sharing ideas and immersing themselves in a wide range of new experiences.
Reflectors	They like to observe others and assimilate as much information as possible before coming to a conclusion.
Theorists	They like to explore how new information fits in with their existing framework of understanding.
Pragmatists	They like to investigate and make use of new ideas.

Learning style	What's difficult for them
Activists	Coping with work that is routine and repetitious.
Reflectors	They can be painstakingly slow in making decisions.
Theorists	They can get impatient with others who don't agree with their ideas.
Pragmatists	They lose interest when things don't work.

In the classroom

- Accept that in any group of learners, there will be a range of different learning preferences.
- Don't prepare learning materials that cater for only one style of learning.
- Encourage learners to come out of their comfort zones and try out different styles of learning.

Critical Perspective

What do you think of the critics of learning style theory who argue that there is too vast a difference in the literature on what learning styles an individual can possess to be useful when practically applied?

For more on learning styles preferences, read:

Honey, P. and Mumford, A. (1986) *Manual of Learning Styles* (2nd edn). London: P. Honey.

Gregorc's defined learning styles as consisting of a set of distinctive behaviours which serve as indicators of how a person learns from and adapts to their environment. Within this model, there are four combinations of behaviours based on perceptual qualities: the means by which you grasp information (*abstractly* or *concretely*) and ordering abilities: the way that you arrange, systemise, record and dispose of information (*sequentially* or *randomly*).

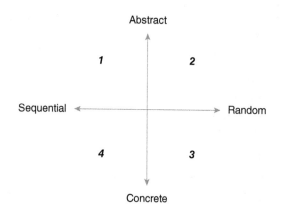

His four learning styles can be summarised as:

1. **Abstract-Sequential** learners are logical, analytical and well-organised. They may be too mechanistic and have a dislike for the unpredictable.
2. **Abstract-Random** learners are sensitive and spontaneous. They may be too emotional in responding to situations and have a dislike for detail and working to deadlines.
3. **Concrete-Random** learners are intuitive, curious and creative. They may be too impulsive in how they react to situations and have a dislike for keeping records and working to deadlines.
4. **Concrete-Sequential** learners are ordered, practical and thorough in their approach. They may be obsessive as they strive for perfection and have a dislike working with abstract ideas.

Gregorc argued that although everyone can make use of all four styles, people have a natural inclination towards one or two of them.

How to use it

The Gregorc's Style Delinator (GSD) is a self-assessment questionnaire in which respondents can get an idea of which learning style they have an inclination towards. In the GSD, there are 15 sets of four words. People are asked to indicate which two words in each set best describe them. Here are a few tips to help you out with planning approaches that cater for people with each preference.

Learning style	How they learn
Abstract–Sequential	By researching ideas and using their research to prove or disprove theories. They like lectures and learn better by watching rather than doing.
Abstract–Random	By listening to others and empathising with their views. They enjoy tackling assignments and learn best through working in groups.
Concrete–Random	Through independent learning and being original and creative. They learn best through trial and error and by being encouraged to use insight and instinct.
Concrete–Sequential	By applying ideas in a practical way. They prefer to be directed and need order and quiet to complete tasks.

Learning style	What's difficult for them
Abstract–Sequential	Adhering to specific rules and regulations. Being asked to work with people who don't share their ideas. Expressing emotions.
Abstract–Random	Concentrating on one thing at a time and working on their own in a restrictive environment with time limits.
Concrete–Random	Working where there are restrictions and limitations on their learning. Keeping records and producing formal reports.
Concrete–Sequential	Working in groups and engaging in abstract discussions. Following incomplete or unclear instructions and using their imagination.

In the classroom

- Accept that in any group of learners, there will be a range of different ways of thinking.
- Don't teach in a way that caters for only one style of thinking.
- Encourage learners to come out of their comfort zones and try out different ways of thinking about a subject.

Critical Perspective

What value is there in encouraging learners to come out of their comfort zones and try out different ways of thinking about a subject?

For more on Gregorc's ideas, read:

Gregorc, A.F. (2006) *The Mind Styles Model: Theory, Principles and Practice*. Columbia, OH: Gregorc Associates.

The Myers-Briggs Type Indicator (MBTI) was developed by Myers and Briggs in the 1960s. It is built on four different scales, first suggested by Carl Jung, as a way to describe personality types. The scales can be summarised as:

The **Extrovert (E)-Introvert (I)** scale explores how people respond and interact with the outside world. Extroverts are usually action-orientated and enjoy frequent social interaction whereas Introverts are thoughtful thinkers who enjoy solitude.

The **Sensors (S)-Intuitors (N)** scale explores how people gather information from the outside world. Sensors focus on facts and details and enjoy hands-on experiences whereas Intuitors pay more attention to patterns and impressions and enjoy speculating and imagining future possibilities.

The **Thinkers (T)-Feelers (F)** scale explores how people make decisions from the information they gather. Thinkers place emphasis on facts and objective data and tend to be consistent, logical and objective when making decisions whereas Feelers are subjective and consider people and emotions when making decisions.

The **Judges (J)-Perceivers (P)** scale explores how people tend to deal with the outside world. Judges prefer structure and order whereas Perceivers are more flexible.

By using the MBTI, Myers and Briggs maintain you gain an indication of where you stand on each of the four scales. Myers and Briggs also indicate that the MBTI is not a test and there are no right or wrong answers. All types have equal value and there are no norms against which a personality type could be compared.

How to use it

In the MBTI there are four questions. Each question has two columns made up of a number of statements. The person is asked to choose which column best describes them. The responses indicate which end of the scale the individual's personality fits (E/I, S/N, T/F and J/P). These are then categorised into one of 16 personality types. For example people with preferences for being *Extroverts, Sensors, Thinkers* and *Judges* are categorised as *ESTJ*.

Doing one of these tests yourself before getting others to do it is a good start. Here are a few tips to help you out with planning approaches that cater for people with each personality type.

Personality type	Preferred learning style
ESTJ	Following directions to the letter and complete assignments on time.
ESTP	Learning about real things – sights, sounds and experiences.
ESFP	Trusting their instincts and abilities when solving problems.
ESFJ	Being in situations where things are certain or controlled.
ENFP	Not having to deal with routine and uninspiring tasks.
ENFJ	Speculating on how others may be affected.

Personality type	Preferred learning style
ENTP	Generating new ideas and theories rather than detail.
ENTJ	Avoiding confrontation or heated discussion.
ISTJ	Working with clearly defined schedules and assignments.
ISTP	Learning and understanding how things work.
ISFP	Working on concrete information rather than abstract theories.
ISFJ	Sitting back and observing others.
INFP	Solving problems based on their personal values rather than logic.
INFJ	Expressing themselves on paper.
INTP	Being encouraged to share their thoughts with others.
INTJ	Working by themselves rather than in groups.

Although the MBTI is a useful tool in helping to forecast how someone's personality may affect their thinking, it's not infallible.

In the classroom

- Understand that in any group of learners, there will be a range of different personalities.
- Don't prepare learning materials that cater for only one personality type.
- Accept that you may not be able to change a person's personality so may have to work around this as their teacher.

Critical Perspective

Critics of the MBTI claim that it mistakenly assumes that personality falls into mutually exclusive categories. For example, you are *either* an extrovert *or* an introvert, but never a mix of the two. How do you feel about this?

For more on Myers–Briggs' ideas, read:

Briggs, K. and Myers, I.B. (1975) *The Myers-Briggs Type Indicator*. Palo Alto, CA: Consulting Psychologist Press.
Briggs, K. and Myers, I.B. (1980) *Gifts Differing*. Palo Alto, CA: Consulting Psychologist Press.

Sternberg used the terms *thinking* and *learning* synonymously. He proposed a model for thinking/learning styles based on a metaphor of mental self-government. In the metaphor, peoples' minds are described as systems that need to be organised and governed in much the same way as society needs to be.

There are 13 thinking/learning styles in this model: four are based on forms of government; three on functions of government; two on levels of government; two on scope of government; and two on political leanings. The styles are generally categorised as:

Government styles:

- **Monarchic**: single-minded and determined, they like to focus on one thing at a time.
- **Hierarchic**: systematic and organised, they like to do many things at the same time.
- **Oligarchic**: flexible but have difficulty in prioritising which things to do and when to do them.
- **Anarchic**: like to challenge authority and dislike systems, guidelines and constraints.

Government functional styles:

- **Legislative**: like to do things their own way and set their own rules.
- **Executive**: like to follow directions and do what they are told to do.
- **Judicial**: like to judge and evaluate people and things.

Levels of government styles:

- **Global**: abstract thinkers who like to deal with the big picture.
- **Local**: concrete thinkers who like to deal with details.

Scope of government styles

- **Internal**: introverted and self-sufficient.
- **External**: extroverted and relies on the support of others.

Leaning of government styles:

- **Liberal**: pushes boundaries and defies conventions.
- **Conservative**: adheres to rules and follows conventions.

Sternberg argues that most people tend toward one style in each category, although these preferences may vary with the task or situation.

How to use it

The *Mental Self-Government (MSG) Thinking Styles Inventory* has around 100 statements relating to different scenarios. It uses a Likert Scale from 1 (doesn't fit me well at all) to

7 (fits me extremely well) to determine how people react to each scenario. From this, a picture begins to emerge of how people's minds are governed when faced with a learning situation.

Here are some tips to help you with planning approaches that cater for people with each thinking/learning style.

- *Hierarchic* and *oligarchic* learners respond better to formal instructions; whereas *monarchic* and *anarchic* learners learn better from project working.
- *Judicial* learners enjoy analytical work whereas *executive* learners thrive on your direction and *legislative* learners like to be creative.
- *Global* learners like to work on abstract ideas whereas *local* learners prefer concrete ideas.
- *Internal* learners prefer working independently whereas *external* learners enjoy group activities.
- *Liberal* learners will challenge you whereas *conservative* learners are likely to agree with your viewpoint.

The key to effective teaching is variety and flexibility so, in order to accommodate an array of thinking and learning styles, systematically vary your teaching and assessment methods to reach every learner.

In the classroom

- Do the test yourself.
- Get your learners to do the test.
- Accept that there will be a number of different learning styles in any group and have materials and teaching methods that cater for this.

Critical Perspective

Is it your responsibility to cater for the different array of thinking styles within your class or is it their responsibility to adapt their style of thinking to take account of your teaching style?

For more on Sternberg's ideas, read:

Sternberg, R. J. (1990) Intellectual styles: Theory and classroom implications. In R. McClure (ed.), *Learning and Thinking Styles: Classroom Interaction*. Washington, DC: National Education Association.
Sternberg, R.J. (2016) *Cognitive Psychology* (7th edn). Belmont, CA: Thomson Wadsworth.

Section 2.3: Motivation

Motivation is a complex issue to get to grips with. Definitions will vary from it being an external action (*the thing you do to get others to do something*) to being an inner force (*something that happens inside people that gets them to do something*).

If you want to become a good teacher, recognise that people will only be motivated to learn if they:

- accept they have a need to learn
- believe they have the potential to learn
- put learning as a priority.

If there is a blockage at any of the three points, you need to address this as any further attempts at teaching may be futile.

This section consists of three famous theories on motivation which will help you to ensure your learners have the right level of motivation to want to learn. The principles on which all three are based are that the people you are teaching will be more disposed to learn if you:

- have good classroom facilities and equipment available
- let learners have a say in the design and delivery of the lesson
- are knowledgeable and enthusiastic about the subject
- act in an approachable but professional manner
- set challenging but realistic learning objectives
- give feedback on work in a timely, positive and helpful manner.

Poor motivation may not just affect a learner's capacity to learn but may also contribute to any disruptive behaviour they may display. Generating good motivation may prevent you having to deal with disruptive behaviour.

Alderfer maintained that human motivation could be separated into three distinct categories: *existence*, *relatedness* and *growth*. He argued that there was a progression from *existence* to *growth* through *relatedness* driven by satisfaction and a regression in the opposite direction driven by frustration.

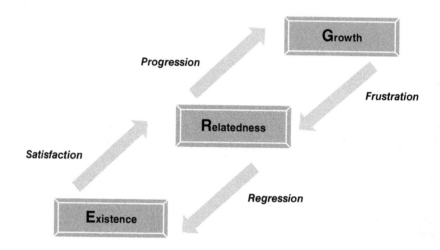

Each of these categories can be summarised in respect of teaching and learning as:

- **Existence**: this is where learner satisfaction can be achieved through survival or physiological well-being. These are where the basic needs such as comfort, heating and lighting are being met.
- **Relatedness**: this is where satisfaction can be achieved through good interpersonal and social relationships within the classroom. The emphasis here is on psychological well-being and a sense of belonging.
- **Growth**: this is where learner satisfaction can be achieved through the attainment of respect and self-actualisation. The emphasis here is on personal development.

Alderfer claims that, although there is a progression from *existence* to *growth*, the likelihood of regression shouldn't be ignored and in some instances may be necessary to ensure learners are given every opportunity for personal growth.

How to use it

The main difference between this model and Maslow's hierarchy of needs (see Theory 26) is that Alderfer stresses the importance of addressing all three needs simultaneously and accepts that regression to a lower level might not be a bad thing.

One of the greatest footballers of all time, in my opinion, was George Best. George had it all: incredible ball skills, good looks, fame and fortune. Inevitably, there was a flaw in his character and his struggle to handle his alcohol addiction and subsequent death at the age of 59 has been well-documented elsewhere. The lack of people around him to support him when he needed to regress back to physiological well-being may have been a major factor in this.

Here are some tips as to how to use the ERG model:

- Ensure your learners' basic needs are being met. These are issues that are sometimes taken for granted such as heating and ventilation in the classroom, comfortable seating, learning aids that cater for learners with hearing or visual disabilities and a generous helping of comfy breaks.
- Encourage social interaction within the class. Start any new programme with an ice-breaker. Make sure that in any small group activities, you mix the learners around so that they are given an opportunity to work with each other.
- Accept that, unlike the first two stages, you may only have a limited amount of control over whether or not your learners achieve self-actualisation. Acknowledging effort as well as achievement will go a long way to helping them on the journey to self-actualisation.
- Remember that there may be points on the journey when your learner needs to turn back or regress to one of the lower levels. If this happens, work with them to ensure they don't regress beyond the point of no return. This will require some understanding on your part and acceptance that you may have to do something to support them.

In the classroom

- Ensure learners' basic physiological and psychological needs are being met.
- Acknowledge your learners' efforts as well as their achievements.
- Accept that some learners may have to go back to the lower levels before they can progress towards self-actualisation.

Critical Perspective

Alderfer argues that ice-breakers are a good way of promoting good interpersonal and social relationships in the classroom. Make a list of useful ice-breakers and their pros and cons.

For more on the ERG model, read:

Alderfer, C.P. (1972) *Existence, Relatedness, and Growth; Human Needs in Organizational Settings.* New York: Free Press.

Alderfer, C.P. (1977) Improving organizational communication through long-term intergroup intervention. *Journal of Applied Behavioral Science, 13,* 193–210.

Vroom's expectancy theory is based on the belief that a person will behave in a certain way based on their belief (expectation) that a specific act will be followed by a desired reward (valence) once the act has been completed satisfactorily (instrumentality). Vroom expresses his theory in terms of a mathematical equation:

Motivation = Expectation x Valence x Instrumentality

The terms in this equation can be summarised as:

- **Expectation**: this is a subjective measure of the learner's belief in themselves and their confidence in being able to achieve the results expected of them.
- **Valence**: this measures the value the learner attaches to a given reward.
- **Instrumentality**: this measures the extent to which the learner believes their teacher will deliver the rewards promised.

Vroom argues that the lower any of the factors on the right hand side of the equation are, the lower the level of motivation will be, and, if either of the factors on the right hand side of the equation equals zero then the resulting motivation will be zero.

How to use

Although your learners won't consciously attach scores to each of the factors on the right hand side of Vroom's equation, they will be thinking in terms of: 'Can I do this?', 'How much do I want it?' and 'Will you do what you've said you'll do when I've done it?' Here are three trainee teachers all enrolled on the same course:

- Darren's opening retort when I asked him why he wanted to do the course was that he didn't want to be there and was only doing the course because he needed the qualification to be able to carry on with his job.
- Leoni desperately wanted to be a teacher but lacked the basic confidence in her ability to stand in front of people.
- Katie had such a bad experience at school, where her dyslexia wasn't diagnosed, that she mistrusted teachers.

Here are some tips to help you keep a healthy right hand side of the equation:

- Strengthen the **valence** link by finding out what it is that your learners want out of the session. This will help you to create the rewards they really cherish. Be prepared for some learners to be driven by extrinsic rewards (qualifications, career enhancement) and others by intrinsic rewards (self-esteem, recognition). Avoid being critical if their drivers aren't compatible with your beliefs about what the teaching is intended to achieve.
- Strengthen the **expectation** link by supporting your learners to believe in themselves (see Theory 3). Make sure you acknowledge effort just as much as you do achievement.

- Strengthen the **instrumentality** link by keeping your promises (see Theory 43). Never make promises that you cannot keep. Telling someone they will pass the course is wrong – there are many factors that may influence this.

Remember that it will be no good delivering fully on two of the three components if you fail to deliver on the third. Luckily I had read Vroom's theory before teaching Darren, Leoni and Katie as all three passed the course and are now successful teachers.

In the classroom

- Make sure the rewards on offer are things the learner really desires.
- Encourage your learners to believe in themselves.
- Always keep your promises and distance yourself from those who don't.

Critical Perspective

There are three factors on the right-hand side of Vroom's equation. Think about a group or individual learner that you are teaching at the moment. Which do you think is (a) the most and (b) the least important to them?

For more on expectancy theory, read:

Vroom, V.H. and Yetton, P.W. (1973) *Work and Motivation, Leadership and Decision Making.* Pittsburgh: University of Pittsburgh Press.
Vroom, V.H. and Jago, A.G. (1988) *The New Leadership.* London: Pearson.

McGregor's theory was originally used to categorise managers. It can however be applied equally well to learners and teachers. The theory is based on a set of assumptions that represents an extreme view. The extremes can be summarised as:

- **Theory X learners** dislike work and will avoid it if possible. They lack interest in the subject and are unambitious. They prefer to be told what to do.
- **Theory Y learners** find work stimulating and interesting. They are fascinated by learning new subjects and are keen to use newly acquired skills and knowledge. They work well on their own initiative.
- **Theory X teachers** rely on coercion and external stimuli to promote a change in behaviour. They believe it is their responsibility to structure learning programmes and energise their learners.
- **Theory Y teachers** rely on their learners to have the inner desire to want to learn. They believe it is their responsibility to create the climate where self-motivated learners will flourish.

In this interpretation, it is important to stress that not all *X-rated* teachers are bad and not all *Y-rated* teachers are good. There's room for both approaches, given the nature of the learners and the context in which learning is taking place. Other issues such as the subject matter and the timeframe for learning need to be taken into account.

How to use it

Let's go to the movies to try to make sense of this:

Theory X Teachers - Theory X Learners

X meets X has been the plot of a number of recent movies, such as *Bad Teacher* and *Rewrite*. In most instances, the teachers were just in it for the money and the learners were there out of some statutory obligation to attend. I guess a typical start to any lesson would be 'neither of us wants to be here so let's get on with it'.

Theory X Teachers - Theory Y Learners

This is typified by Michael Caine's role as the disillusioned teacher in *Educating Rita*. He meets Rita, played by Julie Walters, and her love of learning turns a hopeless situation into a meaningful teacher–learner relationship.

Theory Y Teachers - Theory X Learners

In *To Sir, with Love*, Sydney Poitier plays an enthusiastic black teacher, teaching in an inner-city school where the pupils are disruptive and have no interest in learning. He wins them over with his liberal approach to teaching and his genuine interest in his learners.

Theory Y Teachers - Theory Y Learners

Films such as *Beautiful Minds* and *Dead Poets Society* come to mind where both teachers and learners share a love of the subject.

Here are some tips:

- Don't assume that your default position as a teacher should always be to embrace Theory Y to the total exclusion of Theory X. The reality is that you may have to deal with learners who need to be directed and, on occasions, coerced.
- If this does happen, your style will be about command and control. Try not to let this slip into intimidating or threatening. You may get a quick result from this but you can forget any long-term development.
- The other side of the coin is the danger you run of being seen as weak and a bit of a pushover if you are too compliant with the needs of your learners.
- It may be that the ideal is an approach somewhere between the two extremes where cooperation and compromise dovetail with command and control.

In the classroom

- Don't think that you must always revert to type as an X- or Y-rated teacher.
- Take into account the characteristics of your learners and the context that learning is taking place in when deciding which approach works best.
- Always have a set of ground rules that both you and your learners sign up to.

Critical Perspective

Do you consider that you have a tendency to be more of an X-rated or a Y-rated teacher? What are the factors that lead you to make this consideration of yourself?

For more on McGregor's ideas, read:

McGregor, D (1985) *The Human Side of Enterprise.* New York: McGraw Hill.
Petty, G. (2014) *Teaching Today: A Practical Guide* (5th edn). Oxford: Oxford University Press.

McClelland argued that individuals are motivated by one of three needs: *achievement, power* or *affiliation*.

Each of the needs can be summarised as:

- **Achievement (N-Ach)**: this is the learner's desire for recognition of work well done. N-Ach positives are that they are highly motivated. The downsides may be that they have a fear of failure.
- **Power (N-Pow)**: this is the learner's desire to be in charge. N-Pow positives are that they drive others to high performance standards. The downsides are that they may be detached and driven too much by personal ambition.
- **Affiliation (N-Aff)**: this is the learner's desire for friendly interaction and to be accepted by others. N-Aff positives are that they are loyal and good team players. The downsides are that they may lose focus on tasks if social events take over.

McClelland suggested that, although one need may dominate, some individuals will also need to satisfy elements of the other two.

How to use it

Let's take a trip to the movies to see McClelland's need theory in action.

The one thing the UK has an abundance of is great actresses; and one of the very best is Maggie Smith. Arguably her best role was as Jean Brodie in the film *The Prime of Miss Jean Brodie*. In the film, she plays a slightly eccentric teacher at a Scottish girls' school who ignores the curriculum to influence her impressionable 12-year-old pupils in the worlds of love, politics and art. Three of her class include: Eunice (*N-Ach*), a talented athlete who craves recognition for her abilities; Sandy (*N-Pow*), who tries to emulate her respected teacher; and Joyce (*N-Aff*), a new pupil at the school who desperately wants to be part of the set. Brodie believes that she has 100% support from her pupils but one betrays her because she believes Brodie can no longer satisfy her needs. Which one? Watch the film, it's great.

Once you have identified what needs learners have, here are some tips to help you satisfy these needs:

- Give *N-Ach* learners as much personal responsibility as you feel comfortable giving them but be aware that their fear of failure may inhibit them. If they do make mistakes, reassure them that failing an assignment doesn't make them a failure.
- Keep a watchful eye on the *N-Pow* learners. Don't stifle their commitment but don't allow them to get carried away with their own importance if this is having a negative effect on the rest of the class.
- It's always good to have some *N-Aff* learners in the class but make sure they don't let their desires to want to be liked affect their capacity to learn.

This is arguably one of the more difficult models to actually apply in the classroom. You want to treat all learners in a fair and equitable manner, whilst recognising they have individual needs that should be satisfied. Getting the right balance will take time and application.

In the classroom

- Reassure people who make mistakes that they can bounce back.
- Don't let the people who crave power undermine your authority.
- Encourage learners not to let their desires to have good social relationships in the class undermine their studies.

Critical Perspective

How difficult is it going to be for you to strike a balance between treating all learners in a fair and equitable manner whilst recognising that they have individual needs that need to be satisfied?

For more on McClelland's ideas, read:

McClelland, D.C. (1965) Toward a theory of motive acquisition. *American Psychologist*, 20(5), 321-333.

McClelland, D.C. (1988) *Human Motivation*. Cambridge: Cambridge University Press.

Curzon's interpretation of educational theory and its application to teaching practice makes him one of the most respected writers on the subject. His 14-point plan for motivating learning is taken from some of the great thinkers in the field of education. The 14 points can be summarised as:

- Each learner's motivation and goals should be understood.
- Goals that are too hard or too easy to attain have no motivational value.
- Short-term goals should be explained to the learner in relation to desired long-term outcomes.
- Lessons should be planned by the teacher as part of a scheme of work that will lead to desired outcomes.
- Tasks set by the teacher should reflect the learner's level of ability.
- Attainment of a required level of competence should be perceived by the learner as part of the learning journey, not the destination.
- Lesson material and teaching ought to be meaningful and presented enthusiastically.
- Learners should be able to understand what the teacher is telling them.
- Teaching and learning activities should be varied so as to prevent learners becoming bored.
- Don't just rely on rewards and punishments to motivate learners.
- Use frequent assessment to test whether or not learners are taking in what you are teaching them.
- Give learners feedback on performance as soon as possible.
- Effort and achievement should be acknowledged as often as possible.
- Let learners know that if they have failed a test, they need to learn from the failure.

Curzon argues that a learner's attitude to learning is often dictated by their motivation, which in turn will determine the style, nature and direction of their approach.

How to use it

Here are some steps to follow:

- Take time out to discuss with each learner what they expect from your teaching and what you expect from them. Match the learning goals to these expectations. Don't make the goals too hard as to dishearten them or too easy as to make them complacent.
- Show the learner how each lesson objective dovetails with the long-term learning intentions as set out in the course aims and scheme of work.
- Set challenging but achievable tasks. Aim for one level above that of the learner's current level of ability but explain to the learner that this is only part of the learning journey, not the ultimate destination.
- Make your learning materials interesting and meaningful but not beyond the learners' level of understanding. Use formative assessment throughout the lesson to confirm understanding.

- Present the material with enthusiasm and in a way that will excite or stimulate your learners' curiosity. Do this by involving them in group activities and presenting them with problems to solve.
- Let your learners know how they have done on tasks as soon as possible after the task has been completed. Don't rely on rewards or punishments for success and failure. Make sure that you acknowledge effort as well as achievement.
- Let learners know that if they have failed a test, they are not a failure but that they need to learn from the failure.

In the classroom

- Make sure that you and the learners fully appreciate what's expected of each other.
- Set challenging but achievable tasks.
- Give feedback on effort as well as achievement as soon as possible after the task has been undertaken.

Critical Perspective

A key theme throughout Curzon's points is the need to involve learners in the design of their learning programmes. To what extent do you agree with this?

For more on motivation ideas, read:

Curzon, L.B. (2013) *Teaching in Further Education* (7th edn). London: Continuum.

Dweck is Professor of Psychology at Columbia University. She has developed a well-respected theory of learner motivation based on the learner's own beliefs about their ability to accomplish tasks, achieve goals and function successfully in life. She suggests that people have two extremes of belief about themselves:

- People who believe their ability is fixed and there is very little they can do to improve it.
- People who believe their ability is enhanced by learning.

She argues that about 20% of learners are in the middle of these extremes and that the rest are equally divided between the two extremes. She categorises the extremes into **fixed mindsets** (intelligence is static) and **growth mindsets** (intelligence can be developed).

Dweck identifies a number of interventions that she feels will motivate learners towards developing *growth mindsets*. These can be summarised as:

- **Intelligence**: demonstrate that this isn't fixed and can be developed through hard work and the accumulation of knowledge and understanding.
- **Potential**: convince the learner that full potential can only be reached through constant learning.
- **Validation**: show the learner that they can become whoever they wish and should never have to try to justify themselves to others.
- **Challenge**: get them to welcome challenge and be willing to take reasonable risks to overcome this and improve.
- **Learning**: get them to value learning for what it will do for them.

Dweck argues *growth mindset* learners are motivated by inner desires to improve rather than by external stimuli. In this respect, none of the above interventions will work unless the learner is intrinsically motivated to want them to work.

How to use it

As teachers, we often assume that learning will inevitably lead to achievement and is therefore worth the effort. According to a number of research reports, nearly half of learners at all levels don't share this view.

At a recent international conference on offender learning, one of the delegates was dismissive about her organisation's efforts in supporting offenders on training programmes. She told the audience that none of the dozen offenders they had been working with had gained a qualification. I told her that if the only measure of success was related to the achievement of qualifications, then she had every right to be critical of the organisation's performance. I advised her that what she really needed to be measuring was the journey travelled by each offender in terms of improvements in self-esteem and confidence in their approach to learning.

Here are a few tips if you want to motivate your learners to have a growth mindset:

- Praise effort as much as you praise results.
- Don't make praise person-centred as this implies it's a fixed mindset attribute. Sell them the idea that success comes from hard work.
- Don't teach them that failure is down to personal weaknesses. Teach them to interpret failure in terms of lack of effort.
- Impress on them that knowledge and skills can be cultivated and that effort is required for learning.
- Make use of analogies, metaphors and role models to demonstrate just what can be achieved through hard work and effort.
- Don't allow learners to blame you or the assignments you set as the reason they may have failed the assignment. Get them to reflect on the effort they put in or the strategies they adopted to prepare for the assignment.
- Convince your learners that every setback is a challenge and that failure is the ultimate challenge. In this respect, every challenge should be viewed as an opportunity to improve.

In the classroom

- Make sure that you praise effort as much as you praise results: use phrases such as 'you really tried hard there' rather than 'you're naturally good at this'.
- Don't allow learners who fail to consider themselves a failure. Get them to analyse what went wrong and put it right next time.
- Encourage the use of self-assessment and peer assessment.

Critical Perspective

Do you agree that the journey travelled on a learning experience is more important than the destination?

For more on Dweck's ideas, read:

Dweck, C.S. (2000) *Self-theories: Their Role in Motivation, Personality, and Development (Essays in Social Psychology)*. Philadelphia: Taylor and Francis.
Dweck, C.S. (2012) *Mindset: How you can Fulfil your Potential*. London: Robinson.

SECTION 2.4: BEHAVIOUR MANAGEMENT

Read through the following scenarios and see which one applies to you the most:

- Scenario A: You feel completely relaxed and comfortable during lessons and able to undertake any form of lesson activity without concern. Class control is not really an issue as you and your learners are working together, enjoying the experiences involved. You are completely in control of the class but may need to exercise some authority at times to maintain a calm and purposeful working atmosphere. This is done in a friendly and relaxed manner and is no more than a gentle reminder to your learners. **You believe that teaching is a great profession.**
- Scenario B: Learners determine what goes on in the lesson. The use of resources is largely ignored by learners. When you write on the board, items are being thrown around. You go into the room hoping they will chat to each other and leave you alone. Sometimes your entry into the room is greeted by derision and abuse. There are so many rules being broken you feel it is difficult to know where to start. You start to turn a blind eye to appalling behaviour because you are afraid that any intervention could lead to confrontation or escalation of the problem. **You wish you hadn't gone into teaching.**

If it's always Scenario A, I guess you can skip this section. If it's always Scenario B, you may need to do some serious thinking about your future in teaching. The likelihood is that you will flit between these two extremes depending on how both you and your learners are feeling on a particular day. Now, there's an interesting suggestion that a learner's bad behaviour could be as much a result of your actions as it is of theirs.

In this section, I've included six lines of thought which offer a different perspective on behaviour management, varying from the suggestion that teacher-learner relationships are based on mutual trust and respect to the belief that all learners are psychopaths.

anter argued that the rights and needs of teachers and learners are best met when both the teacher and the learner clearly communicate their expectations to each other and consistently follow up with appropriate action that never violates the best interests of the other person. He believed that uncertainty over expectations would often lead to passive or aggressive behaviour on the part of the teacher or learner which in turn would fail to create an optimum teaching or learning environment.

The consequences of acting passively, aggressively or assertively can be explained as:

Canter's ideas on the expectations of teachers and learners in respect of classroom discipline can be expressed as:

Teachers have the right to:

- establish classroom rules and procedures that are in their interests as well as their learners
- insist on reasonable levels of behaviour by their learners
- expect support when imposing discipline or sanctions.

Learners have the right to:

- have teachers who will help them to limit their inappropriate behaviour
- have teachers who will encourage them to display their appropriate behaviour
- choose how to behave in full knowledge of the consequences of their actions.

Canter argues that compliance to rules has evolved from the authoritarian approach of the twentieth century, in which ground rules were imposed, to a more democratic and cooperative approach, in which ground rules are agreed.

How to use it

Let's be clear about this - you have rights just as much as your learners. In the same way that learners have an expectation that you will behave in a professional manner, so you should expect that no learner should be allowed to prevent you from teaching or keeping another learner from learning.

ASSERTIVE DISCIPLINE

Darren taught IT to a group of 16–18-year-olds. One of his learners, Jacob, a quiet hard-working member of the class, wore his hoodie during lessons. Darren was constantly asking Jacob to remove the hoodie and, frustrated by his refusal, excluded Jacob from the class. Darren's line manager explained that excluding Jacob would result in the organisation losing funding and asked that he be allowed to return to class. Jacob returned and continued to wear his hoodie.

This is a common situation that could have been the learner chewing gum or using a mobile phone. Before responding to the situation, you need to know what your organisation's policies are on discipline.

Here are some tips for applying *assertive discipline* in the classroom:

- Discuss with your learners which rules you all feel comfortable with.
- Have a small number of *given rules* such as non-threatening behaviour and respect for others' views that you had prepared earlier.
- Be willing to compromise on rules that learners might feel unreasonable.
- Agree what are acceptable negative consequences (sanctions) for non-compliance with the rules.
- Agree what are acceptable positive consequences (rewards) for compliance with the rules.
- Write up the rules and give everyone (including your line management) a copy and/or display these in a prominent position.
- If anyone infringes the rules, make them aware that it is *their* rules they are breaking.
- Don't forget to catch someone out doing something good.

In the classroom

- Involve learners in setting the ground rules.
- Agree what are acceptable consequences for compliance or infringement of the ground rules.
- Have some ground rules where no tolerance is given but also have some on which there is some compromise.

Critical Perspective

What do you think about the way that the situation between Darren and Jacob was handled? Have you encountered similar problems? How did you deal with them?

For more on Canter's ideas, read:

Canter, L. and Canter, M. (1992) *Assertive Discipline*. Los Angeles: Canter and Associates.

Kounin studied the approaches of a number of teachers who were regarded as outstanding by their peers. His research indicated that it wasn't the teachers' abilities to deal with misbehaviour that was important but in how they prevented learners misbehaving in the first place. He identified three key actions that contributed to this:

Reacting to learners - these are the signals that teachers give out to their learners and include:

- the *ripple effect*, where the reaction of the teacher to an individual's behaviour impacts on the wider group, not just the individual it is aimed at
- *withitness*, which refers to the teacher needing to be aware of what's going on, and for learners to be aware of this
- *overlapping*, where the teacher tends to two or more events in the classroom simultaneously, rather than focusing on one at the expense of the other(s).

Movement management - this is defined as the extent to which a lesson proceeds smoothly without digressions, diversions or disruptions and includes:

- *smoothness*, which involves keeping the lesson moving and avoiding abrupt changes
- *momentum*, which refers to maintaining an appropriate pace and progression throughout the lesson.

Group focus - this involves keeping the whole class engaged and interested in the subject matter and includes:

- *group alerting*, where the whole group becomes engrossed in the subject matter
- *group accountability*, which involves the teacher making the class aware that their understanding of the subject matter will be tested.

Kounin claims that as well as engaging learners in the lesson, teachers need to tackle both the signs that are the basis for the cause of the undesired behaviour and the pay-offs for good and bad behaviour in order to keep behaviour problems to a minimum.

How to use it

Moussa is 10 and has severe behavioural issues. When one of his classmates, Sadiq, enters the room, Moussa goes into an uncontrollable frenzy, shouting and waving his arms. There doesn't appear to be any history of antagonism between Moussa and Sadiq, and Sadiq is a mild individual who does nothing to provoke Moussa. The only redress that Moussa's teachers have is to remove him from the class to what they call the *zone*. This is a quiet area away from the main classroom where pupils are encouraged to reflect on their action. After about an hour of reflection, Moussa usually returns to the classroom as if nothing has happened. At his appraisal, with teachers and parents, Moussa's mother asked if he could be allowed more time in the *zone* as he preferred this to being in class.

To make use of Kounin's model:

- Assess the extent of the undesired behaviour. Maintain a stage of relaxed vigilance and decide what impact this is having on others.
- Be aware that learners will pick up on any signs of you not being 'with it'. Dealing with issues too aggressively will damage the rapport you may have with your learners. Being too passive may give them the impression that you are weak. Try to go for an 'I win – you win' situation (see Theory 58).
- Don't allow your focus to be dominated by having to deal with one event at the expense of others. You will have to deal with Moussa's outbursts but need to maintain a watchful eye on the rest of the group.
- Make sure your lessons flow well and your learners are engaged. It's often when uncertainty and boredom set in that misbehaviour occurs.
- Determine what the desired behaviour is going to be like. Look for the signs that may be triggering the undesired behaviour. Focus on signs not causes and make sure that the pay-off is going to be a deterrent rather than an encouragement for undesired behaviour. Have a plan for changing the pay-off if it's not working.

Moussa's teachers had spent so much time trying to rationalise why he reacted so badly to Sadiq that they missed the now obvious point that it was the pay-off that caused the undesired behaviour not the signs. Once Moussa realised the pay-off was not what he wanted, he no longer reacted so badly to Sadiq.

In the classroom

- Assess what impact the undesired behaviour is having on the class.
- Look for the signs that may be triggering the behaviour.
- Make sure pay-off will actually deter the undesired behaviour.

Critical Perspective

What do you think about the way that Moussa's teachers dealt with his behaviour towards Sadiq? Have you encountered similar problems? How did you deal with them?

For more on Kounin's ideas, read:

Kounin, J.S. (1970) *Discipline and Group Management in Classrooms*. New York: Holt, Reinhart & Winston.

Hattie believed that how learners see themselves, and what they perceive as most important in terms of their learning and their desired outcomes, would have a significant effect on their motivation to learn and subsequent behaviour in class. He argued that research on the subject was divided into understanding the *structure* of self-concept (how we see ourselves) and the *processes* of self-concept (how we use what we find out about ourselves). He uses the metaphor of the *rope* to bring the strands together.

In the *rope model*, Hattie argues that there is no single strand underlying an individual's self-concept but many overlapping concepts of self. He categorises these as:

- **Self-efficacy**: this is the confidence, or strength of belief, that learners have in themselves that they can achieve the desired outcomes.
- **Self-handicapping**: this occurs when learners allow self-imposed obstacles to get in the way of their achieving.
- **Self-motivation**: these can be intrinsic or extrinsic factors that drive the learner towards achieving the desired outcomes.
- **Self-goals**: these could include mastery goals (something they can achieve through increased effort); performance goals (demonstrating expertise); or social goals (interacting and relating to their peers).
- **Self-dependence**: this occurs when learners become dependent on directions from their teacher and lack the capacity to regulate or evaluate their own performance.
- **Self-discounting and distortion**: this is when learners disregard positive and negative feedback from their teachers as not being worthwhile.
- **Self-perfectionism**: this is when learners set standards for themselves that may be too demanding and see it as failure when these aren't met.

Hattie suggests that the strength in the rope lies not in any single strand but in the combination of many overlapping strands. He claims that, when any of the strands become weak, the learner will start to experience such a sense of helplessness that they feel they can't cope with the learning. The result is that they disengage with learning activities and turn to challenging behaviour as a protection measure against being looked on by their peers as the class failure.

How to use it

Hattie talks a lot about his work with offenders in prison or under probation orders. The National Offender Management Service (NOMS) views education, training and employment as being a contributory factor of 25% towards someone not reoffending and the raising of self-esteem a further 15%.

YSS are a charity based in Worcestershire. They work with young offenders or young people at risk of offending. Their ethos is based on the importance of young people having self-belief in themselves and offering support to help the young person overcome barriers that are imposed by society or self-imposed. One of the young people they have helped commented that 'the probation service tell you what to do, YSS support you to do what you need to do'.

The key aspect of YSS' work, and the reason why their patron is HRH Princess Anne, is that the learners are given the freedom to choose which courses of action are important to them. In this respect, as Hattie claims, they impose some sense of order, coherence and predictability in their lives. Hattie's use of the *rope* metaphor is a powerful way of emphasising that there are overlapping concepts of self. Here are some tips to help spot when one of the strands of self-belief is beginning to weaken. The learner will:

- tend to avoid taking on difficult tasks, has little commitment to achieving goals and sees failure as a chance to dwell on personal deficiencies
- have little motivation towards undertaking tasks, choose easy achievable goals and exaggerate obstacles to success
- not see ability as something that can be developed by increased effort
- will only do what the teacher asks them to do
- dismiss feedback from the teacher or their peers as not valuable or worthwhile
- look for signs of weaknesses in others as a means of enhancing their own poor sense of self-worth.

These are self-concepts that can be worked on with the learner by encouraging them to be more pro-active in seeking learning opportunities, responding positively to feedback, setting themselves challenging goals and viewing learning as a positive experience.

In the classroom

- Look for any signs of lack of self-belief in your learners.
- Analyse the cause of the lack of self-belief.
- Work with the learner to improve their self-belief.

Critical Perspective

Hattie's rope model suggests that there are seven factors governing how learners see themselves that will determine how well they engage with learning. Look at some of your learners who are not engaging and see what, if any, of the seven factors are appropriate.

For more on Hattie's ideas, read:

Hattie, J. (2012) *Visible Learning for Teachers*. London: Routledge.
For more on YSS google their website: yss.org.uk.

Willingham's response to the question of why students don't like school, or more broadly why learners don't enjoy learning, is that teachers often overload learners with the irrelevant and unimportant and fail to direct learners' attention to what really matters.

As a cognitive scientist, Willingham argued that insight into how the mind works, and how memory functions, was the foundation for effective teaching. This insight would then provide the basis for engaging with learners and generating a genuine desire in them to want to learn. His ideas can be summarised as:

- *The mind has the capacity for working and long-term memory*: working memory has a limited capacity which can be easily overloaded. Long-term memory is a bank of almost unlimited capacity which draws its data from the working memory.
- *Memory is the residue of thought*: encouraging learners to think about a subject in a way they find interesting will enhance their capacity to remember the subject.
- *Critical thinking requires background knowledge*: analysis of a subject requires sufficient background knowledge of issues related to the subject to enable comparisons to be made.
- *Abstract concepts can be understood by comparing with concrete examples and analogies*: abstract ideas can be rationalised in the context of things already known and understood by the learner.
- *Learning is impossible without practice*: practice reinforces basic skills and protects against forgetting.
- *Novices can't learn like experts*: novices absorb and comprehend learning; experts create it.
- *Learning styles are futile*: effective teaching focuses on the content of the lesson, not differences in the learner's preferred style of learning.
- *Hard work improves intelligence*: good teachers acknowledge effort not just results.

Willingham advocates that learners' enjoyment of learning can be increased through the use of questions, case studies, stories, analogies and practice.

How to use it

Time for a confession:

I'll be honest, I didn't like school; or more precisely, I didn't like education because I felt that I was being spoon-fed stuff that had no relevance to me. It wasn't until I was in my mid-40s when, needing a management qualification to back up over 20 years' experience of managing in the Civil Service, I chose to do a Diploma in Management Studies (DMS). The course was designed to make you think; everything was built around the need to analyse case studies and solve problems. I was also introduced to the wonderful world of metaphors. To say that all of this awakened a desire to want to learn more is an understatement.

Here are some useful tips when trying to make sure your learners enjoy, and therefore get the best out of, their learning experience:

- Don't overload your learners with a mass of irrelevant or unimportant trivia. You may think that you are being clever by imparting all of this information but their working memory which has to process this information will not function effectively if you do this.
- Make sure that you organise ideas in the lesson so that learners find them interesting and easy to understand. The things that will go through the working memory into the long-term memory are the things that have had an impact on the learner, either because they were relevant or attention grabbing.
- Use things such as questions, examples, anecdotes, metaphors or mnemonics to make a topic memorable.
- Test your learners' prior knowledge of a subject and build on what they already know as a way of helping them to understand new material.
- Avoid focusing on your learners' individual learning styles and concentrate on the required learning outcomes when making decisions about how to teach.

In the classroom

- Focus only on issues that are relevant and important to the learners.
- Organise ideas so that learners will find them interesting and easy to follow.
- Test your learners' understanding of a subject and build on this.

Critical Perspective

Do you agree with Willingham's argument that students don't enjoy learning because teachers overload them with irrelevant and unimportant facts?

For more on Willingham's ideas, read:

Willingham, D. (2009) *Why Don't Students Like School*. San Francisco: Jossey Bass.

Although the title of Cowley's book may compel some people to buy it (and possibly others not to buy it), there are some interesting ideas in her work that earn her a place as an influential contemporary thinker on what to do when encountering misbehaviour in the classroom. One of the basic premises is that it is the frequency and nature of low-level incidents of misbehaviour that cause much of the stress in teaching. It's within the context of dealing with lower-level incidents of misbehaviour that Cowley would suggest her ideas can be best appreciated. A summary of her advice for teachers is:

- *Knowledge is power*: whatever system your organisation has in place for dealing with disciplinary matters, make sure that you fully understand it.
- *Arm yourself for the battle(s) ahead*: if you are uncertain about what is and isn't allowed, learners will sense your weakness and exploit it to their advantage.
- *Keep calm and consistent*: accept that your patience will be tested, and sometimes to the limit. Remember that you need to remain calm and consistent when this happens.
- *Give them structure*: give learners a clear, unambiguous explanation of what you expect from them in terms of their behaviour. The consequences of them falling short of these expectations should be spelt out as early as possible.
- *Be positive*: once you have established order within the classroom, try to catch your learners out doing something good.
- *Be interested*: developing a good relationship or rapport with your learners will influence them towards better behaviour in the classroom.
- *Be flexible*: learn when it may be appropriate to bend the rules a bit.
- *Be persistent*: if at first you don't succeed then persevere.

Cowley argues that there may be times when it seems appropriate to ignore minor behaviour problems. Doing this too often however could result in chaos breaking out. She suggests that with experience, a teacher will be able to judge each situation on its merits.

How to use it

Reflecting back over the many years that I spent in school and further education, I've tried to make sense of why the same group of learners (including me) were impeccably behaved in teacher A's geography class and awful in teacher B's English class. Teacher B seemed to welcome confrontation; often using sarcasm as his main weapon. I felt that he would often pick his fights with the wrong person, for the wrong reason at the wrong moment; resorting to imposing sanctions when he was losing. I can't ever remember teacher A acting in that way. A look from him was sufficient to stop even the most unruly member of the class in their tracks. He was also quick to praise effort, even when someone got the answer wrong but had at least tried.

Here are some key tips for *getting the buggers to behave*:

- If you are a new teacher (or even an experienced one), some learners will 'try it on' with you. If you are uncertain about what is and isn't allowed, learners will sense your weakness and exploit it to their advantage. Accept that your patience will be tested, and sometimes to the limit. When this happens, remember that you need to remain calm and consistent.

- A clear, unambiguous explanation of what you expect from your learners in terms of their behaviour and the consequences of their falling short of these expectations should be spelt out as early as possible. This will create a sense of order within the class. Once you have established this, try to catch your learners out doing something good. Always be on the lookout for good behaviour and acknowledge this by praising it in front of others.
- Take an interest in your learners' lives. Developing a good relationship or rapport with learners will influence them towards better behaviour in the classroom.
- Learn when it may be appropriate to bend the rules a bit. You don't want to come over as being a control freak who only does things by the book. Trust your instincts and judge each situation on its merits.
- If at first you don't succeed then persevere. Don't expect that behaviour management techniques will always work immediately; give them a chance before abandoning all hope or trying something completely different.

Oh, by the way, never call them a *bugger* to their face.

In the classroom

- Make sure you know your organisation's policies regarding discipline.
- Accept that some learners will try and test you out. Keep calm if they do.
- Don't be afraid to compromise if it's appropriate to do so. This will earn you respect rather than expose a weakness.

Critical Perspective

Do you agree with Cowley's statement that it is the frequency and nature of low-level incidents of misbehaviour that causes much of the stress in teaching?

For more on Cowley's ideas, read:

Cowley, S. (2014) *Getting the Buggers to Behave* (5th edn). London: Bloomsbury Education.

Hare developed the Psychopathic Checklist (PCL) as a means of diagnosing psychopathic traits in individuals for clinical, legal or research purposes. Here is a summary of how I have adapted Hare's theory, using my own headings, to show how the key traits could be found in the people that you are teaching.

- The **seducer**: the learner who charms others in a glib and superficial manner and tries to be in charge.
- The **ego-maniac**: the learner who has an exaggeratedly high estimation of their ability and refuses to accept criticism.
- The **sponge**: the learner who constantly needs to be stimulated and disrupts sessions that they feel are not challenging enough.
- The **procrastinator**: the learner who always comes up with excuses for not meeting assignment deadlines.
- The **shell**: the learner who shows no remorse or guilt if they offend you or other learners through inappropriate comments.
- The **unmovable rock**: the learner who displays callousness and a lack of empathy with other learners who may not share their point of view.
- The **parasite**: the learner who lives off the knowledge and skills of their peers and falsely claims credit for others' ideas.
- The **deflector**: the learner who fails to accept responsibility for their own actions and tries to blame others when things go wrong.
- The **results merchant**: the learner who lacks any drive for long-term development and is just obsessed with passing assignments.
- The **disrupter**: the learner who acts impulsively and irresponsibly and causes disharmony within the class.
- The **delinquent**: the learner who has poor control over their behaviour and frequently annoys or upsets their peers.

The model is only used here for illustrative purposes and serves to highlight extremes in people's behaviours that you may encounter.

How to use it

Should you encounter people displaying these traits in your class, I would advise you to:

- Assume that they will always do the worst thing possible within their trait characteristic.
- Have a strategy in mind for handling the worst possible scenario.
- If they don't do the worst thing possible, celebrate with a quiet drink and save the strategy for next time.
- If they do the worst possible thing, keep a clear head and follow the old boxing maxim of defending yourself at all times. Implement the planned strategy and keep a record of everything that was said or done. You can still have a quiet drink, but this time to relax.

- Make sure that you follow the rules and regulations set down by your organisation or licensing body for dealing with people. Even if you were in the right, failure to adhere to correct procedures could result in litigation against you or your organisation or disciplinary action.

It's worth making the point here that you will also almost certainly display some of these traits. You need to reflect on this and explore the impact that you have on others.

In the classroom

- Assume the psychopaths in your class will always do the worst you think they are capable of doing.
- Have a strategy for dealing with this.
- Accept that you will also display psychopathic tendencies.

Critical Perspective

I have suggested that any class that you are teaching has a mixture of students displaying psychopathic tendencies. What do you feel about this arguably contentious statement?

For more on the psychopaths, read:

Hare, R.D. (2003) *The Psychopathic Checklist – Revised* (2nd edn). Toronto: Multi-Health Systems.

Section 2.5: Coaching and Mentoring

So far, the emphasis has been on teaching. If the purpose of your involvement with the learner is to support the person to move towards achieving their learning outcomes, then you may be expected to act out the role of coach or mentor. You might think that coaching, mentoring and teaching are the same thing. It's important therefore that I discuss the differences in each of the approaches in terms of relationships, time, structure and outcome.

Teachers are usually trained professionals who work with people on developing their understanding of an issue. Coaches are also usually trained professionals but focus more on helping the person to develop specific skills. Mentors are usually experienced individuals who share knowledge and experiences with a less experienced person.

Teaching and coaching can be as short as a single session or part of a session that may be necessary for the person to develop understanding or a particular skill. Mentoring requires time to develop a relationship of mutual trust in which both partners can learn about one another and feel safe in sharing the real issues that the person is facing.

Teachers will respond to the individual's needs but may have a set structure to their approach. Coaches set the topic, the pace and the learning methods to help develop specific skills. Mentors will tailor their approaches to meet the individual's needs.

Teaching and coaching are task oriented with the focus on concrete issues and easy-to-measure performance outputs. Mentoring is relationship oriented with the focus on mutual development.

The one thing that unites each of the above interventions is that they seek some form of positive outcome for the learner. The thing that differentiates them is the level of challenge and direction that takes place: challenge in respect of getting people to deliver the desired outcomes; direction in terms of telling them what to do or getting them to think and do for themselves. This can be represented as:

Whitmore suggests that the GROW model is a simple but powerful way of structuring a coaching session. He likens it to thinking about planning a journey in which you decide where you are going (the *Goal*), establish where you are at present (the *Reality*), explore the various routes (the *Options*) and be committed to reaching your destination (the *Will* to succeed).

Watch the Growth

Establish the Will

Explore the Options

Examine the Current Reality

Establish the Goal

The various constituents of the model can be summarised as:

- *Establish the goal*: look at what the learner wants to achieve and express this in terms of what they will be like when they have achieved it.
- *Examine the current reality*: encourage the learner to avoid trying to solve problems before considering where they are at present.
- *Explore the options*: after exploring the reality, turn the learner's attention to determining what is possible.
- *Establish the will*: now that the options are clear, get the learner to commit to specific actions in order to move forward towards achieving their goal.

Whitmore stresses the importance of the coach not considering themself to be an expert in the other person's predicament and not trying to solve their problems for them. He describes the ultimate role of the coach as being a facilitator who helps the person to select the best options.

How to use it

The GROW model is relatively straightforward and the metaphor of organic growth is a good way of thinking about the model. The essence of good coaching, using this model, is asking good questions. Here are some useful questions that you could ask your client in each stage:

- **Establishing the goal**: to make sure that their goal is specific, measurable, achievable, realistic and time-bound (see Theory 111) ask them: 'How does this relate to your learning objectives?', 'When will you know that you have achieved your goal?', 'How confident are you that you can achieve this objective?', 'What is a realistic schedule for achieving the objective?'
- **Examining the reality**: to make sure that they don't start coming up with solutions before they've even considered where they stand at present ask: 'What is happening to you now?', 'How do you feel about what is happening?', 'What have you been doing to date to address the issue?', 'How does this issue impact on other issues you are facing?'
- **Explore the options**: avoid coming up with the options. Remember these may be your options as to how you would tackle the situation. You should however get the learner to consider the viability of each option by asking: 'What are the possible repercussions of adopting this option?', 'What could you do if something goes wrong?', 'What factors do you need to consider when weighing up an option?'
- **Establish the will**: having explored the options, you now need to get the learner to commit to specific courses of action by asking 'What will you do next?', 'When will you do it by?', 'How will you know that it's been done?'

Notice that all of the questions asked are open questions. Try to avoid asking closed questions that just require a 'yes' or 'no' answer. Make sure that when the person that you are coaching responds to your question, you listen in an attentive and non-judgemental manner. In this respect your body language may be more important that what you actually say.

In the classroom

- Make sure you set SMART lesson objectives.
- Get learners to reflect on where they are at present.
- Get learners to choose the most suitable option and get them to commit to it.

Critical Perspective

How important do you think it is for the coach to be an expert in the subject matter that they are coaching?

For more on the GROW model, read:

Bates, B. (2015) *The Little Book of Big Coaching Theories*. London: Pearson.
Whitmore, J. (1998) *Coaching for Performance*. London: Nicholas Brealey.

The *COACHING* model was developed by Bates after a comprehensive review of 76 theories and models related to coaching. Bates uses the acronym *COACHING* to represent eight key elements that he argues should be present in any coaching programme. Here is a summary of the elements:

- **Clarify the role**: establish who does what, when, where and how.
- **Organise goals and objectives**: get the people you are working with to have a vision about what they could be and set goals that will help them to achieve this vision.
- **Act with conviction**: choose the most appropriate method for coaching an individual/ group and see it through with conviction and commitment.
- **Confirm that expectations are being met**: elicit feedback not just on the outcome but on the process undertaken and be prepared to make changes if necessary.
- **Have a strategy for dealing with setbacks**: accept that bad things happen and deal with them.
- **Inspire creative thinking**: encourage the person you are coaching to be willing to think outside of the box.
- **Never be afraid of failure**: if the person you are coaching fails at a task, it doesn't mean that you or the individual is a failure; it simply means that they have failed the task.
- **Get to know the person you are coaching**: build a relationship that is based on respect and trust.

Bates suggests that the thing that differentiates coaching from other measures is the level of challenge and direction that takes place: challenge in respect of getting people to deliver the desired outcomes; direction in terms of telling them what to do or getting them to think and do it for themselves.

How to use it

Here are some tips in how to apply the model:

- Discuss what expectations you and the learner have of each other. Agree the ground rules and boundaries for the coaching relationship.
- Get your learner to have a vision about what they could be and set sessional and long-term goals that will help them to achieve this vision. Make sure the goals are *SMART* (see Theory 111).
- Whatever coaching method you choose, see it through with enthusiasm, conviction and commitment.
- Get feedback to confirm that expectations are being met. Don't do this just at the end of the coaching session; do it frequently throughout a session. Get feedback not just on the outcome but on the process undertaken and be prepared to make changes if necessary.

- Accept that bad things happen. It's how you deal with these setbacks that will define you as a person as well as a coach.
- Encourage the person you are coaching to be willing to think outside of the box. Great ideas or learning experiences rarely happen as a result of people doing the same thing over and over again. Coaching people to be competent is okay but supporting them to be creative is where the real value lies.
- Never be afraid of failure. If the person you are coaching fails at a task, it doesn't mean that you or the individual is a failure; it simply means that they have failed the task. Get them to analyse why they failed the task and what they can do differently next time.
- Build a relationship that is based on respect and trust. If you have this relationship, you can challenge someone, set difficult tasks or ask provocative questions, secure in the knowledge that this is being done with good intent.

In the classroom

- Agree who is responsible for doing what in the coaching relationship.
- Review progress frequently and adjust coaching methods if necessary.
- Advise the person you are coaching not to be afraid of failure.

Critical Perspective

What are the consequences for the coach and the person being coached if they don't have a clear understanding of the rules and boundaries of the coaching relationship?

For more on coaching, read:

Bates, B. (2015) *The Little Book of Big Coaching Models*. London: Pearson.

Bell devised a questionnaire for the purpose of determining whether or not some-one had the qualities to be a good mentor. The questionnaire (obtainable online) is based on a series of 39 questions with two possible answers. The individual is asked to indicate which of the two answers fits them best.

Examples of the questions and responses include:

- People see me as..... (a) Hard-nosed (b) A Soft-touch
- When it comes to social situations, I.....(a) Hold back (b) Jump in
- Work days that I like most are.....(a) Unpredictable (b) Well-planned
- My approach to planning my personal activities is.....(a) Easy-going (b) Orderly
- I prefer to express myself to others in ways that are.....(a) Indirect (b) Direct

Bell argues that the responses to these questions measure, at a given moment in time, the mentor's capacity for *sociability*, *dominance* and *openness*. These can be summarised as:

- **Sociability**: this relates to the mentor's preference for being with or apart from others. People with high sociability scores will find the rapport-building and dialogue-leading dimensions of mentoring easier.
- **Dominance**: this relates to the mentor's preference for being in charge. This is a major issue in mentoring, where the relationship is built on shared power. People with high dominance scores may be reluctant to share control.
- **Openness**: this relates to the mentor's capacity to trust others and to generate their trust in them. People with low openness scores are likely to be cautious, guarded and reluctant to show feelings.

Bell argues that the *mentor scale* is not there to judge or criticise someone as a person but to help evaluate their strengths and areas for development and to tease out any blind spots they have in terms of their ability to be a mentor.

How to use it

Although I have been fortunate to have had a positive influence on a number of peoples' lives, it's the few disasters that I have encountered that seem to stick in my mind. Harold was a skilled engineer who, like many of his contemporaries, was experiencing difficulties in the early 1970s in finding work in engineering. I had trained as an employment counsellor and was working with Harold to help him find work. I knew what was right for him and con-vinced him to switch from working in engineering to the service sector where there were jobs. I was notified of a job as a shop floor attendant with a major DIY store. I badgered Harold into applying. He went for an interview. He didn't get the job and shortly afterwards committed suicide.

I felt that I had built up an excellent relationship with Harold and that he trusted my judgement. Where I realise now that I went wrong was that I assumed the dominant role in the relationship; it was my solution to the problem, not his. Here are some tips to helping you become a better mentor:

- Take time getting to know one another. Draw up a picture of the person that you are working with through meaningful conversation. Establish rapport and identify areas of mutual interest.
- Discuss the purpose of the interaction. Find out what previous experience they have had of being mentored. Share some of your own experiences of mentoring or being mentored. This will demonstrate that you are able to understand and empathise with their feelings.
- Determine the individual's goals and what they want to get out of the relationship. Be absolutely sure about what they need from you.
- Describe what you feel you can and can't do. Don't build up a level of expectation of support that you can't provide.
- Share your assumptions, needs and limitations candidly.
- Discuss what opportunities and options exist and the most useful kind of assistance you can provide.

Telling the person that you are mentoring what to do may not be the best thing for them. Supporting them to decide for themselves will give them ownership of the issue.

An interesting corollary to Bell's mentor scale is that if you score low on the mentor scale, you may actually be more suited to being a coach.

In the classroom

- Take time to get to know the person you are mentoring.
- Find out what the mentee wants out of your mentoring.
- Be honest in what you feel you can, or can't, achieve with your mentee.

Critical Perspective

What do you think are the critical differences between a coach and a mentor?

For more on the mentor scale, read:

Bell, C. (2002) *Managers as Mentors*. San Francisco: Berrett-Kochler.

Costa and Kellick describe a *critical friend* as 'a trusted person who asks provoca-tive questions, provides a different perspective on an issue facing someone and critiques their actions with good intent'. They argue that it is the inherent tension within the term – friends bringing a high degree of unconditional positive regard, and crit-ics being negative and intolerant of failure – that makes it a powerful idea. They outline a six-stage process for the interaction that can be depicted as:

Each stage of the process can be summarised as:

- **Engagement**: the learner outlines the problem and asks the teacher for feedback.
- **Questioning**: the teacher as a critical friend asks questions in order to understand the roots of the problem and to clarify the context in which the problem is occurring.
- **Desired outcomes**: the learner is encouraged to set the desired outcomes for the interaction, thus ensuring they are in control.
- **Feedback**: the teacher provides feedback on what seems to be significant about the problem. This feedback should be more than a cursory look at the problem and should provide an alternative viewpoint that helps address the problem.
- **Reflection**: both parties reflect on what was discussed.
- **Recording**: the learner records their views on the points and suggestions raised. The teacher records the advice given and makes a note of what follow-up action they need to take.

Costa and Kallick describe the ideal for critical friendship as a 'marriage of unconditional support and unconditional critique'.

How to use it

San Patrignano is a village in eastern Italy. Just over 1300 people live there. What is unu-sual about the village is that over 80% of its residents are rehabilitating drug addicts. When I first encountered the village, I was amazed to find that there is no formal policing and hardly any crime. Law and order is maintained through a process of critical befriending, in which former addicts work on a one-to-one basis with new residents questioning and challenging their behaviour. Since its inception in 1978 with a handful of addicts living in a communal house, the village now has 250 employees, 100 volunteers, a school, hospital, restaurants and Italy's fourth best-rated pizzeria.

Here are some tips to helping you become a good critical friend with your learners:

- Don't allow your friendship with the learner to obscure the real issue that they are faced with. Placing too much stress on the friendship side of the role may compromise the need for a deep and critical exchange of views.
- Sympathising with their plight will get you nowhere and may even have a detrimental effect on coming up with a solution. The aim is for you to stimulate divergent thinking by introducing different views and fresh insights.
- Have a clear understanding of the boundaries that exist in the relationship.
- Set clear objectives of who will do what and by when.
- Review progress on the objectives at regular intervals.
- Reflect on the nature and appropriateness of the relations: do they need revising?
- Provide honest and critical feedback to your learner.
- Be willing to accept honest and critical feedback from your learner.

If you take on the role of critical friendship, remember it is less formal than mentoring or coaching and can be best described as a professional undertaking based on mutual regard and a willingness to question and challenge. If you are unable to function in either respect, don't assume the role.

In the classroom

- Make sure both you and the mentee understand where the boundaries are in the relationship.
- Never allow any sympathies you have for their plight to affect your objectivity.
- Be willing to give and accept honest feedback on what's taken place.

Critical Perspective

What do you think that Costa and Kallick meant when they described critical friendship as a 'marriage of unconditional support and unconditional critique'?

For more on critical friendship, read:

Costa, A. and Kallick, B. (1983) Through the lens of a critical friend. *Educational Leadership*, *51*(2), 49–51.
For more on San Patrignano, google their website: sanpatrignano.org.

SECTION 2.6: TEAMWORKING

I'm going to suggest that teachers are not, by nature, good team members. Watch a pack of wolves in one of David Attenborough's wonderful wildlife series isolate a weaker member of a herd of buffalos and move in for the kill and you may think that we could learn much about how other animals work as a team. See the same pack fight viciously over a small morsel of food and you may think otherwise.

Before I get hate mail from teachers who think that I'm likening them to scavengers fighting for meagre resources let me say that I'm suggesting nothing of the sort. We all know that the majority of teachers love sharing their learning materials, enjoy their work being critiqued by their colleagues and always put the interests of the team above any personal needs. Sadly, the *majority* doesn't mean all teachers subscribe to this view.

In order for people to find a reason to work as a member of a team, they need a common purpose and a sense of identity. Put a group of people in a lift together and they think and act as individuals. Create a crisis situation (a breakdown or fire) and the need for survival becomes the common purpose, with each individual assuming a role (leader, comforter, problem solver, etc.). Moving from mere survival as a team to effective operation and optimum performance is a process that requires understanding, commitment and great leadership.

In this section I want to consider the team as being either a departmental team or a group of learners. I look firstly at two theories related to team development: Tuckman's theory about the process that a team needs to go through to become effective and Wheelan's thoughts on how a group matures. The section is completed by a look at Buckley's ideas on the value of team teaching. Understanding how these theories work and how they could be used in tandem to create effective team working is going to bring on board those teachers who are not natural team players.

Tuckman's first names are Bruce and Wayne. His group development model has secured him a place as a superhero in team-building parlance. His model is based on the notion that groups go through a four-stage developmental process (*forming, storming, norming* and *performing*) before they become a fully operational performing team. He later added a fifth stage (*adjourning*) as an essential part of the process.

Each of these stages can be summarised as:

*   **Forming**: this is where members start to interact with each other and work out what is expected of them. Some members of the group will feel excited and enthusiastic in this stage, whilst others will feel afraid and uncertain.
*   **Storming**: as people start to mingle, conflict occurs as personal agendas start to emerge. Some members will assert themselves and begin to question authority, whilst others will go along with what's being said.
*   **Norming**: as the members of the group find ways of resolving conflict they begin to emerge as a cohesive unit. Criticisms are constructive and the team members start to work cooperatively with one another.
*   **Performing**: as confidence and trust in each other begin to grow, performance increases.
*   **Adjourning**: as the task has been completed, the group dissolves. At this stage, team members will either feel a sense of satisfaction or loss, depending on the outcome. Other emotions may include relief or sadness.

Tuckman stressed the importance of providing guidance to the team at the very outset of the team formation. He argued that determining what the group's objectives and roles were would be a major factor in determining whether the group approached initial tasks with anticipation or trepidation.

How to use it

In the film *Cool Runnings*, John Candy plays Irv Blitzer, the leader of the Jamaican bobsled team. Look at how the film mirrors Tuckman's model:

Blitzer pulls together an unlikely cast of characters, mostly made up of sprinters, to make up the Jamaican bobsled team to compete in the 1968 Winter Olympics (*forming*). There's a lot of animosity amongst members of the squad stemming from a number of incidents that occurred when they were sprinting against each other (*storming*). None of the characters have any real aspirations to be Olympians and treat the event as a bit of a joke (*norming*). Their early runs prove to be an embarrassment as they finish last each time. They start to work cooperatively when their efforts are ridiculed by other competing countries. Eventually, as they start to resolve conflict within the team, they begin to operate as a cohesive unit and come close to breaking the world record (*performing*). The team returns home to Jamaica as heroes (*adjourning*).

Here are some tips as to how you, as the teacher or team leader, should react in each stage of the team formation process.

- As the group begins to *form*, meet with the group members to discuss ground rules. Suggest that each member explains what it is that they expect from the team.
- In the *storming* stage, expect conflicts over values and challenges to authority. If disagreements get too heated then remain calm and deal with incidents assertively as they occur, as acting aggressively or passively will not achieve much.
- If you have dealt effectively with the *storming* phase, team members will enter the *norming* stage and begin to develop their own ways of dealing with disagreements. This is the time to start backing off.
- If all has gone according to plan, the team will start *performing* as a cohesive unit. Keep a watchful eye on proceedings but allow the team space. Don't be concerned if the team makes mistakes but support them to learn from the mistakes.
- Once the task has been completed, celebrate the team's achievements and acknowledge everyone's contribution; efforts as well as achievements.

It shouldn't be too difficult to see how the principles behind this theory can be applied within the classroom with the learners as the group members and you, the teacher, as the group leader.

In the classroom

- Establish the ground rules through discussion rather than imposition.
- Allow friction to occur but make sure this is resolved.
- Acknowledge everyone's efforts.

Critical Perspective

What do you think about Tuckman's assertion that the team needs to experience and resolve conflict before they will perform well as a team?

For more on Tuckman's ideas, read:

Tuckman, B.W. (1965) Development sequences in small groups. *Psychology Bulletin*, 3(6), 384-399.

Wheelan argues that teams mature simply through a process of interaction. She claims that the length of time a team work together will have a significant impact on how they function as a team. She uses a life-growth model to describe this process. The model can be depicted as:

| **Infancy** Conforms to norms | **Adolescence** Challenges authority | **Adulthood** Bonding | **Maturity** Confidence & self-belief |

Each of the phases in the model can be summarised in respect of teaching as:

- *Infancy*: this is where learners are dependent on the teacher's direction and support. They have a tendency to conform to classroom norms and react badly to criticism from both the teacher and their peers; no matter how well-intentioned.
- *Adolescence*: this is the rebellious stage when the teacher's authority may be challenged. There may also be conflict with other members of the class as disagreements occur and cliques begin to be formed.
- *Adulthood*: this is where roles and structure become more formalised as the team starts to bond. The team may make mistakes but have to learn from this if they want to mature.
- *Maturity*: this is where the team become clearer about their roles and responsibilities. They now have the confidence and self-belief to tackle even the most challenging tasks.

Wheelan devised a Group Development Observation System (GDSO) to indicate at which stage in the process group members considered the team to be.

How to use it

I love the metaphor of the stages of life that Wheelan uses. Here's an example of how I went through a complete life cycle in the space of three days.

In 1993 I enrolled on a two-year Diploma in Management Studies (DMS) course. The group that I was in were given a task and, remembering the way we had all been taught previously, waited to be told what to do (*Infancy*). When these instructions never came, and silence prevailed, we started to become frustrated and challenge our lecturer's authority. When this got us nowhere, one member of our group got up and left (*Adolescence*). With our lecturer still not giving us any guidance we decided to work on the task on our own. Each of us took it in turns leading the group and acting as scribes. When our lecturer did eventually say something (he muttered 'complacency'), it was to warn us that we were going off task. We quickly learned from this (*Adulthood*). By the end of the third day, we started to have confidence in each other's contribution and belief in our ability to complete the task (*Maturity*).

Here are some tips on how to use Wheelan's model as a teacher:

- Whichever approach you adopt in the first two stages make sure that what you do is consistent and that you stick to your guns. Failing to see through on threats or promises will diminish your credibility enormously.
- Be aware of any frustration that your learners may feel if you are critical of any aspect of their work. Taking these frustrations out on you is bad but taking them out on other learners is worse. Make sure that you resolve any conflicts that do arise quickly and effectively (see Theory 44).
- As they progress onto the third stage, don't start to relax because they have started bonding as a learning group. This is where they will make mistakes, and quite possibly big ones that may haunt them for some time. Reassure them that making mistakes doesn't make them a failure, it just means they have made a mistake; it's what they learn from their mistakes that's important.
- As they become more mature, don't be afraid to back off. You may still want to keep a watchful eye on what they're doing in case they need your support and guidance.

In the classroom

- Understand at which stage in the model your group is at.
- Adapt your teaching strategies to reflect this.
- Don't be afraid to cut the apron strings when you feel your group have reached maturity.

Critical Perspective

There is a critical third stage in Whelan's model where she claims that the team will make mistakes. Do you agree with her claim that these present the teacher with great learning opportunities?

For more on Wheelan's ideas, read:

Wheelan, S.A. (2013) *Creating Effective Teams*. London: SAGE.

Team teaching happens when two or more teachers cooperate, deliberately and methodically, in the teaching process. Buckley suggests that this would involve jointly: setting the course goals, designing a scheme of work, preparing lesson plans, selecting materials, teaching the lesson, assessing learning and evaluating each other's performance.

Buckley claims that team teaching:

- improves the quality of scholarship and teaching through more interaction between teachers.
- allows for the sharing of insights and challenging of long-held assumptions.
- encourages teachers to learn new approaches to their teaching from observing others.
- prevents boredom and the mental fatigue that can arise from teaching the same material in the same way.
- creates more time for lesson planning by spreading the responsibility for planning.
- energises teachers by showing them new approaches.
- provides opportunities for teachers to form deep working relationships with their colleagues.
- stimulates learners by offering contrasting viewpoints.

Buckley argues that a well-coordinated team will use the expertise and knowledge of its members to promote effective learning and expose learners to a variety of different teaching styles. He also warns of the extra pressure that may be placed on teaching and support staff through having to function as a team.

How to use it

It's important to emphasise a point that Buckley makes about *team teaching* not being a cure-all remedy. An energetic, insightful and committed team will contribute significantly to helping learners achieve their learning outcomes. A lazy, dysfunctional and self-interested collection of individuals will have the opposite effect.

Here are some tips to help you towards effective team teaching:

- You need to be fully aware of why you are adopting a team teaching approach. Whether this is down to resources, timetabling or the sharing of knowledge and expertise, the question of can you justify it as the most appropriate teaching approach is one that must be answered in the affirmative.
- If you are satisfied that team teaching is the best approach, then make the development of the team a priority. Pick the right people for the team and sort out any issues that arise as early as possible. Expect conflict and have a strategy for dealing with this.
- Don't assume that like *Topsy*, the team will just grow and grow. Like any new venture, it will need nurturing to make it effective.

- Set clear goals for the team and make sure its activities lead to those goals.
- Once the team is up and running, establish a rapport with the other team members. Learners of any age will sense when there is tension or a lack of harmony within a teaching team.
- Identify what the team members' preferred teaching styles are and work out how these can complement each other.
- Don't be afraid to discuss team members' strengths and weaknesses, but do this in an open, transparent manner so that there's no talking behind others' backs. Remember if this is the culture in the team, then they'll be doing the same to you.
- Act as a unified team, be innovative and grow and, most of all, enjoy the experience of working alongside colleagues.

With such a convincing argument in favour of team teaching, why isn't every lesson taught in this way? Well, sadly some teachers have rigid personalities or may be resistant to new ideas, some don't like performing in front of their colleagues for fear of humiliation if things don't go well and some are protective of the materials they have developed and don't like sharing.

In the classroom

- Set clear goals for the team.
- Identify how teachers' preferred teaching styles can be used to complement each other.
- Establish a rapport within the team and enjoy the experience of working together.

Critical Perspective

Buckley makes the point that team teaching doesn't always work because of a lack of resources, teachers with rigid personalities or a fear of being humiliated in front of colleagues if things go wrong. Do you have experiences of any of these happening to you?

For more on team teaching, read:

Buckley, F.J. (2000) *Team Teaching: What, Why and How?* Thousand Oaks CA: SAGE.
Curzon, L.B. (2006) *Teaching in Further Education* (6th edn). London: Continuum.

SUMMARY OF PART 2

Part 2 has set out to cover contemporary thinking on teaching and learning. The six sections include theories and models relating to the personal qualities that teachers need to have to be effective and their ability to think beyond basic teaching strategies as a means of supporting learners. There are also theories and models relating to how learners think and what motivates them to learn. Here are some of the key points to emerge from this part of the book:

- Using the same teaching approaches in the same way year in year out is a recipe for boredom and mental fatigue.
- Having a reputation for delivering on promises and being approachable and welcoming are important qualities in a teacher.
- Knowing how to resolve conflict in class or in teaching teams is a vital attribute for teachers to have.
- Making more emotional withdrawals than deposits will bankrupt an individual's relationship with another person.
- Teaching people to be competent is good but supporting them to be creative is where the added value is.
- People have a preference for the way they learn and respond best either by observing, reading, listening or doing.
- Individuals have their own unique approach to thinking and learning.
- Perception and personality will influence the way that people think and learn.
- Although people may have a learning style preference they won't learn just by adhering to this preference.
- Nobody is perfect.
- Motivation can be intrinsic (driven by inner desire) or extrinsic (driven by external stimuli).
- Motivation can be influenced by the individual's level of belief in themselves, how much they attach to success and the contribution that others can make.
- A learner's needs can be gauged by their desires for: recognition, power or acceptance.
- Intelligence isn't something that is static; it can be developed.
- Teachers have rights as much as learners do.

- Look for the signs that may be causing bad behaviour.
- Make sure that the consequence of undesired behaviour is something the learner fears.
- Make sure that the consequence of desired behaviour is something the learner desires.
- Accept that everyone has the potential for psychopathic behaviour.
- How learners see themselves has a significant effect on their motivation.
- Never overload learners with irrelevant or unimportant information.
- Ignoring too many minor behavioural problems could result in chaos breaking out.
- Encourage the person being coached to come up with their own solutions.
- Never be afraid of failure.
- A good mentor will never judge or criticise the person they are mentoring, but strives to help them evaluate their strengths and areas for development.
- A good mentor will ask provocative questions with good intent.
- Groups need to go through a development process before they mature and become fully operational.
- Team teaching will use the expertise and knowledge of its members to promote effective learning and expose learners to a variety of different teaching styles.

PART 3
AN INTRODUCTION TO EARLY CHILDHOOD AND DEVELOPMENTAL STRATEGIES

INTRODUCTION TO PART 3

Each of the child development theories and strategies in this section makes an important contribution to how teachers can support children to develop and learn. It's critical to appreciate that whatever your role with children is, that there is no one approach that addresses every aspect of the way a child develops. For that reason, it is important to gain insight from each of the entries and understand that children are unique and are influenced by both nature and nurture.

In this part of the book you will encounter eight approaches that look at childhood development from a physical, social, emotional, ecological and moral perspective, a further five that look at strategies for working with children in the classroom, seven that look at strategies for working with children with additional needs and six approaches from schools around the world.

The section complements entries that appear earlier in the book which look at the development of learning theories from the philosophical through to the early psychological studies to a more contemporary neuroscientific approach to the subject. Whereas the earlier entries were not age-specific, the entries in this section focus more on explaining how children change and grow over the course of their childhood and the factors that influence this growth.

As you can see throughout the book, some of psychology's best-known thinkers have developed theories to help explore and explain different aspects of child development. While not all of these theories are fully accepted today, they all had an important influence on our understanding of child development. You may be surprised therefore to see that I have omitted Freud's thoughts on child development occurring in a series of stages focused on different pleasure areas of the body. During each stage, Freud claimed that the child encounters conflicts that play a significant role in the course of their development. His theory suggested that the energy of the libido was focused on different erogenous zones at specific stages. He claimed that failure to progress through a stage can result in a fixation at that point in development, which Freud believed could have an influence on adult behaviour. I chose to omit Freud's theories, not because I disagreed with them, indeed throughout the book I have chosen not to express support or dissent on any of the theories (I've challenged you to do that), but because there is already enough written on Freud.

Section 3.1: Children and Society

Children start to develop their social skills from a very early age. The demanding and egocentric nature of the under-threes gives way to a more considerate approach that is largely influenced by a complex array of factors including the interactions they experience as members of a social setting that includes family, friends, nursery and school. In this section, I want to look at four theories relating to children and the impact that these interactions have on them.

I start with two theories which deal with the crises that children experience and need to resolve as part of their social development. The first entry deals with the distress that infants often experience when separated from their primary care giver. This is then followed by a look at a further series of psychosocial crises that children and young people have to experience which could have a positive or negative outcome for personality development.

The section is completed by a look at two theories that cover the wider impact that society has on influencing the child's social development and capacity to learn. The first of these deals with children who engage in a process of collective learning in a shared domain of human endeavour. The second entry sees the world in which the child grows as having a major influence on their development.

Although I have included the work of Jean Piaget in another part of the book (see Theory 20), his theories of cognitive development are seminal to any discussion on the social development of children.

Bowlby observed that children became increasingly distressed when separated from their primary care giver with a pattern emerging that starts with angry protest followed by despair. Apathy and listlessness follow with a period of quiet detachment and if separated long enough, lack of interest in, and withdrawal from, the missing care giver. This is represented as a lateral progression.

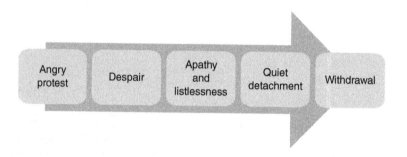

Bowlby believed this to be an evolving need which could be divided into the following stages:

- **Pre-attachment** (birth-6 weeks): during this stage, babies recognise their primary care giver but do not yet have an attachment. Their crying and fussing draws the attention and care of the parent, which is rewarding to both the child and the care giver. As this stage progresses, infants begin to recognise the parent more and develop a sense of trust.
- **Indiscriminate attachment** (6 weeks-7 months): infants begin to show a distinct preference for the primary care givers as well as certain secondary care givers in their lives.
- **Discriminate attachment** (7 months-1 year): attachment is established and the infant prefers their primary care giver over anyone else, and experiences separation anxiety when they leave.
- **Multiple attachment** (1 year +): as language develops, separation anxiety declines and a sense of security begins to develop. The infant can now understand when their primary care giver is leaving and when they will be coming back.

Mary Ainsworth (1913-1999) supported Bowlby's concept of a mother-baby attachment process and conducted further research in this area. Ainsworth, through her research referred to as *Strange Situations*, looked at the attachment process in both African and American cultures, in which she identified the characteristics of a secure and insecure attachment between mother and baby and provided the first empirical justification for Bowlby's theories.

How to use it

Bowlby suggests that there is a critical period for developing an attachment (birth-5 years). If an attachment has not developed during this period, then the child will suffer irreversible

ATTACHMENT THEORY

developmental consequences, such as reduced intelligence and increased aggression. If you believe in Bowlby's ideas then an understanding of the following states of attachment is critical:

- **Secure attachment**: children feel secure and happy. They are eager to explore their surroundings. They know they could trust their primary care giver to be there for them. Although distressed at their absence, they are confident that they will return.
- **Anxious avoidant attachment**: children do not trust their primary care giver to fulfil their needs. They act indifferent to their primary care giver's presence or absence, but are anxious inside. They are not explorative, and are emotionally distant.
- **Anxious resistant attachment**: children show a mixture of anger and helplessness towards their primary care giver. They act passively, and feel insecure. Experience has taught them that they cannot rely on their mother.
- **Disorganised/disoriented attachment**: children who do not fit into the other categories are included in this fourth form of attachment. These children could act in a depressed, angry, passive, or apathetical manner.

The above stress the importance of the teacher and parent working together to support the child through what Bowlby claims is arguably the most critical stage in their development.

In the classroom

- Make sure that you offer early intervention and support to families where attachment needs are not being met.
- Encourage the child's primary care giver to stay with their children for short periods of time during the settling-in period.
- Work with the child's primary care giver to ensure that their behaviour is consistent and sensitive to the needs of their child.

Critical Perspective

Critics of attachment theory argue that parents do not shape their child's personality or character and that a child's teachers and peers will have more influence on them than their parents. Where do you stand on this?

For more on attachment theory, read:

Ainsworth, M.D. (1989) Attachment beyond infancy. *American Psychologist*, 44(4), 709-716.
Bowlby, J. (2008) *Attachment*. New York: Basic Books.

Erikson proposed a psychoanalytic theory of psychosocial development comprising eight stages from infancy to adulthood. During each stage, Erikson claims that the person experiences a psychosocial crisis which could have a positive or negative outcome for personality development. The crises are represented as a series of dilemmas:

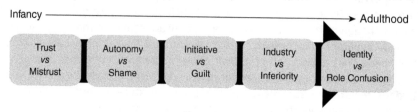

The stages can be summarised as:

- Stage 1 (0-2 years): **Trust vs Mistrust** - Trust comes from the consistent meeting of needs. An infant who can trust their primary care giver (PCG) to meet their needs, will take from this stage a basic sense of trust in the world which helps the acceptance of limits and boundaries.
- Stage 2 (2-4 years): **Autonomy vs Shame** - A child of this age is beginning to explore the world at will. This is the age commonly known as the 'terrible twos'. The very young child learns by feeling with all the senses, and an expression of autonomy in this process seems very relevant to the child's growth. If this autonomy is thwarted, three consequences may ensue: a sense of shame develops, which prevents a healthy acceptance of limits, resulting in the child feeling devastated by small crises.
- Stage 3 (4-6 years): **Initiative vs Guilt** - The child in this stage is beginning to make decisions, and carry them out, primarily through play activities. Imagination is the key mover. A sense of purpose develops when they are able to envision something in their imagination and pursue it.
- Stage 4 (6-12 years): **Industry vs Inferiority** - These are the years when a child can begin to work hard academically and gain competence in various areas of activity.
- Stage 5 (12-17 years): **Identity vs Role Confusion** - The questions arising at this stage are, 'Who am I?', 'What are my values?', 'What is my identity?' Identity is defined as the ability to exercise choice.

Erikson advocates that there are three further stages of psychosocial development beyond schooling that include 'intimacy vs isolation' (18-35 years), where people build close relationships and experience love; 'generativity vs stagnation' (35-60), where contributions are focused on the needs of future generations; and 'ego-integrity vs despair' when people reflect on their lives and express feelings of satisfaction or dissatisfaction. He argued that we achieve a sense of completeness and 'personal wholeness' in later life in direct proportion to the degree to which we successfully negotiate earlier stages.

How to use it

Erikson claims that his stages of the psychosocial crises are 'plausible and insightful descriptions of how personality develops'. Helping the child through the various stages and the positive learning that should accompany them is a complex and difficult task. Here are some suggestions.

- **0-2 years**: this is when the child begins to recognise what's right and what's wrong. Getting them to trust you by not making promises that you can't keep will help the process of acceptance of limits and boundaries.
- **2-4 years**: this is the age when feelings are beginning to be expressed. It is important not to condemn feelings such as anger or jealousy that the child may hold, but to help the child to be sensitive to their behavioural expressions in a particular situation.
- **4-6 years**: this is the age when children must be allowed room for the expression of imagination. This can be achieved by providing them with plenty of opportunity for them to participate in activities such as playing with various natural, simple materials, and role-playing. Stories and songs that stimulate the imagination can also be introduced in this stage as well as real-life activities like preparing and serving food.
- **6-12 years**: it is vitally important in this stage to help the child feel that they can pursue a task and do it well. Set small learning targets in a variety of areas and celebrate achievements of these targets. Don't just focus on the end result, but on the processes the child has undertaken.
- **12-17 years**: this is when children develop a coherent sense of who they are. Encourage them to reflect on 'Who are you?', 'What are your values?', 'What is your identity?' 'What choices do you have in life?'

Erikson argues that helping the child to understand what's right and wrong, allowing them freedom of expression, encouraging them to be imaginative, to feel confident in undertaking tasks, and to develop their ability to exercise the right choice is a critical part of your role as a teacher that will help ensure that the child has a unified sense of self that will equip them for a happy and productive adulthood.

In the classroom

- Make sure that you fulfil any promises that you make to students.
- Have a range of activities that will spark your students' imagination.
- Encourage students to discuss what makes them tick – their principles and values in life.

Critical Perspective

How does Erikson's theory of psychosocial development differ from Sigmund Freud's psychosexual theory?

For more on psychosocial development, read:

Erikson, E.H. (1964) *Insight and Responsibility*. New York: Norton.
Erikson, E.H. (1968) *Identity: Youth and Crisis*. New York: Norton.

Although Lave and Wenger, individually, have made useful contributions to our understanding of social learning theory, it is their collaboration on the subject of *situated learning* that has been their most important work to date.

Combining their expertise in social anthropology and neuroscience, Lave and Wenger suggested that *socially situated learning* takes place by people who engage in a process of collective learning in a shared domain of human endeavour, what they refer to as a *community of practice*. They use the examples of 'a tribe learning to survive, a band of artists seeking new forms of expression, a group of engineers working on similar problems, a clique of pupils defining their identity in the school, a network of surgeons exploring novel techniques, a gathering of first-time managers helping each other cope'.

A classic example of socially situated learning is that of the kibbutzim (collective farms) of Israel. The most striking feature of kibbutz education, especially in the early days of the kibbutz, was that the parents forego rearing and educating their offspring themselves and instead hand the children over to professional educators, sometimes immediately after birth. Although the kibbutzim type of education developed for both social and economic reasons, four educational considerations gained prominence:

- The kibbutz way of life makes for complete equality of the sexes.
- The education of children in special children's houses is the best way of perpetuating the kibbutz way of life.
- Collective education is more 'scientific' than education within the family, in that children are reared and trained by experts in an atmosphere free of the tensions engendered by family relationships.
- Collective education is more democratic than traditional education and more in keeping with the spirit of cooperative living.

Much of what is evident in kibbutzim education underpins Lave and Wenger's theories of socially situated learning with the emphasis on students being actively involved in addressing real world problems. As the practice implies, the student is 'situated' in the learning experience and knowledge acquisition becomes a part of the learning activity, its context, and the culture in which it is developed and used.

Lave and Wenger argue that students form or construct their own knowledge from the experiences that they bring to the learning situation. In this respect, the success of situated learning experiences relies on social interaction and practical activity.

How to use it

Socially situated learning suggests that learning takes place through the relationships between people and through connecting prior knowledge with authentic, informal, and often unintended contextual learning. In this situation, a student's role changes from being a beginner to an expert as they become more active and immersed in the social community where learning is often unintentional rather than deliberate. If you want to follow the ideas of Lave and Wenger accept that knowledge needs to be presented in authentic contexts, so:

- organise field trips where your learners can have the opportunity to actively partici-pate in an unfamiliar environment
- foster a sense of cooperative education and work place experiences in which students are immersed and physically active in an actual work environment
- don't rely on teaching subjects such as music and art from text books, and in the classroom focus on practices which replicate the actual setting of these events, e.g., orchestras, studios, galleries
- select situations that will engage the learners in complex, realistic, problem-centred activities that will support the desired knowledge to be acquired
- change your role from transmitter of knowledge to that of a facilitator of learning by tracking progress, assessing products produced by learners, building collaborative learning environments and encouraging reflection
- assess the intellectual growth of the individual and the community of learners through discussion, reflection, evaluation, and validation of the community's perspective.

Whatever methods you use, the situated learning experience should encourage students to tap their prior knowledge, search out real world learning opportunities and to not be afraid to challenge others in their community.

In the classroom

- Encourage your learners to view their lives and the world as being meaningful.
- Place your learners in authentic learning situations where they are actively immersed in an activity.
- Be a facilitator of learning, not just a transmitter of knowledge.

Critical Perspective

Socially situated learning is based on the premise that knowledge should be presented in an authentic context. Critics argue that this premise discounts the notion that learning in abstraction can be of use. What do you think about this?

For more on Lave and Wenger's ideas, read:

Lave, J. and Wenger, E. (1991) *Situated Learning: Legitimate Peripheral Participation.* Cambridge: Cambridge University Press.
Wenger, E. (1998) *Communities of Practice: Learning, Meaning and Identity.* Cambridge: Cambridge University Press.

When Bronfenbrenner developed the Ecological Systems Theory (EST), he emphasised a balance between nature and nurture, otherwise known as heredity and environment. To illustrate his theory, the child is placed in the middle of concentric circles surrounded by a variety of different factors which all influence the child.

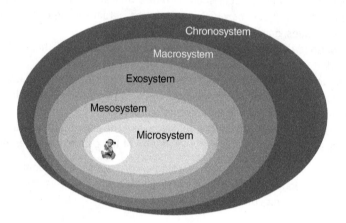

The five sections are described as the:

- **Microsystem**: individuals who have a direct influence on the child are included in this system (e.g. the child's family and friends).
- **Mesosystem**: in this system the broader surroundings and direct influences on the child's development are taken into account (e.g. education and health care).
- **Exosystem**: in this system there is a broader circle of people who indirectly influence the child (e.g. colleagues and friends of their family members).
- **Macrosystem**: this is an even broader system that includes the values, customs and attitudes of the cultural group the child belongs to.
- **Chronosystem**: this system acknowledges that the child's biological hereditary make-up combines with environmental forces to mould their development.

Bronfenbrenner sees the world in which the child grows as having a major influence on their development. He describes this as a two-way influence, in which the personality and behaviour of the child will influence the way people in the environment will interact with that child. He also believes that the interactions between environmental factors could affect the child's development. For instance, it is not just the influence of the parents or the childcare centre on the child but the way the parents and childcare centre staff get on.

How to use it

Bronfenbrenner claims that his theory helps teachers understand the importance of fostering positive relationships with children and their families and to appreciate that the way they interact with and support those families will affect the child's development. He also claims that it heightens teacher's awareness of the variety of different factors which all influence the child to ensure that they organise learning experiences that reflect the needs and expectations of the society, culture and community in which their learners live.

If you want to follow the ideas of Bronfenbrenner, appreciate:

- that the child's first transition from home to school could influence their future outlook on education so make sure that it is a positive one by creating a safe, nurturing environment in which students can feel comfortable enough to take risks in learning and feel support when they struggle
- that if there are subsequent transitions, for example, class to class, school to school, etc. that you make sure you pass relevant information about the child to key personnel in the new setting
- the importance of being a positive role model for the child
- the necessity of listening to what they have to say and following through on any commitments that you make to help them in times of distress
- the importance of encouraging the child's parents or primary care givers to participate in the child's learning experiences and achievements. Setting aside a night when children present their projects to their parents or primary care givers is a good way of doing this.

In the classroom

- Appreciate that students may struggle with the transition from home to school, class to class and school to school.
- Be a positive role model for your students.
- Encourage parents of students to be part of their child's learning.

Critical Perspective

What do you think of the critics of ecological systems theory who argue that with so much information collected in regards to all of the spheres of influence exerted on an individual, how can this information be classified in terms of hierarchical importance and impact: for example are the child's relationships in their microsystem having a stronger influence than those in his mesosystem?

For more on Bronfenbrenner's ideas, read:

Bronfenbrenner, U. (1979) *The Ecology of Human Development*. Cambridge, MA: Harvard University Press.
Bronfenbrenner, U. (2007) *Making Human Beings Human*. Thousand Oaks, CA: Sage.

Section 3.2: Emotional Growth

This was arguably one of the most difficult parts of the book to research and write. There is so much written on the subject of the emotional growth of children and so many theories on the factors that influence this that choosing a small number to focus on was very difficult.

I wanted something that emphasised that each child has a unique genetic and biological make-up that determines their rate of emotional development and that dealt with the impact that nature and nurture (see Theory 4) has on this.

I chose the first entry because although Gesell admits that the environment (nurture) had an influence on development it was biology (nature) that was, in his opinion, the biggest influence. I then balanced this with Coles' view of the powerful social and economic forces that influence a child's emotional growth.

I was aware that I was still unable to resolve the nature-nurture debate so I switched my attention to theories that covered two aspects of emotional development that seemed prominent in most of the books that I was reading on the subject – identity and morality. I felt that any consideration of emotional behaviour had to start from the perspective of the child's sense of self-being and self-worth.

Children often build their senses of identity and moral reasoning through how other people react to them. They are for example more aware of racial differences of skin colour when they live in a diverse neighbourhood. I was therefore drawn to Banks' arguments that children in diverse neighbourhoods identify with certain groups to experience a feeling of belonging and have a strong need to belong to groups. It's this notion that identity and morality is not something that can be taught or imposed on children but is developed through their interaction with others that Kohlberg explores through moral reasoning in the final entry in this section.

It's also well worth reading the entry on Jane Elliot's work with children (see Theory 9) in which she exposes children to the issues of identity and morality and the impact that this has on the children as they grow up.

Gesell was one of the first psychologists to systematically describe children's physical, social and emotional achievements. He based his theory on three major assumptions:

- Development is orderly, sequential and predictable and builds on earlier learning, skills or behaviours.
- Children develop individually and at their own pace but every child follows the same sequence.
- Certain aspects of development happen at specific times and can lead to states of equilibrium or disequilibrium.

The following diagram is a snapshot from two to eight years of age and indicates predictive behavioural patterns in half-yearly cycles:

Disequilibrium

7.5 years: *Neurotic compatibility*

6.5 years: *Inwardising*

5.5 years: *Break-up*

4.5 years: *Neurotic compatibility*

3.5 years: *Inwardising*

2.5 years: *Break-up*

Equilibrium

8 years: *Smooth*

7 years: *Expansion*

6 years: *Sorting out*

5 years: *Smooth*

4 years: *Expansion*

3 years: *Sorting out*

2 years: *Smooth*

A summary of each aspect of the maturational timetable is:

Behaviour	Ages 2–5	Ages 5–8
Smooth	Loving and affectionate but needy	More calm but may become withdrawn
Break-up	Rigid, inflexible, domineering, demanding, prone to tantrums	Complains a lot and is often moody
Sorting out	Less rigid, more flexible and seeing others' points of view	Positive, cheerful, able to empathise with others
Inwardising	Emotionally insecure and more demanding	Tense, negative, becoming disobedient and withdrawn
Expansion	Height of imagination, silly actions and prone to outbursts	Friendly, loving, caring and optimistic
Neurotic compatibility	More developed language and fine motor skills	Enthusiastic, outgoing but prone to excessive self-criticism

Gesell clearly believed that each child's unique genetic and biological make-up determines the rate of development and that although the environment (nurture) had an influence on development it was biology (nature) that was the biggest influence. He therefore argued that it was the environment that should be changed and adapted to meet the individual genetic prearranged timetables.

MATURATIONAL THEORY

How to use it

Gesell's observations of children allowed him to describe a series of developmental milestones in ten major areas that will impact on the normative behaviours of the child. Summaries of these milestones and what you can do to support children to reach them are:

- *Motor characteristics*: bodily activity including hand and eye coordination. Include plenty of practical activities in your lesson planning.
- *Personal hygiene*: attention to daily health routines including eating, sleeping, bathing and dressing. Keep a look out and report any concerns that you have about the child's lifestyle.
- *Emotional expression*: developing affective attitudes including laughing, crying, assertion and anger. Encourage them to be expressive in acting or role plays.
- *Fears and dreams*: the ability to deal with anxieties and complexes. Listen to them if they start to express any concerns. Seek professional help if you feel the child is developing emotional problems.
- *Self and sex*: the development of confidence and relationships. Praise the child when they do something good. Focus on effort not just results.
- *Interpersonal relations*: the importance of love and friendship. Encourage plenty of interaction and team work in the class.
- *Play and pastime*: hobbies; reading, music, art and cinema. Encourage them to discuss their hobbies with the rest of the class. Have 'tell-and-show' lessons where children bring in samples of their hobbies.
- *School life*: adjustment to school; classroom demeanour and attention to lessons. Encourage cooperation not competition in class activities.
- *Ethical sense*: a sense of what's good and what's bad, and responses to instruction, punishment, praise and reason. Allow them an opportunity to consider the consequences of their behaviour.
- *Philosophical outlook*: able to express thoughts on emotive subjects such as war, death, religion and culture. Have plenty of opportunity to discuss issues of the day.

Through his research Gesell concluded that although the environment has some effect on a child's development it is the child's DNA that is the main factor that will determine whether or not they suffer from any developmental problems.

In the classroom

- Support the child to develop physically and emotionally.
- Help them to resolve any issues that they have with anxieties, complexes and relationships.
- Encourage discussion and debate on emotive issues.

Critical Perspective

Gesell's belief that early childhood development is guided by heredity has been questioned by critics who claim that he focuses too much on motor and intellectual development and almost completely ignores the child's emotional development. What do you think about this criticism?

For more on maturational theory, read:

Gesell, A., Ilg, F., Bates Ames, L. and Bullis, G. (1977) *The Child from Five to Ten*. New York: Harper and Row.
Also see: https://gesellinstitute.org/pages/gesell-theory

The core of Coles' social psychiatry is that it shows not only the mental stresses and strains in children's lives but the way in which powerful social and economic forces impinge on those lives and how they respond: well and poorly; emotionally and stoically; in resistance and defeat. Storytelling is at the heart of Coles' method, which involves finding in the words of his subjects stories that display prominent elements of human nature.

His work is based on his beliefs that:

- The best learning occurs through a study of life's stories.
- Children possess a keen moral sensitivity to ideas and values, an appreciation of what is right and wrong, and to the reasons underlying what people do, feel and think.
- Children are concerned morally with issues linked to their everyday lives.
- Children determine what is right and wrong based on their observations of life around them.
- Moral standards come to be set aside as children reflect the values of society.
- Children's political lives come to merge with their moral lives.

Coles argues that, 'Morality defines not only how we get along with the world and one another, and the rules of life; it characterizes our very nature.' He further argues that, 'Morality has to do with human connection: The kind of connection that responds to others, and in turn earns the caring response of others.' 'If we are deprived of our morality', he says, 'we're deprived of an essential part of ourselves; the factor that defines the quality of our lives as human beings.'

As in any aspect of education, the early years in the school and with the parents and the family can have a great impact on the cognitive, social, emotional and moral development of the child. Coles claims that though aspects of each of these faculties are influenced by inherited qualities from genetic endowments, they are shaped, realised and developed through interaction with the environment. He further argues that in our present society, it seems the moral aspects of child rearing and education are less emphasized than in the past, leaving children less well equipped to deal with the challenges of life and living, and educators are often left with the task of compensating for faulty, poor or missing early training.

How to use it

Coles credits children with teaching him, arguing that we vastly underestimate the wisdom that resides in children. Here is a story that he tells people to prove this. When a seven-year-old black child, Ruby Bridges, was jeered and threatened for wanting to go to a white school in segregated New Orleans in the early sixties, Coles approached her wanting to know what she was thinking and feeling. They talked to each other over several months, and the deeper their conversation went, the more Coles was surprised at what Ruby had to tell him. Here are extracts from Coles' notes on his meeting with Ruby.

She once told me that she felt sorry for those people who were trying to kill her. I asked her, 'You feel sorry for them?' And she looked at me and said, 'Well, don't you think they need feeling sorry for?' Talk about wisdom! And talk about moral intuition. I sat there stunned. I was applying standard psychology, trying to help her realize that she was maybe angry at these people, and bitter and anxious, and she was telling me that she prayed for them. I was struck dumb and I was silent, because I had to reflect upon this child's wisdom. She was smart enough to understand, without taking courses in the social sciences or other fields of inquiry, what happens to people.

Here are some tips on how to apply Coles' ideas in the classroom.

- Listen without passing judgement to any stories that students have to tell you about what's going on in their lives.
- Get them to reflect on any questionable actions they may have taken.
- Provide students with adequate time to review their own reasoning for misbehaving and to come up with a solution for the future.
- Encourage students to see the consequences of their actions through the eyes of others.
- Give students the opportunity to help create a classroom code of conduct. In this way, they will assume ownership of the rules that they set and follow them accordingly, rather than blindly agreeing to standards set by school administrators or other authorities.

In the classroom

- Listen without passing judgement to any stories that students have to tell you about what's going on in their lives.
- Give students the opportunity to help create a classroom code of conduct.
- Allow for students to complete a written self-evaluation of any misbehaving on their part.

Critical Perspective

Do you believe that what you say and do in the classroom will have the greatest impact on your students' moral development or are there other factors that are more important?

For more on Coles' ideas, read:

Coles, R. (1989) *The Call of Stories: Teaching and the Moral Imagination.* Boston: Houghton Mifflin.

Coles, R. (1990) *The Spiritual Life of Children.* Boston: Houghton Mifflin.

Banks' theory on the development of ethnic identity provides a framework for understanding the impact of cultural identity on learning. According to his model, Banks describes six stages of ethnic identity development. These are summarised as:

- Stage 1: *Cultural psychological captivity* - this is when individuals internalise the negative stereotypes and beliefs about their ethnicity. This is often when people are younger and don't really realise the differences between different races or cultures. They are also not terribly aware of their own backgrounds. This can result in social withdrawal, inferiority symptoms and further impact negatively on a person's self-esteem.
- Stage 2: *Cultural encapsulation* - this is characterised by the individual's voluntary separation from the dominant culture as they develop a defensive attitude towards their culture resulting in the belief that some cultural groups are inferior and ethno-centric. As a result, they can unknowingly become culturally isolated by the dominant culture. Banks observed that these often result in emotions such as self-rejection and low self-esteem.
- Stage 3: *Cultural identity clarification* - here, individuals are able to clarify their personal attitudes and cultural identity and to develop clear and positive attitudes toward their cultural group. As this happens, an individual learns and accepts both the positive and negative attributes of their culture. They also replace rejection, fear and hate of external cultures by a genuine pride and acceptance of their own traditions.
- Stage 4: *Biculturalism* - individuals in this stage possess a healthy sense of ethnic identity and a respect for other cultures. They begin to develop positive psychological characteristics and the skills necessary to successfully participate in their own and other cultures.
- Stage 5: *Multiculturalism and reflective nationalism* - this is where they have an idealised goal for citizenship identity within a culturally diverse nation. They have developed the ability to function, albeit at minimal levels, within several cultural communities. They can understand, appreciate and share the values, symbols and institutions of several cultures.
- Stage 6: *Globalism and global competency* - they now possess an open mind while actively seeking to understand cultural norms and expectations of others. They have the knowledge, skills and attitude needed to function effectively within their own cultural communities, within other cultures and in the global community.

Banks argues that students identify with certain groups to experience a feeling of belonging and have a strong need to belong to groups, because groups provide a source of motivation.

How to use it

Banks suggests that every student comes to the classroom with a set of behaviours and characteristics that are shaped by group norms that may be influenced by race, social class or religion and that will subsequently affect their academic achievement. He claims that to enhance academic success, teachers should use information about cultural identity to create learning environments that recognise the cultural contributions of students.

Here are some tips on how to foster cultural identity in the classroom:

- Make use of socialising agents, such as peer groups, media, parents and teachers to influence the development of a positive or negative student self-concept.
- Develop a classroom environment that models tolerance and appreciation of student differences by viewing students as cultural beings, embracing student diversity and validating the cultural identity of students.
- Be aware that your teaching practices, your every interaction with students and your own ideas about identity will influence the academic success and social development of your students.
- Encourage students to discover and share their cultural identities through writing projects that focus on their cultural heritages.
- Actively engage them in learning by developing lessons that highlight students' cultures and experiences.
- Help students to feel comfortable with their cultural identity and assist them in their learning by using a multicultural teaching approach that embraces diversity in the classroom.
- Get to know students on a personal level, building teaching around the students' interests when possible, and showcasing the talents of students and using these as teaching tools.
- Empower students to succeed by providing them with a learning environment which respects their culture, embraces their diversity and celebrates their differences.

In the classroom

- Students' cultural identities must be validated through lessons and teaching practices.
- Make sure that students have a sense of belonging, are valued and appreciated on a daily basis.
- Celebrate cultural diversity.

Critical Perspective

Do you believe that a strong sense of their cultural identity is essential for an individual's overall well-being in a community?

For more on cultural identity, read:

Banks, J.A. and Banks, C.A. (2009) *Multicultural Education: Issues and Perspectives* (7th edn). New York: Wiley.

Banks, J.A. (2008) Diversity, group identity, and citizenship education in a global age. *Educational Researcher,* 37(3), 129–139.

Kohlberg's theory on moral development tracks an individual's level of moral reasoning by assigning them to one of three levels. Each level encompasses two stages, making six stages in all. These are summarised as:

- **The pre-conventional level**: this level of moral thinking is that which is generally found at primary school level.
  1. The first stage of this level is where children behave according to socially acceptable norms because they are told to do so by some authority figure (e.g., parent or teacher). This obedience is compelled by the threat or application of punishment.
  2. The second stage of this level is characterised by a view that the right behaviour means acting in one's own best interests.
- **The conventional level**: this level of moral thinking is that which generally starts in adolescence and continues into early adulthood.
  3. The first stage of this level is characterised by an attitude in which young people seek to do what will gain the approval of others.
  4. The second stage is one oriented to abiding by the law and responding to the obligations of duty.
- **The post-conventional level**: this level of moral thinking is one that starts with adulthood but one which Kohlberg felt is not reached by the majority of adults.
  5. The first stage of this level is where people develop an understanding of social mutuality and a genuine interest in the welfare of others.
  6. The second stage is based on respect for universal moral principles and the demands of an individual's conscience.

Kohlberg believed that individuals could only progress through these stages one stage at a time; that is, they could not jump stages and could only come to an understanding of a moral rationale one stage above their own.

How to use it

According to Kohlberg, it was important to present students with moral dilemmas for discussion which would help them to see the reasonableness of a 'higher stage' morality and encourage their development in that direction.

One example that Kohlberg used was the 'Heinz Steals the Drug' scenario. In this, a woman has terminal cancer and her doctors believe that only one drug might save her. This drug had been discovered by a local pharmacist who was able to make it for $200 per dose and sell it for $2,000 per dose. The woman's husband, Heinz, could only raise $1,000 to buy the drug. He tried to negotiate with the pharmacist for a lower price or to be extended credit to pay for it over time. The pharmacist refused to sell it for any less than the retail price or to accept partial payments. Rebuffed and desperate, Heinz instead broke into the pharmacy and stole the drug to save his wife. Kohlberg asks, 'Should the husband have done that?'

Kohlberg was not interested so much in the answer to the question of whether students considered Heinz to be right or wrong but in the reasoning for each student's response. In this respect, he believed that morality is not something that can be imposed on children but is developed through their interaction with others. As an educator, consider where your student's moral development lies in terms of Kohlberg's six stages:

- **Stage 1**: They know that if they do something wrong, they will be punished.
- **Stage 2**: They know that if they do something right, they will be rewarded.
- **Stage 3**: They know that people will like them if they do something good for others.
- **Stage 4**: They know that it is important to respect authority and follow the rules.
- **Stage 5**: They understand the importance of considering the various opinions and values of other people before coming up with decisions on the morality of their action.
- **Stage 6**: They appreciate the need to allow their own conscience to be the ultimate judge of what's right and what's wrong.

In the classroom

- Present students with moral dilemmas for discussion.
- Encourage them to respect other's views and opinions on the issue.
- Allow students the opportunity to explain why they did something wrong and that they understand the consequences for this.

Critical Perspective

What would your response be to what Heinz did? How did you arrive at that decision?

For more on Kohlberg's ideas, read:

Kohlberg, L. (1973) The claim to moral adequacy of a highest stage of moral judgment. *Journal of Philosophy*, 70(18), 630-646.

Kohlberg, L. (1984) *The Psychology of Moral Development: The Nature and Validity of Moral Stages*. New York: Harper & Row.

SECTION 3.3: CLASSROOM STRATEGIES

Throughout this book, I've looked at theories about how people think and learn and the factors that influence this. Although the entries in this section have a strong emphasis on childhood developmental strategies, I would argue that many of the principles and practices can be equally applied to adult learning. I wanted to include in this section therefore five teaching strategies specifically designed for children that didn't lie easily in other parts of the book but which would have been remiss of me not to include.

The entries range from one more established theory which is based on the principles of early childhood specialists which in turn became the foundation for kindergartens (literally translated as child's garden) everywhere to four more contemporary approaches which speculate that we are all born with a predisposition to learn language, that literacy can be best taught in early childhood learning through synthetic phonics and that learning through play allows children to experience and put together everyday objects in a manner that they find exciting and stimulating. The final entry in this section argues that the traditional concept of education is not fit for purpose in preparing children to deal with the challenges, complexities and expectations of the twenty-first century.

Frobel created a programme based on principles of early childhood specialists which became the foundation for kindergartens (literally translated as child's garden) everywhere, as well as several educational philosophies which are the basis of many preschool and early education methods today.

Froebel believed that young children possess unique capabilities and needs, and that adults should serve as the 'gardeners' of children's potential. Froebel asserted that young children, up to the age of seven, could learn best in an atmosphere that provided a stimulating and prepared environment where they could explore and learn from their own perspectives. The key features of Froebel's kindergartens are:

- That parents are the first educators for children and that there should be close links between home and school.
- The main goal is to teach the whole child in all developmental areas: socially, academically, emotionally, physically and spiritually.
- There are four main components of the Froebel approach: motor skills expression, social participation, free self-expression and creativity.
- Children learn to be more independent since they are used to solving problems that arise during their play. This encourages them to feel confident in their ability to handle issues as they arise.
- The Froebel classroom develops fine motor skills in children, which aids them with later learning and activities, such as writing and advanced art skills.

The Froebel philosophy stresses that children who attend a Froebel kindergarten learn to see problems from many angles and to solve them independently. Froebel argues that as children work with materials, they gain perseverance as they attempt to figure out how to manipulate them to create the output they want.

Froebel referred to this approach as *Gifts and Occupations*. The *gifts* are a series of specially designed materials which provide hands-on exploration of solids, surfaces, lines, rings and points and which children use to explore principles of movement, maths and construction. The *occupations* are a series of activities designed to provide further hands-on explorations and practice with skills like clay work, wood work, weaving, drawing and cutting. Froebel argues that this approach is designed to allow children uninterrupted periods of play where they construct their own meaning of how things work.

How to use it

If you believe in Froebel's assertion that, 'play is the highest expression of human development in childhood; for it alone is the free expression of what's in a child's soul', and want to follow his ideas, then accept that:

- Play meets the biological need to discover how things work and thrives in a culture where imagination and creativity are valued.
- An atmosphere of playful nonsense can be an important way of building close relationships.

- Children make stories everywhere, with natural materials, small worlds, blocks, sand and water, and much more.
- Classrooms should be very carefully prepared, presenting children with the tools and materials that are optimal for their level of development.
- Movement is imperative for young learners so lessons should be alive with dance, play and all other forms of movement.
- Children develop differently and should be allowed to learn at their own developmental pace.
- Teachers should not be viewed as the keepers of knowledge, but instead as guides who can help lead a child to understanding.

Froebel argues that if children can develop a sense of wonder about nature, can see the effect of their actions on things around them and can get to know their own small garden (i.e. the way they grow) in deep ways, then they are much more likely to want to help shape a sustainable future.

In the classroom

- Cater for the individual learning needs of children wherever possible.
- Encourage children to be imaginative and creative in their play activities.
- Use materials and activities that will encourage the child to develop their fine motor skills and to explore the world around them.

Critical Perspective

Critics of Froebel's approach believe that the focus on fine motor skills in pre-school education should be supplemented with more academic subjects such as the 3Rs. Do you feel that there is too much or not enough emphasis on teaching reading, writing and arithmetic in pre-school education?

For more on Froebel's ideas, read:

Tovey, H. (2017) *Bringing the Froebel Approach to your Early Years Practice* (2nd edn). London and New York: Routledge.
Wollons, R.L. (ed.) (2000) *Kindergartens and Cultures: The Global Diffusion of an Idea*. New Haven, CT: Yale University Press.

American-born linguist Noam Chomsky believes that we are born with a predisposition to learn language. The essence of his theories of language acquisition claim that, although a child's environment, notably who they listen to and speak to, supplies the content of the language, all children are born with the innate ability – what he refers to as a *language acquisition device* (LAD) – to learn any human language.

Chomsky believes that all children are pre-wired by the LAD to learn language and are born with the basic rules for language intact – a concept that he refers to as *universal grammar*. Although he accepts that many of the unique details of any specific language, such as the words, tone and accent, are heavily influenced by the environment, according to Chomsky, the human brain is ready-made to structure words so that they make grammatical sense. This can be represented as:

Chomsky bases his claim on a number of principles:

- Every human language appears to have certain universal elements.
- Culture and intelligence play little part in the acquisition of some grammatical principles.
- Children have a critical learning age (birth to puberty) and an optimal learning age (between 3 and 10 years old) when they learn to become fluent in the language.
- Children do not need a trigger to learn a language; it comes naturally to them.
- Parents and teachers do not need to coax a child to speak.
- Even if a child is corrected, they will often still speak in the same way that they spoke before being corrected.

Prior to Chomsky, it was widely agreed by theorists, such as the behaviourist B.F. Skinner, that language acquisition was mostly a process of stimulus-response and developed through children watching and learning from their parents. Chomsky's notion that the brain is pre-wired for language was quite a contrast to the accepted beliefs of the time. In this respect Chomsky claims that language growth, like other bodily growth functions, such as puberty, is another genetically programmed inevitability of human development.

How to use it

Chomsky argues that the value of education should be placed on developing students' critical thinking skills and the process of gaining useful and applicable knowledge. In terms of language development, Chomsky cites the case of a child living in a remote forest who is taken from birth to live in an American city. He claims that despite no training in grammar or verbs, the child's innate ability to process language will speed up their ability to acquire knowledge of their new language.

If you want to follow the ideas of Chomsky then you have to believe that:

- Children do not simply copy the language that they hear around them.
- They deduce rules from it which they can then use to produce sentences that they have never heard before.
- They do not learn a repertoire of phrases and sayings, but a grammar that generates an infinite number of new sentences.
- Children are born with the LAD wired into their brains.

Okay, let's pause here for a moment. I know that if I go to Germany and want a nearby chemist, the structure of my question would be *'Gibt es in der Nähe eine Apotheke'* ('is there near to here, a chemist?'). In France I would say, *'il y a un chimiste près d'ici?'* ('there is a chemist near here?'). What does this mean in terms of my overworked LAD?

Chomsky explains that some languages have a basic Subject Verb Object (SVO) structure. Three quarters of the world's languages such as English, French and Vietnamese use either this structure or Subject Object Verb (SOV), while others prefer Verb Subject Object (VSO) or Verb Object Subject (VOS). From this we can see that the components within the structure are fundamentally the same, it is merely the sequence in which they appear that differentiates the language. I should add that Object Subject Verb (OSV) is very rare but you will find an example in the sayings of the Jedi Grand Master, *Yoda*, who complements *Luke Skywalker* by telling him, 'Strong with the force you are'.

In the classroom

- Trust in the notion that the child's capacity to speak fluently will develop naturally.
- Don't rely on rote learning.
- Don't rush to correct language errors.

Critical Perspective

Although the notion that children are born with the capacity to formulate and understand all kinds of sentences, despite never having heard or learned them, has gained considerable popularity, there is no biological evidence to support this theory, and Chomsky's claim that all children have an innate knowledge of language that is not deeply influenced by their parents is highly controversial. How do you stand on this issue?

For more on Chomsky's ideas, read:

Chomsky, N. (1966) *Topics in the Theory of Generative Grammar*. London: Walter de Gruyter.
Chomsky, N. (1986) *Knowledge of Language: Its Nature, Origin and Use*. New York: Praeger.

Jolly Phonics was developed by Lloyd and Wernham in 1977 for working with a small group of children who were having difficulty with their reading. It is a child-centred approach to teaching literacy though synthetic phonics, and probably the most popular of the teaching-through-phonic approaches in the UK, being used in about two-thirds of UK primary and special schools.

It is based on teaching five key skills for reading and writing:

- **Learning the letter sounds**: children and young people are taught the 42 main letter sounds that include the letters of the alphabet plus digraphs such as sh, th, ai and eu.
- **Learning letter formation**: using different multi-sensory methods, they are then taught how to form and write the letters.
- **Blending**: they are then taught how to blend the sounds together to form new words.
- **Segmenting**: the next stage is to improve spelling by identifying the sounds in words.
- **Tricky words**: learning irregular spellings such as through and dough.

The sounds are not introduced alphabetically but are presented in seven groups as follows:

1. s, a, t, i, p, n
2. c, k, e, h, r, m, d
3. g, o, u, l, f, b
4. ai, j, oa, ie, ee, or
5. z, w, ng, v, *oo*, oo
6. y, x, ch, sh, *th*, th
7. qu, ou, oi, ue, er, ar

Phonics are now a standard part of early-years education and for working with children and young people who have difficulty in learning how to read and write. Lloyd and Wernham claim that it is a fun way of learning that can be implemented with minimal cost or training.

How to use it

There is a list of actions that can accompany the teaching of phonics that can be fun and particularly useful for visual and kinaesthetic learners. Here is an example for the first group:

- **s**: Weave hand in an *s* shape, like a snake, and say *sssssssss*......
- **a**: Wiggle fingers mimicking ants crawling up your arm and say *a, a*....
- **t**: Turn head from side to side as if watching a tennis match and say *t, t, t*......
- **i**: Wriggle fingers at the end of the nose and pretend to be a mouse by saying *i, i, i*.....
- **p**: Pretend to blow out candles and say *p, p, p*.......
- **n**: Hold out arms and pretend to be a plane by saying *nnnnnnnnn*...........

A list of all of the phonics and actions can be found in Sue Lloyd's handbook (see below). Here are some more ideas:

- Give each child a clipboard with some phonemes on. Encourage them to find objects in the outdoor area that begin with that phoneme.
- Chalk a hopscotch grid onto the playground and fill the squares with phonemes. Encourage the children to say the phonemes as they land on them. Give the children chalks so that they can try making their own grids.
- Have a number of beanbags marked with phonemes and a large bucket. Encourage the children to say the phoneme printed on the beanbag as they throw it into the bucket.
- Use chalk to write some phonemes on a surface in your outdoor area. Give the children a spray bottle filled with water and ask them to find and spray the phonemes.

In the classroom

- Make the learning fun.
- Encourage children to design their own phonic games.
- Don't confine learning to just the classroom; there is a whole world outdoors that can be explored.

Critical Perspective

What do you think of the critics of *jolly phonics* who argue that it is a poor replacement for the traditional way of teaching the alphabet and does very little to help children to develop their literacy skills?

For more on jolly phonics, read:

Lloyd, S. (1992) *The Jolly Phonics Handbook*. Chigwell, Essex: Jolly Learning Ltd.
Wernham, S. (2010) *Jolly Phonics Teacher's Book in Print Letters*. Chigwell, Essex: Jolly Learning Ltd.

According to Goldschmeid, *heuristic learning* is learning through play that allows children to experience and put together everyday objects in a manner that they find exciting and stimulating.

The five key principles of heuristic learning can be summarised as:

- *Equipment*: this should be variable and consist of objects with different properties such as wood, metal, plastic and paper. There should be large and small objects, heavy and light, and clear and opaque. A prime consideration should always be the safety of the child and objects that may be a health hazard must be avoided.
- *Teacher*: the teacher's role is to set up the play experience, position themselves so as to not be directly included in the play and observe what goes on. The teacher should only intervene when there may be a health and safety issue.
- *Timing*: heuristic play will only work if the child is feeling comfortable and energetic enough to participate.
- *Set-up*: the heuristic play area should be away from other distractions and noise; preferably screened off from the main play area.
- *Availability*: there needs to be a good supply of equipment so that children don't have to share items and arguments are avoided. As children develop, social skills, such as sharing and negotiating, can be introduced into heuristic play.

Goldschmeid argues that through heuristic learning, children will have the opportunity to make their own discoveries and be given the freedom to determine their own actions and make informed choices.

How to use it

In the Castle Business Academy, the school works with children with special needs. Their heuristic play sessions are called *junk modelling* and their treasure trove of play items is called the *junk box*. The junk box is just that – a collection of everyday items that seem to have no use or purpose to anyone. That is except to children like Paulo. Paulo has limited cognitive ability but a very fertile imagination. What may appear to many to be a box of cornflakes, some cotton wool and an empty plastic squeezy bottle to Paulo becomes a train.

Here are some tips on how to set up a heuristic play session.

- Find an area that is separate from the main play area. This needn't be a separate room provided the children are not distracted by other people, objects or noise. A sign on the entrance to the area asking other people not to intrude will prevent unnecessary interruptions to the child's concentration.
- Don't overwhelm the children but choose a number of everyday objects that they can investigate safely and without too much physical effort. Pick things that vary in shape, size, weight, colour, texture, smell.

HEURISTIC LEARNING

- Allow children about 40 minutes play time. If you allot 10 minutes for setting up and 10 minutes for clearing up, this should make a nice one hour session. Keeping play to around 40 minutes will be sufficient and prevent the child from getting bored.
- Don't interfere during the session unless there are health and safety issues or arguments start breaking out. With slightly older children, you may want to see how they resolve conflict, thus developing their social skills.
- How you end the session will depend on the ages and maturity of the children. Don't rush the clearing up part, as getting the children to name the objects as they put them away is a good part of the learning process and thanking them for helping does wonders for their self-esteem.

Just look at what you can achieve through heuristic play: enjoyment, exploration, active learning, creativity, critical thinking and social skills. Wow, now look to see if you can use this method with older children and adults.

In the classroom

- Make sure the items are varied but safe to use.
- Avoid any distractions that may disrupt the child's concentration.
- Assume the role of observer and don't interfere in the play unless necessary.

Critical Perspective

Heuristic learning consists of offering a group of children, for a defined period of time in a controlled environment, a large number of objects and receptacles with which they play freely without adult intervention. Do you agree with critics who argue that heuristic play is just an excuse for lazy teachers not teaching in a traditional manner?

For more on heuristic learning, read:

Goldschmeid, E. and Jackson, S. (2004) *People Under Three: Young Children in Day Care* (3rd edn). London: Routledge.

Claxton challenged the traditional concept of education as not being fit for purpose in preparing children to deal with the challenges, complexities and expectations of the twenty-first century. He was critical of the government's emphasis on examination results and league tables and advocated that building confidence and character was more crucial to the student's development.

He developed the concept of *building learning power* (BLP) that he claimed would develop the whole child. Claxton suggested that BLP was more than just a child acquiring knowledge or learning a skill but was about enjoying the learning experience, having a learner identity and seeking out opportunities for learning. In order to achieve this, he argued that children needed to work on what he described as '*the four Rs*'. This can be summarised as the student having:

- **Resilience**: not being deterred from seeking out and taking up learning opportunities.
- **Resourcefulness**: not being afraid to come out of their comfort zone and being prepared to learn in different ways.
- **Reflectiveness**: having a learning plan and monitoring and adapting this in light of new experiences.
- **Reciprocity**: balancing having confidence in themselves as a learner with the need to collaborate and learn from others.

Although Claxton is critical of government policy on education he doesn't completely dismiss the importance of not jeopardising a child's performance on more conventional success measures. In this respect, he suggests that the *four Rs* should be there to complement and not replace the need to gain subject-specific knowledge and complete tasks. He also argues that effective implementation of BLP will not require a radical change in teaching methods.

Claxton is firm in his belief in the importance of interactive and collaborative learning as the basis for building effective learning power. He suggests that this can be achieved by teachers explaining, commenting, orchestrating and modelling the *four Rs* from the perspective of the subject under investigation.

How to use it

In an interesting guide that he presents to teachers and parents, Claxton describes developing a child's learning power as being 'comparable to developing their muscles'. He advocates that to do this, teachers need to encourage their learners to:

- Ask questions, to be curious and to be playful with ideas.
- See the connections between events and their own experiences.
- Use their imagination and intuition to explore new possibilities.
- Use their powers of logic and reason to work things out methodically.
- Capitalise on the vast array of resources that are available to support their learning.
- Know where they are going and what they need to do to get there.

- Review how things are going and change plans in light of changing circumstances.
- Draw out the lessons from experiences and reflect on their learning.
- Get to know themselves as a learner and what works best for them.
- Recognise and respect other viewpoints and learn from these.
- Adopt the habits and values of other people who they respect.
- Listen to and empathise with other people.
- Know when it is appropriate to learn separately or with others.
- Recognise and reduce distractions and create the best environment for learning.
- Keep going in the face of adversity and learn how to deal with difficulties.
- Learn how to concentrate and become absorbed in what they are doing.
- Notice subtle pattern and nuances in their experiences.

Claxton claims that encouraging children in this way will create classroom cultures that cultivate the habits and attitudes of curious, confident and independent learners, captures the richness of learning, make the *how* of learning explicit, grow high-value learning characteristics and equip children with the learning habits and the qualifications to thrive in the twenty-first century.

In the classroom

- Tell children about the need to develop their learning powers and allow them to discuss their thoughts on this.
- Select activities and arrange the learning environment that will help children to develop their resilience, resourcefulness, reflectiveness and reciprocity.
- Role model what it means to be an effective learner.

Critical Perspective

What do you think Claxton meant when he wrote that 'many children often underachieve not because they don't know what to do, but because they don't do what they know'?

For more on building learning power, read:

Claxton, G. (2018) *The Learning Power Approach: Teaching Learners to Teach Themselves.* Carmarthen, Wales: Crown House Publishing.

Also see: www.great-chart.kent.sch.uk/wp-content/uploads/2014/11/BLP-Parent27s-Guide.pdf

SECTION 3.4: WORKING WITH CHILDREN WITH ADDITIONAL NEEDS

In this section, I want to look at one of the most challenging aspects of teaching: working with children whose learning is hampered by the existence of a neurological or psychological condition. I have chosen classroom teaching techniques such as Makaton, communication tools such as Mindfulness, NLP and Transactional Analysis and use of therapies such as CBT and MBT to demonstrate how teachers can overcome some of the difficulties created by these conditions.

Neurology and psychology are closely related in that they are disciplines that focus on the functions and disorders of the brain. The disorders arising from each can be distinguished however by the following definitions:

- A **neurological** disorder is when something happens to hinder or prevent the development of areas of the brain that control movement or sensory perception. This includes conditions such as Down syndrome, autism and dyslexia.
- A **psychological** disorder is a disorder of the mind involving thoughts, behaviours and emotions that cause either self or others significant distress. This includes conditions such as schizophrenia, attachment disorder and depression.

Both sets of disorders can be wide ranging, affecting someone's physical, cognitive, emotional or behavioural states. They have various causes, complications and outcomes. Some disorders can be treated, others are permanent. Some disorders are present at birth (congenital), others emerge during infancy and adolescence whereas some remain dormant until adulthood. Some disorders may be very limited in their functional effects, while others may involve substantial disability and subsequent support needs.

Identifying psychological disorders in children or young people can be difficult with many conditions, such as ADHD and autism not being diagnosed until later childhood. In some cases, identifying the cause of a disorder can be complicated because they have a variety of symptoms that make it difficult to associate with any one condition. There are examples of psychological disorders being misdiagnosed. A recent TV documentary, *Girls with Autism*, highlighted the case in the 1980s of several teenage girls with autism who were diagnosed as having other conditions and incorrectly treated for these conditions.

The word *neurodiversity* is an umbrella term referring to a group of neurological development disorders which share common features, in particular differences in how people learn and process information. It was first introduced in the late 1990s by Judy Singer, a sociologist who had autism, in an attempt to argue that neurological conditions should not be seen as problematic, but as alternative, acceptable forms of human chemistry. According to Singer, the neurodiversity movement was necessary because of negative attitudes towards people who had neurological development disorders such as autism, dyspraxia, ADHD and Down's syndrome. This could include any of the following:

- Intolerant attitudes toward neuro diverse behaviour that may be perceived as odd or unusual.
- Intolerance toward difficulties that neuro diverse people often have.
- Discrimination against people for being neuro diverse or because of neuro diverse traits or behaviours.
- Lack of accommodation for difficulties associated with neuro diversity.
- Attitudes that neuro diverse people are inferior, or that there is something wrong with them; or that they have a disease that needs to be cured.
- Institutions designed without consideration of neuro diverse children (for example, schools with heavy demand on social skills that may be hard for them).
- Barriers to participation in society due to difficulties associated with autism that could have been accommodated (for example, a technically competent neuro diverse person may lose a job because of social awkwardness or may never get past the interview stage).
- Lack of protection for a neuro diverse person in equal employment opportunity legislation.

Singer claims that the potential is great for the neurodiversity movement to create significant social transformation and that it will help combat the belief that people who are considered disabled should be discriminated against or condescended to. Singer also claims that some parents of children with a neurological development disorder also support neurodiversity and the view that the condition is a unique way of being, rather than a disease to be cured. Such parents say they value their children's individuality and want to allow their children to develop naturally.

How to use it

By using the concept of neurodiversity to account for individual neurological differences, teachers can create a situation whereby people labelled with a specific condition or disability may be seen in terms of their strengths more so than their weaknesses; for example people with dyslexia, such as Steven Spielberg, who can be seen in terms of their visual thinking ability and artistic ability; people with ADHD, such as Olympic swimming champion Michael Phelps, who can be regarded as possessing an obsessive desire to succeed; individuals on the autistic spectrum, such as Albert Einstein and Mark Zuckerberg, who can be looked at in terms of their ability to work with systems such as computer programming or mathematical computation.

To support your work with children with neurological development disorders:

- **Talk to others**: there is a potential army of people out there who can give you advice and support when working with the child.
- **Encourage the child to be ambitious but realistic about what's achievable**: if the child who you are teaching is destined to sweep floors for a living, encourage them to be the best floorsweeper that ever lived.
- **Accept that you won't get a quick fix when working with children with needs**: success usually comes in the form of a series of small gains, often achieved over a long period of time.
- **Consider the child, not the disability**: adopt the philosophy that they are abled, but in a different way.
- **Have a positive approach to teaching children with disabilities**: there will be dark days when you feel that you are not making any progress with them, and want to give in. Do this and your negativity will rub off on them.
- **Empathy, not sympathy, is required**: not all children want someone's pity: they may need help and support but very often sympathy is the last thing they want.
- **Realise that others have needs to**: this includes you as well. Give the child who you are teaching your best shot, but not at the exclusion of others in the class.

In the classroom

- Have a positive approach to teaching children with disabilities but accept that you won't get a quick fix when working with them.
- Consider the child, not the disability; encourage them to be ambitious but realistic about what's achievable.
- Stress the importance of respect and use examples of famous people who are neurologically different but have achieved great things.

Critical Perspective

Do you agree with critics who argue that neurodiversity is just another bandwagon that minority groups jump onto?

For more ideas on neurodiversity, read:

Armstrong, T. (2011) *The Power of Neurodiversity*. Philadelphia: Da Capo Press.
Bates, R. (2016) *A Quick Guide to Special Needs and Disabilities*. London: SAGE.

Although *mindfulness* is based on some of the principles of Buddhism, it was the work of Kabat-Zinn in the 1990s that popularised it as a developmental tool. According to Kabat-Zinn, *mindfulness* is about dealing with thoughts in a detached, de-centred and non-judgemental manner. The main characteristics when working with children with additional needs are:

- **Be non-judgemental**: don't allow your own goals and values to affect your judgement on what's happening to the child. The temptation is to judge each action by the individual as good or bad. By letting go of these judgements, you will see things as they are, rather than filtering them through your own personal belief system.
- **Focus on purpose**: learn to manage the discomfort of uncertainty. Don't get sidetracked when things don't go right. Stay focused on the task in hand. Accept that there will be dark moments when you feel there is little hope. If you allow this negativity to take over completely, however, the child will pick up on this and both of you will get into a downward spiral.
- **Live in the present moment**: learn to slow down, ignore negative brain chatter about the child's condition and experience the event for what it is. Being in the *here and now* means that you experience things for what they are and not what they have been or might be.

Central to Kabat-Zinn's theory is the notion of using meditative techniques to stay in the body and to observe what thoughts are going on in the mind but not to identify with them. Gandhi once told his followers that if you can't find 20 minutes to meditate each day, find an hour. Kabat-Zinn argues that most people accept that taking time over their hygiene (showering, brushing teeth, etc.) or exercising is essential but ignore the care and attention needed for their greatest asset – their mind. He suggests that the mind can be the source of happiness or despair, creativity or self-destruction, or problem-solving or problem-making. This is particularly important when working with children with additional learning needs as a result of them having a neurological disorder.

How to use it

As well as being a useful tool for parents and teachers, mindfulness can also be used to improve the child's ability to concentrate on tasks and to stay calm when things aren't going well, or when they are having problems concentrating or conceptualising something:

- **Mindful listening**: use a tuning fork (a bell or some chimes will do) and ask them to listen to the tone. Ask them to think of something wonderful while they can still hear the tone and to raise their hand when the tone disappears. This is useful when you want them to relax after an exercise.
- **Mindful breathing**: ask them to lie down and place their favourite stuffed toy on their stomach. Ask them to rock it to sleep by breathing in and out.

- *Mindful eating*: give them a piece of fruit and ask them if they were being visited by someone from another planet how they would describe the fruit by using all of their senses (sight, smell, feel, touch and taste). This is a good exercise for getting them to savour their food and, by extension, the present moment.
- *Mindful time*: make time to connect with them. This shouldn't necessarily involve a trip to the cinema or fast food restaurant where there are distractions but something as simple as a stroll round the school or local park. A fun activity is to try to notice sights or sounds that neither of you have seen or heard before.
- *Mindful tasks*: don't make these habitual or too complicated but something simple like when they are feeling stressed or anxious about a task to get them to do a scan of their body from toes to nose, thinking about each part of their body in turn and how good they feel about it.

Kabat-Zinn claims that activities like this will help to focus the child or young person's mind on events that are happening now and at the same time be fun.

In the classroom

- Don't allow your own beliefs and values to affect your judgement on what's happening to the child.
- Don't get side-tracked when things don't go right.
- Accept that you need to experience things for what they are and not what they have been or might be.

Critical Perspective

Although it's been around now for a few years, mindfulness has begun to become popular in teaching and therapy work. Critics of mindfulness argue that it is just a fad and that claims about its behaviour-changing potential are just a marketing ploy to sell more books on the subject. What are your views on this?

For more on mindfulness, read:

Hanh, T.N. (2011) *Planting Seeds: Practicing Mindfulness with Children*. Berkeley, CA: Parallax Press.
Kabat-Zinn, J. (1994) *Wherever You Go, There You Are*. New York: Hyperion.

Transactional *Analysis* (TA) was developed by Eric Berne in the 1960s. Berne suggested that the state of mind we are in when we communicate with others will influence how the individual receives, interprets or acts on the communication. He proposed five states of mind, or *ego states*, that people use when communicating.

Here is a summary of how TA can be interpreted for teachers communicating with children:

- The **critical parent** state: this is where the teacher is overbearing towards the child and tells them what to do because they believe their way is the only correct one.
- The **nurturing parent** state: this is where the teacher expresses concern for the child and offers advice and support.
- The **free child** state: this is where the teacher is not afraid to share their feelings with the child.
- The **adaptive child** state: this is where the teacher feels inhibited in expressing themselves in front of the child.
- The **adult** state: this is where the teacher acts by expressing themselves in a calm and rational manner.

Berne stresses that the terms *parent*, *child* and *adult* have nothing to do with age or relationships but act as metaphors to describe the state of mind people adopt. He also argued that, although behaving in the *adult* ego state is generally the most effective practitioner approach, there may be times when being in the *parent* or even the *child* ego state may get results.

How to use it

Berne claims that transactional analysis is a powerful means of communicating effectively with individuals. Here are a few tips if you are going to use Berne's model when communicating with your students:

- Analyse what ego state you are in when dealing with them (this could be any one of the five ego states).
- Recognise that you have the ability to adopt any ego state.
- Appreciate that:

  o *Parent* to *child* or *child* to *parent* may get short-term results but may lead to problems later on.
  o *Parent* to *parent* may result in friction, especially if both are in *critical parent* mode.
  o *Child* to *child* may result in inertia, especially if both are in *adaptive child* mode.
  o *Adult* to *adult* is the best for long-term results.

- Start any interaction with words like 'How', 'What', 'When' and 'Why'. I promise you that this will get you to *adult* to *adult*. It may need perseverance but you will get there eventually.

TRANSACTIONAL ANALYSIS

Berne claims that transactional analysis is a very powerful tool to have when dealing with challenging children.

In the classroom

Ask yourself:

- Am I sure that I am in the right frame of mind when I am about to communicate with them?
- Do I appreciate what frame of mind they are in?
- Have I chosen the right ego state for the communication that will achieve a long-term satisfactory outcome?

Critical Perspective

What do you think of critics of transactional analysis who claim that it is grounded on the assumption that we make current decisions based on past experiences and the outcome of actions that were at one time important in our lives but that may no longer be valid?

For more on transactional analysis, read:

Berne, E. (1964) *The Games People Play: The Psychology of Human Relationships*. London: Penguin Books.

Steiner, C. (1994) *Scripts People Live: Transactional Analysis of Life Scripts*. New York: Grove Press.

The concept of Neuro-Linguistic Programming (NLP) was developed in the early 1970s by Bandler and Grinder as a methodology to understand and change unwanted human behaviour patterns.

The breakdown of the term defines what NLP is all about:

- **Neuro**: is how you use your senses to make sense of what's happening, which in turn influences how you feel and what you say and do.
- **Linguistic**: is the language and communication systems that you use to influence yourself and others.
- **Programming**: is a succession of steps designed to achieve a particular outcome.

Bandler and Grinder modelled some of their techniques on the work of a number of therapists who were achieving excellent results with clients. They then presented these techniques under what is known as the four pillars of NLP:

- **Setting your goal**: knowing what you want in any situation.
- **Using your senses**: paying close attention to the world around you.
- **Behaving flexibly**: keep on changing what you do until you get what you want.
- **Building relationships**: being aware of the contribution that others make to help you achieve your goal.

Bandler and Grinder emphasise that NLP is not a process for bending minds but a collection of tools that teachers - in fact anyone involved with the child or young person - can use to have a positive influence on them and that will enhance their interpersonal effectiveness and classroom delivery. They also claim that NLP will enable teachers to discover how language and their internal processing affects the behaviour of others around them, learn to communicate in ways they never thought possible both inside and outside the classroom and take their communication skills to the next level.

How to use it

Here are some important principles should you choose to use NLP when working with students:

- **The map is not the territory**: accept that, if the territory represents reality, the map is merely the student's representation of that reality. Some students have incredibly complex maps, others have very basic maps.
- **Respect the other person's map**: acknowledge that a student responds according to their individual map and may act in ways that you find unhelpful or unacceptable.
- **Seek to be understood not just heard**: instead of blaming the students for misunderstanding your meaning, accept total responsibility for your communication. Always make sure when you talk to them that you get them to give you feedback that they have understood what you wanted them to do.

- **Every behaviour has a positive intention**: appreciate that their behaviour is their response to what they perceive to be the reality currently being experienced by them. Remember that although you may not share their sense of what's real, this doesn't make it any less real for them.
- **Accept the person; change the behaviour**: understand that their behaviour is not who they are, but a reaction to the challenges they are facing. Accept them for who they are, but support them to change their behaviour if it's inappropriate.
- **There is no failure, only feedback**: reassure them that if they haven't succeeded in overcoming their challenges, they haven't failed, they just haven't succeeded yet. Support them to vary their behaviour and find different ways of achieving their desired outcomes.
- **If you always do what you've always done, you'll always get what you've always got**: this is sometimes referred to as Ashby's Law of Requisite Variety. Recognise that by having greater flexibility of thought and behaviour you are more likely to be able to influence the student's reaction to how they feel about themself.

In the classroom

- Observe your students carefully and you will get some interesting information about their state of mind.
- Your body language is important and will tell students a lot about the way you feel.
- Your students' body language is important and will tell you a lot about the way they are responding to your teaching.

Critical Perspective

Some people are wary about NLP because they think it is a way of bending minds and manipulating people. What are your thoughts on this?

For more on NLP, read:

Churches, R. and Terry, R. (2007) *NLP for Teachers: How to be a Highly Effective Teacher*. Carmarthen, Wales: Crown House Publishing.

Beever, S. (2009) *Happy Kids, Happy You: Using NLP to bring out the best in ourselves and the child we care for*. Carmarthen, Wales: Crown House Publishing.

Cognitive Behavioural Therapy (CBT) was developed by Dr Aaron Beck in the 1960s. It differs from the more traditional behavioural therapies in that it focuses primarily on the thoughts and emotions (the causes) that lead to certain unwanted behaviours rather attempting to eliminate the symptoms (the effects) of unwanted behaviour. Over the past 50 years there has been significant growth in the use of CBT, especially in the prison and education systems. It is now widely used in the treatment of depression, anxiety and other neurological development disorders, and as an anger management tool. Although it was originally intended to just deal with adults, CBT practices have been widened over the past 20 years to include working with children and young people.

People who have become stigmatised and even traumatised through having a condition that made them different from their peers are often racked with self-directed messages of inadequacy and self-doubt. CBT therapists work with the client to get them to:

- *reflect* – reconsider their assumptions about themselves
- *recognise* – identify the thoughts and emotions that are causing the unwanted behaviour
- *react* – to see that, by changing the way they view themselves and their environment, they can improve their condition.

Beck argued that, in order to be effective, CBT therapists need to encourage the client to open up about what's affecting their thoughts and emotions and to generate more positive thoughts about their situations and their ability to cope with them. This may prove challenging as many children and younger clients with psychological disorders may feel overwhelmed by their conditions and see improvement as impossible. Beck claims that CBT attempts to deal with this by breaking down the improvements into bite-sizable, manageable steps.

How to use it

Peter was considered a brilliant pupil by his teachers. He passed four A levels with outstanding grades and the Oxbridge entrance exams. His potential was recognised early by the school, but so was his disruptive behaviour. When he was in year 13 he had rigged a minor explosion in a chemistry class that destroyed equipment and came close to hurting someone. He had avoided being excluded from school due to the prestige his achievements gave the school. Peter was an exceptional pupil but sacrificed a lot of his formative years in his attempt to get outstanding grades. Peter is now in his mid-thirties. After spells of homelessness and a caution for shoplifting, he is now in a stable relationship and works in a charity shop. He appeared to be at a very content phase in his life.

If you are having problems with a student like Peter, here are some thoughts about how a trained CBT therapist would go about working with them:

- **Engagement:** they would meet with Peter and his teacher and parents to assess the extent and nature of their concerns about his behaviour and the outcomes that they expect from the therapy.

- **Formulation**: once the student has identified possible outcomes and demonstrated a willingness to engage with the CBT process, a plan is formulated to deal with the issues facing them.
- **Reappraisal**: the therapist works with the individual to help them reappraise their thoughts and negative assumptions about themselves and to develop alternative and more positive assumptions about their learning.
- **Consolidation**: the therapist will work with the individual to help them to consolidate more positive assumptions about themselves and their learning and have a strategy for dealing with any relapses.

Beck claims that using CBT focuses specifically on problems being experienced in the here and now, not the past.

In the classroom

- Look out for students who are displaying persistent erratic behaviour.
- Determine whether or not you need to seek professional help for them.
- Discuss with an educational psychologist whether CBT will help.

Critical Perspective

What do you think about Peter's school's actions in failing to deal with his disruptive behaviour because of the prestige that his academic achievements gave them?

For more on CBT, read:

Fitzgerald, S. (2013) *The CBT Workbook*. London: Hodder & Stoughton.
Stallard, P. (2005) *A Clinician's Guide to Think Good - Feel Good: Using CBT with Children*. Chichester, England: John Wiley & Sons Ltd.

Mentalisation-Based Treatment (MBT) was developed by Bateman and Fonagy in the 1990s. It differs from the more traditional behavioural therapies in that it focuses primarily on encouraging individuals to examine their own thoughts or beliefs about themselves and their relationships with others.

MBT was originally designed for working with people with borderline personality disorder (BPD) but can also be used to work with anyone who has problems sustaining any form of meaningful relationship due to anger issues or have conditions such as eating disorders, depression or PTSD.

The major goals of MBT involve:

- **Better behavioural control**: understanding the contributions made to the problems and conflicts they are experiencing with others. This will help children and young people understand which thoughts, interactions and circumstances are causing them to have challenges in their lives and feel more in charge of their own lives and behaviour.
- **Increased affect regulation**: changing their impulsive, automatic, and/or addictive responses to a particular challenge and developing the ability to calm down when upset or affected by these.
- **More intimate and gratifying relationships**: relating to other people with empathy and compassion by being aware of the mental states of others and appreciating that all may not be as it appears to them.
- **The ability to pursue life goals**: taking a step back and reflecting on the validity of existing goals.

The theories that underpin the process of mentalisation are that: everyone has the ability to ascribe intentions and meaning to human behaviour; it is predicated on the belief that ideas shape interpersonal behaviour; it shapes our understanding of ourselves and others and it is central to human communications and relationships.

How to use it

Connor was 12 when Vic started teaching him. There was something about Connor that disturbed Vic. It wasn't fear but that sense of dread that you get when you think something bad is going to happen. Vic wasn't alone in this respect; other teachers had similar feelings towards Connor. It wasn't that people particularly disliked Connor and nothing untoward had happened in the first term to cause Vic to impose any sanctions on him. Connor didn't have any close friends in the class and preferred to work on his own. On the occasions when he was asked to work with others, he became agitated and Vic noticed Connor constantly tapping his toes on the floor. When one of his classmates said that he'd got something wrong, Connor left the room. He returned after a few minutes and when the same classmate made a derisive comment about his absence Connor just flew at him, with a flurry of punches. Vic had to restrain Connor and remove him from the class.

If you are having problems with a student like Connor, here are some thoughts about how a trained MBT therapist would go about working with them:

- The therapist will focus on Connor's difficulty in recognising the effects that his behaviour has on other people and his inability to empathise with others.
- They will try to get Connor to take a step back from his thoughts about himself and others and to mentalise or rationalise whether these thoughts are valid.
- They will then get Connor to reflect on his current interpersonal interactions and relationships – a process that is described as one of curious exploration and investigation.

Bateman and Fonagy claim that the essence of MBT is *thinking about thinking* and is the best way of someone examining their own thoughts and beliefs.

In the classroom

- Look out for students who are displaying persistent erratic behaviour.
- Determine whether or not you need to seek professional help for them.
- Discuss with an educational psychologist whether MBT will help.

Critical Perspective

Have you had to deal with someone with anger issues like Connor? If so, what do you think about the appropriateness of therapies like MBT in dealing with this?

For more on MBT, read:

Bateman, A. and Fonagy, P. (2006) *Mentalization-Based Treatment for Borderline Personality Disorder: A Practical Guide*. Oxford: Oxford University Press.

Allen, J.G. and Fonagy, P. (2006) *Handbook of Mentalization-Based Treatment*. Chichester: John Wiley & Sons.

Makaton was developed in the 1970s by Margaret Walker, a speech and language therapist, with the help of Kathy Johnston and Tony Cornforth. The term was invented by using the first syllables of their names. It has remained one of most pervasive and influential pedagogical approaches for children with severe learning difficulties and is being used in special needs schools in over 40 countries.

Makaton is designed to support communication with a series of signs and symbols that are used in conjunction with speech in much the same way as sign language is used for people who are profoundly deaf. This helps provide extra clues about what someone is saying. Their designers claim that using signs in this way can help people who have no speech or whose speech is impaired.

The Makaton designers also claim that, for those who have experienced the frustration of being unable to communicate meaningfully or effectively, Makaton takes away that frustration and enables individuals to connect with other people and the world around them. They further claim that the Makaton process is extremely flexible and can be personalised to an individual's needs and used at a level suitable for them, and can be used to enable the child or young person to:

- share their thoughts, choices and emotions
- take part in games and songs
- listen to, read and tell stories
- find their way around public places.

Most people start using Makaton as children then naturally stop using the signs and symbols as they no longer need them to communicate. Today it is estimated that over 100,000 children and young people use Makaton symbols and signs to help them to communicate.

How to use it

The designers of Makaton argue that using symbols that are a simplified version of sign language can help children and young people who have limited learning abilities and speech, and those who cannot, or prefer not to, use sign language. There are also examples of schools, such as the ARK Rose Primary School in Birmingham, where children whose first language isn't English and who had little or no understanding of English, are being taught Makaton to help them to communicate with teachers and other students. The school found that within two months after starting to learn, most children were able to have meaningful conversations with others in the class.

To be effective in teaching Makaton to children with communication difficulties, teachers need to:

- focus on what the child needs to be able to communicate, i.e. their wants and needs
- find out what motivates them to sign, e.g. their likes and hobbies
- be wary of overloading learners with too many signs at any one time
- use singing and signing to enforce learning

- use pictures, gestures and photos and don't rely solely on Makaton for communication purposes
- use the materials available on the Makaton website.

In the classroom

- Determine what the child needs to communicate such as their wants and needs.
- Determine what motivates them to sign, such as their interests and hobbies.
- Determine how you can use other media tools to enhance Makaton.

Critical Perspective

Do you agree with the critics of Makaton who argue that it is merely a watered down version of sign language and can actually discourage children from developing their ability to speak?

For more on Makaton, read:

Walker, M. (2015) *Animal Signs*. Farnborough: The Makaton Charity.
There are a number of books and free downloadable materials available on the Makaton website: www.makaton.org/shop

SECTION 3.5: DIFFERENT SCHOOL APPROACHES

The purpose of this section of the book is to explore some pertinent and particular models of educational practice and provision from around the world. I've chosen just a small sample from the many different approaches worldwide because I think that they address the question of whether education is a preparation for employment or a lifelong process without a finite goal with something in between.

The first two examples originated in Europe in the early part of the twentieth century. The Montessorian approach believed in the importance of educating the senses before educating the intellect and the Summerhill School approach was based on the belief that children should be given a sense of personal freedom through guidance and support rather than control.

More contemporary approaches discussed in this section include: the Steiner approach which emphasises the importance of the use of practical, artistic and conceptual elements in education; the Reggio Emilia approach which focuses on what children know, are curious about and what challenges them; the Forest Schools approach which concentrates on developing children's enthusiasm for education through an appreciation of nature; and *Te Whāriki* which is founded on the mission to ensure that children will grow up as 'competent and confident learners and communicators, healthy in mind, body and spirit and in the knowledge that they make a valued contribution to society'.

It's important that I make two points here. Firstly, that I don't discount the value that religious-based schools have to play in their respective communities, and secondly, that there are some really innovative projects related to the teaching of new technologies. They are not included here, partly because of space and partly because I just don't know enough about them and their educational value to be confident in their inclusion.

Montessori believed in the importance of educating the senses before educating the intellect. Her theories developed as a result of her time as a physician working with children categorised as *uneducable*. She rejected the behaviourist approach to teaching skills through repetition and focused on developing exercises that prepared people to learn new skills by first educating their senses.

Her theories are based on a series of observations of children during which time she discovered:

- Younger learners (from birth to around age six) in particular have an 'absorbent mind', during which time their motivation to learn new things is limitless.
- There are a number of 'sensitivity periods' of development during which time a learner's mind is open to learning new skills or knowledge.
- Movement enhances thinking and learning.
- People learn better when learning is relevant to them.
- All learners are capable of self-directed learning.
- Learning is improved if there is a sense of control or order within the classroom.
- Learners learn best from self-discovery and making mistakes.

Montessori suggested that the focus on self-realisation through independent activity, the concern with attitude, the focus on the teacher as a facilitator and the creation of a stimulating learning environment would create a more meaningful learning experience.

How to use it

It's difficult not to get carried away with some of the philosophical ideas that underpin Montessorian education. Tell my mate Glen, a bricklaying tutor at a local college, that all of his learners 'hold within them something wonderful, something so special that it could be the key to changing the world', and he'll think you've been off with the fairies again. There is however something wholesome in what Montessori is advocating.

To become a *Montessorian*:

- Appreciate that people thrive on order and structure so ensure that everything has its place and that the learning environment is as accessible as possible for people to work in.
- Be aware that individuals will have peaks and troughs in their responses to your practice. Don't assume that everyone is learning at the same intense rate as others. Have a strategy for dealing with both the high and low intensity individuals in the same group.
- Make your learning materials appeal to as wide a range of senses as possible. A maths teacher I once observed brought several different boxes of a well-known sweet (cones, boxes, cylinders, etc.) into class. She used them to teach size, shape, volume, even statistics by looking at the frequency of colours of sweets in each packet. Learners were allowed to eat the sweets afterwards.

- Encourage people to develop as spontaneous, creative individuals by allowing them to view situations from different standpoints (see Theory 8), take risks, make mistakes and follow their natural impulses.
- Allow individuals the freedom to work alone on certain activities but don't forget to get them to share their learning experiences with others. In this capacity appreciate that your role is as the facilitator (see Theory 25) not the classroom controller.

In the classroom

- Make your subject matter accessible to all.
- Have learning materials that appeal to a wide range of senses.
- Encourage learners to follow their natural instincts and not be afraid of making mistakes.

Critical Perspective

What are the dangers of encouraging children to develop as spontaneous, creative individuals by allowing them to view situations from different standpoints, take risks, make mistakes and follow their natural impulses?

For more on Montessori's ideas, read:

Hainstock, E.G. (1997) *The Essential Montessori: An Introduction to the Woman, the Writings, the Method and the Movement*. New York: Plume.

Standing, E.M. (1984) *Maria Montessori: Her Life and Work*. New York: Plume.

Neill opened Summerhill School in the South of England in 1921. The school's philosophy was based on the belief that the happiness of the child should be the prime consideration in their upbringing and education and that this happiness could be fostered by giving them a sense of personal freedom through guidance and support rather than control.

He suggested that this sense of freedom could be developed in line with the following principles:

- People learn better when they are not forced to attend lessons.
- People should be given the opportunity to contribute to determining ground rules.
- People should have an equal say in developing learning routines.
- Externally imposed discipline should be avoided.
- Internal self-discipline should be encouraged.
- Extrinsic motivation (rewards and punishments) should be avoided.
- Intrinsic self-motivation should be developed.

Neill argued that deprivation of freedom to learn during childhood contributed to some of the psychological disorders in adulthood and may be a contributing factor as to why some adults are reluctant to continue into post-compulsory education.

School inspectors and later Ofsted might take a dim view of the educational achievements at Summerhill; maybe even recommend that they go into special measures. Neill countered this by claiming that the children accepted at Summerhill were often from problematic backgrounds and that, although they were less likely to go to university, they were more likely to pass a job interview than someone from a conventional educational background.

How to use it

I'm not sure that, even today, Neill's approach would be acceptable to many who think his theories are too radical; or at best controversial, and a serious threat to social disorder. You have to decide which camp you are in on this. No sitting on the fence!

To give you some food for thought, have a look at the film *To Sir, with Love* and Sydney Poitier's portrayal of a black teacher working in a tough London secondary school. His pupils came from rough homes and enjoyed riding roughshod over their teachers. Poitier's character wins over his pupils by treating them as adults, involving them in deciding on classroom issues and organising activities that are meaningful and fun.

Does he succeed? Watch the film and decide for yourself. In the meantime, here are a few tips for how to emulate Neill:

- Unless it conflicts with the policy of your organisation, allow learners the opportunity to opt out of lessons they feel will not contribute to the achievement of their learning goals. This will allow them to concentrate on the ones that will.

- Give learners the opportunity to contribute to determining ground rules and in developing learning objectives and routines. This will engender a sense of ownership in their learning.
- Avoid externally imposed discipline and encourage your learners to develop internal self-discipline. This will enhance their inner desire to want to learn.

Of course, Neill was the Head of the school and decisions about how much freedom learners had to learn rested with him. You may not be in such a position. Buy the head of your organisation a copy of this book (or maybe one of Neill's books) and stick a bookmark in this page. You never know, it might just spark a *ping* moment (see Theory 18).

In the classroom

- Allow learners to opt out of lessons that have no meaning or relevance to them.
- Give learners the opportunity to contribute to developing ground rules and learning intentions.
- Don't rely on rewards and punishments as a way of motivating your learners.

Critical Perspective

What do you think of Neill's philosophy at Summerhill school which was based on the belief that the happiness of the child should be the prime consideration in their upbringing and education and that this happiness could be fostered by giving them a sense of personal freedom through guidance and support rather than control?

For more on Neill's ideas, read:

Ayers, W. (2003) *On the Side of the Child: Summerhill Revisited.* New York: Teachers College Press.

Neill, A.S. (1960) *Summerhill School: A Radical Approach to Learning.* New York: St. Martin's Griffin.

Reggio Emilia is a small town in Northern Italy that became internationally renowned for its community-based learning provision for children from infancy to six years of age. Professor Loris Malaguzzi, the founder of the Reggio approach to pre-school education, was heavily influenced by the work of another Italian educator, Maria Montessori, and her idea of educating the senses before educating the intellect.

In its most basic form Malaguzzi's approach to teaching, learning and advocacy for children was to observe what children know, are curious about and what challenges them. Teachers are encouraged to record these observations and to reflect on appropriate ways to help children expand their academic and social potentials. In this respect, Malaguzzi argued that:

- Children are capable of constructing their own learning and are driven by their interests to understand and know more.
- Children form an understanding of themselves and their place in the world through their interactions with others.
- The adult is not the giver of knowledge. Children search out the knowledge through their own investigations.
- Children use communication as a way of discovering things, asking questions and using language as *play.*
- Children are listened to with respect, believing that their questions and observations are an opportunity to learn and search together.
- The environment is the third teacher and is recognised for its potential to inspire children.
- The space encourages collaboration, communication and exploration.
- Learning takes a child-led project approach, which isn't planned in advanced but emerges based on the child's interests.
- An emphasis on documenting children's thoughts, and making their thoughts visible in many different ways – photographs, transcripts of children's thoughts and explanations, visual representations (drawings, sculptures, etc.) are all designed to show the child's learning process.

Probably the most well-known aspect of the Reggio Emilia approach is *The Hundred Languages of Children* model and the belief that children use many different ways to show their understanding and express their thoughts and creativity. The model suggests that children have a hundred (or more) different ways of thinking, of discovering, of learning. This can be done through drawing and sculpting, through dance and movement, through painting and pretend play, through modelling and music. Reggio Emilia educators argue that each one of these *Hundred Languages* must be valued and nurtured.

How to use it

The Reggio Emilia approach views children as individuals and responds to them appropriately. Teachers believe that all children have preparedness, potential, curiosity and interest in constructing their learning, in engaging in social interaction, and in negotiating with everything the environment brings to them. To follow these principles:

- Recognise your role as the child's mentor and guide. Observe them, listen to their questions and their stories, find what interests them and then provide them with opportunities to explore these interests further.
- Get to know the child's strengths, needs and personality.
- Document what they do and work closely with other teachers and the child's parents on projects that are based on the child's interests.
- Don't rely solely on written assignments as a means of assessing a child's progress. Allow them to do this through poetry and song, dance and movement, art and media or any medium that they feel comfortable with.
- Act as an advocate for the child with other educators and community members.
- Encourage parents to accept that they are an essential component of the school, and need to play an active part in their children's learning experiences and help to ensure the welfare of all the children in the school.
- Accept that projects provide the backbone of the children's and teachers' learning experiences. They are based on the strong convictions that learning by doing is of great importance and that to discuss in groups and to revisit ideas and experiences is the premier way of learning.

In the classroom

- Get to know the child's strengths, needs and personality and use this as the basis for their learning.
- Don't rely solely on written assignments or SATs tests as a means of assessing a child's progress.
- Encourage parents to play an active part in their children's learning experiences.

Critical Perspective

The main criticism of the Reggio Emilia approach is that it is not a formal learning process with the absence of a defined curriculum and teacher certification. Do you consider that this is a recipe for creativity or chaos?

For more on Reggio Emilia, read:

Abbott, L. and Nutbrown, C. (eds) (2001) *Experiencing Reggio Emilia: Implications for Pre-school Provision*. Buckingham: Open University Press.

Rinaldi, C. (2006) *In Dialogue with Reggio Emilia: Listening, Researching and Learning*. Abingdon, Oxon: Routledge.

The Steiner approach to education emphasises the importance of the use of practical, artistic and conceptual elements in education. This method of education was established by Rudolf Steiner, the founder of a spiritual philosophy called *anthroposophy*, which includes theories about spirits on earth and reincarnation.

The Steiner approach to education is modelled strongly on the work of Jean Piaget and is based on the argument that the role of play and imagination in learning is integral for the development of creative and analytical thinking. The approach therefore is aimed at providing an environment where young people can develop free thinking as the basis for developing their own personalities as responsible individuals.

The key features of Steiner's approach to education are:

- *Children need to learn through all senses* - all lessons in Steiner schools are designed to appeal to the 'head, hands and heart' meaning that it is important to educate the whole child.
- *Imagination is at the heart of learning* - Steiner school classrooms include a great deal of storytelling, fantasy, make-believe play, art, drama and crafts.
- *Life-skills are imperative to a complete education* - children in Steiner school classrooms are taught things like wood carving, sewing, gardening and sculpting. They are offered opportunities to take up things like learning to play a musical instrument or knitting
- *A lifelong love for learning can be achieved through the arts* - Steiner suggested that curriculum subjects such as maths and English can be examined through graphic-arts projects, and a multi-disciplinary approach is desirable.
- *Children need to be surrounded by beauty in an aesthetically pleasing environment* - the Steiner school classroom is a home-like setting filled with natural materials where children have periods of guided free-play which focuses on their developmental needs.
- *Children are taught respect, cooperation, compassion and social responsibility* - ethical ideas and social responsibility are introduced as the young person begins to develop the capacity for making judgements.
- *Students are discouraged from using technology at young ages* - Steiner argues that this lack of exposure to televisions, computers and other forms of technology create students with extended attention spans and contributes to their creative imaginative thinking.

The Steiner approach is used for *Waldorf* schools, which were developed in the early twentieth century at the request of the owner of the Waldorf-Astoria Cigarette Company in Stuttgart, Germany, to serve the children of employees of the factory. The co-educational school was the first comprehensive school in Germany, serving children from all social classes, genders, abilities and interests. There are now well over a thousand Waldorf schools.

How to use it

Steiner believed in educating the whole child, but in a way that was appropriate to their developmental stage and their needs. If you want to follow the ideas of Steiner then consider which of the approaches are appropriate to the children that you are teaching:

STEINER SCHOOLS

Early childhood learning

- Learning in early childhood should be practical activity oriented as the learning in this stage is largely sensory-based.
- The classroom environment should be homelike and include natural materials, and provide examples of productive work in which children can take part.
- There should be lots of outdoor activities accompanied by songs, poems and games.
- There should be specific times set aside for stories and fairy tales to encourage imaginative thinking.
- Exposure to normal media like television and mainstream music should be discouraged.

Primary education

- Elementary education should be more imaginative and artistic so that the child gets an idea of life and the surrounding world, and develops their own ideas.
- There should be an emphasis on activities that involve visual arts, drama, vocal and instrumental music and crafts.
- Lessons should not be based on standardised textbooks but on each child being allowed to create their own list of coursework.
- Each child should be allowed to learn in their own pace to allow the child to grasp the concepts or learn a skill based on their capabilities.

Secondary education

- This should be based on ethical ideas and social responsibility as the young person should begin to develop the capacity for abstract thought and conceptual judgement.
- There should be a higher concentration on academic subjects.

In the classroom

- Early childhood education should be fun and focused on play.
- Primary education should focus on creative activities.
- Secondary education should concentrate on giving the child a sense of social responsibility.

Critical Perspective

The main criticism of Steiner schooling is that children are not taught to read until they are seven or eight years old. Are you someone who worries that Steiner-educated children will fall behind in their education, particularly if they transfer to a more traditional school where reading is taught at an earlier age?

For more on Steiner's ideas, read:

Edmunds, F. (2012) *An Introduction to Steiner Schools: The Waldorf School.* Sophia Books: Forest Row.

Te *Whāriki* (Maori for 'woven mat') is the name given to the pre-school curriculum in New Zealand. It was developed by May and Carr in the early nineties and founded on the mission to ensure that children grow up as 'competent and confident learners and communicators, healthy in mind, body and spirit and in the knowledge that they make a valued contribution to society'.

The four broad principles of *Te Whāriki* are:

- **Empowerment** (Whakamana) - children are empowered to learn and grow at a pace to suit them.
- **Holistic development** (Kotahitanga) - children learn and grow in a holistic way. Their intellectual, social, cultural, physical, emotional and spiritual learning is interwoven across all their experiences.
- **Family and community** (Whanau tangata) - a child's family and community are recognised as part of the learning experience.
- **Relationships** (Nga Hononga) - children learn through positive relationships with people, places and things.

Te Whāriki's four principles are interwoven with these learning strands, learning dispositions and subsequent action and behaviours to produce:

Strand	Learning disposition	Action and behaviours
Well-being (Mana atua)	Trust and playfulness	Being involved
Contribution (Mana tangata)	Fairness and empathy	Taking responsibility
Belonging (Mana whenua)	Courage and curiosity	Taking an interest
Communication (Mana reo)	Confidence	Expressing feelings
Exploration (Mana aotūroa)	Perseverance	Tackling problems

Because *Te Whāriki* places the learning experiences of children in a broader social and cultural context, reciprocal relationships and interactions are of central importance with children actively co-constructing their own knowledge and understandings in everyday social and cultural settings. Such approaches recognise the multiple pathways of development and learning, which underpin principles of diversity and inclusion.

May and Carr argue that because learning happens in this way and all the time, the connections children make about their learning between home and their school setting helps them build strong learning foundations. They further claim that this links completely with the metaphor of the *woven mat* which views the curriculum for each child as a tapestry and emphasises a model of learning for young children as being a mixture of increasing complexity and richness rather than a staircase of accumulated skills and knowledge.

TE WHĀRIKI

How to use it

May and Carr admit that translating the principles of diversity and inclusion embedded in *Te Whāriki* is a challenge to teachers in many centres. Here are some tips on how to respond to the challenge:

- Provide resources, challenges and support for the child's widening interests and problem-solving capacities.
- Allow for creative expression, symbolism and representation, especially through the child's use of storytelling.
- Create opportunities that take the child outside their comfort zone with new and exciting experiences.
- Encourage them to interact with other children.
- Recognise the child's developing personality and sense of humour.

By doing this, May and Carr claim that children will experience an environment where their health is promoted; their emotional well-being is nurtured; they are kept safe from harm; their links with the family and the wider world will be affirmed and extended; and they will experience an environment where there are equitable opportunities for learning, irrespective of gender, ability, age, ethnicity or background.

In the classroom

- Allow children to learn and grow in a holistic way, at their own pace.
- Invite the child's family and community to be part of the learning experience.
- Encourage the child to learn through the relationships they have with people, places and things.

Critical Perspective

Te Whāriki is founded on the mission to ensure that 'children will grow up as competent and confident communicators, healthy in mind, body and spirit and in the knowledge that they make a valued contribution to society'. How important do you think this is where young children are concerned?

For more on *Te Whāriki*, read:

Carr, M. and May, H. (1993) Choosing a model: Reflecting on the development process of Te Whāriki. *International Journal of Early Years Education*, 1(3), 7-22.

May, H. (2009) *Politics in the Playground: The World of Early Childhood in New Zealand.* Dunedin: University of Otago Press.

Although there is a question mark about where and when the concept of Forest Schools was actually first developed and by whom, I've found sufficient evidence in the literature to suggest that it was in Denmark in 1952 where the format for the way that Forest Schools now operate originated, and that Ella Flatau's *Walking Kindergartens* were the first examples of it in practice with younger children.

It is based on the idea that young children can develop enthusiasm for education through an appreciation of nature. It is claimed that in Denmark, Forest Schools have boosted pupils' confidence and improved their behaviour and social skills, and that by participating in engaging, motivating and achievable tasks and activities in a woodland environment participants have an opportunity to develop intrinsic motivation and sound emotional and social skills.

Forest Schools claim that, by using the outdoor environment, usually a woodland setting with other habitats in which to explore and learn, they 'create a unique learning vehicle that is used to encourage a range of individuals, community groups and larger organisations to utilise their local open space for interactive play, health, recreation and personal development uses'. They claim that the outcomes of this are that it:

- gives participants a positive mental attitude, self-esteem and confidence through using their own initiative to solve problems
- improves their cooperation and awareness of others
- improves their motivation and encourages them to have a positive attitude to learning
- encourages ownership and pride in the local environment
- encourages an improved relationship with, and better understanding of, the outdoors
- increases the skills and knowledge of the participants
- teaches them how to manage essential life skills such as risk.

Forest School teachers claim that as a result of these outcomes, learners develop a respect and understanding for the natural world and what it has to offer. In this environment they further claim that learners take their time and begin to realise that making mistakes is acceptable and part of a good learning curve. None of this can be achieved unless each individual is willing to take risks. It may be a personal emotional risk or a physical risk like climbing a tree, and knowing how to take the risk and when to say this is high enough for me.

How to use it

Forest Routes is an organisation based in the UK that has developed the Forest Schools concept for working with children and young people who have learning difficulties or who are disengaging with traditional educational approaches. Nigel Curnow, the CEO of Forest Routes claims that it is the combination of the pedagogy of Forest Schools and practical aspects of bushcraft, such as knife use, that create a supportive and nurturing environment, which often makes the difference for those who find mainstream learning challenging. These type of activities help change how many in society view certain items such as knives, which are no longer seen as a weapon but become an essential tool that can be used to create fire, spoons and musical instruments. Here are some tips from Forest Routes as to how you can make the concept work well in your school:

- **Find a suitable space**: a corner of the school field isn't enough; you need access to green spaces with an abundance of trees. A local park may do but a bit of wild space is better.
- **Ensure that senior managers are on board**: the headteacher and management team must be supportive of Forest School principles.
- **Integrate these principles into the school development plan**: look at how you can make the most of the ethos and facilities within the formal and informal curriculum of the school.
- **Take things gradually**: a school not currently involved in outdoor education should not try to move straight to a Forest School ethos
- **Train in-house Forest School leaders**: if you want to get out into the woods on a regular basis, delving into a lot more of the practical stuff and actually building your own classroom outdoors, then train up a Forest School leader.
- **Don't be daunted by risk**: there is a perception that Forest School is all about knives and fires. As a result, some schools get really scared by the concept.
- **Accept that you won't persuade everybody of the virtues of Forest Schools**: a lot of people, teachers, parents and children aren't outdoor types. Don't try to force anyone to participate but try to win them over by making the activities fun and meaningful.

In the forest

- Make sure that you do a risk assessment.
- Only use tools appropriate to the age group that you are teaching.
- Tell learners not to be afraid of making mistakes and that learning from mistakes is an essential part of growing up.

Critical Perspective

Forest Schools are sweeping the UK with their focus on fresh air, teamwork and child-centred learning rather than testing. But can they prepare children for our technology-obsessed world?

For more on Forest Schools, read:

Knight, S. (2011) *Forest School for All*. London: SAGE.

SUMMARY OF PART 3

In this part of the book, I have included eight approaches that look at childhood development from a social, emotional, ecological, ethical and moral perspective and a further five that look at strategies for working with children in the classroom.

I started by looking at the child and their social development and began with two theories which deal with the crises that children experience and need to resolve as part of their social development. I then looked at two theories that cover the wider impact that society has on influencing the child's social development and capacity to learn.

The next section was arguably one of the most difficult parts of the book to research and write. I wanted something that emphasised that each child has a unique genetic and biological make-up that determines their rate of emotional development and that dealt with the impact that nature and nurture has on this. I built on the Locke–Descartes debate on this in Theory 4 by looking at the thoughts of Gesell and Coles. I then looked at two theories that dealt with the issues of identity and morality and the impact that these have on a child's emotional development.

I then looked at five classroom teaching approaches specifically designed for children that ranged from one more established theory which is based on the principles of early childhood specialists to four more contemporary approaches.

The next task was to look at one of the most challenging aspects of teaching – working with children whose learning is hampered by the existence of a neurological or psychological condition. I began by introducing the concept of neurodiveristy before choosing classroom teaching techniques, such as Makaton, communication tools such as transactional analysis, NLP and mindfulness and use of therapies such as CBT and MBT to demonstrate how teachers can overcome some of the difficulties created by these conditions.

I concluded this part of the book by looking at some models of educational practice and provision from around the world. I chose just a small sample from the many different approaches worldwide because I thought that they addressed the question of whether education is a preparation for employment or a lifelong process without a finite goal through approaches that were something in between.

The key points to emerge from this part of the book are:

- Make sure that you offer early intervention and support to families where attachment needs are not being met.
- Encourage the child's primary care giver to stay with their children for short periods of time during the settling-in period.
- Work with the child's primary care giver to ensure that their behaviour is consistent and sensitive to the needs of their child.
- Make sure that you fulfil any promises that you make to learners.
- Have a range of activities that will spark your learners' imagination.
- Encourage your learners to view their lives and the world as being meaningful.
- Place your learners in authentic learning situations where they are actively immersed in an activity.
- Be a facilitator of learning, not just a transmitter of knowledge.
- Cater for the individual learning needs of children wherever possible.
- Encourage children to be imaginative and creative in their play activities.
- Use materials and activities that will encourage the child to develop their fine motor skills and to explore the world around them.
- Listen without passing judgement to any stories that students have to tell you about what's going on in their lives.
- Give children the opportunity to help create a classroom code of conduct.
- Students' cultural identities must be validated through lessons and teaching practices.
- Make sure that students have a sense of belonging, are valued and appreciated on a daily basis.
- Celebrate cultural diversity.
- Present students with moral dilemmas for discussion.
- Encourage them to respect other's views and opinions on the issue.
- Allow students the opportunity to explain why they did something wrong and that they understand the consequences for this.
- Trust in the notion that the child's capacity to speak fluently will develop naturally.
- Don't rely on rote learning and don't rush to correct language errors.
- Make the learning fun.
- Encourage children to design their own phonic games.
- Don't confine learning to just the classroom; there is a whole world outdoors that can be explored.
- Make sure play items are varied but safe to use.
- Assume the role of observer and don't interfere in the play unless necessary.
- Select activities and arrange the learning environment so that it will help children to develop their resilience, resourcefulness, reflectiveness and reciprocity.
- Have a positive approach to teaching children with disabilities but accept that you won't get a quick fix when working with them.
- Consider the child, not the disability; encourage them to be ambitious but realistic about what's achievable.
- Stress the importance of respect and use examples of famous people who are neurologically different but have achieved great things.

- Don't allow your own beliefs and values to affect your judgement on what's happening to the child.
- Don't get side-tracked when things don't go right.
- Accept that you need to experience things for what they are and not what they have been or might be.
- Observe your learners carefully and you will get some interesting information about their state of mind.
- Your body language is important and will tell students a lot about the way you feel.
- Your students' body language is important and will tell you a lot about the way they are responding to your teaching.
- Look out for students who are displaying persistent erratic behaviour.
- Determine whether or not you need to seek professional help for them.
- Discuss with an educational psychologist whether CBT or MBT will help deal with students who are displaying persistent erratic behaviour.
- Be aware of what the child needs to communicate such as their wants and needs.
- Consider what motivates them to sign, such as their interests and hobbies.
- Have learning materials that appeal to a wide range of senses.
- Encourage children to follow their natural instincts and not be afraid of making mistakes.
- Give learners the opportunity to contribute to developing ground rules and learning intentions.
- Don't rely on rewards and punishments as a way of motivating your learners.
- Get to know the child's strengths, needs and personality and use this as the basis for their learning.
- Don't rely solely on written assignments or SATs tests as a means of assessing a child's progress.
- Encourage parents to play an active part in their children's learning experiences.
- Early childhood education should be fun and focused on play.
- Primary education should focus on creative activities.
- Secondary education should concentrate on giving the child a sense of social responsibility.
- Allow children to learn and grow in a holistic way, at their own pace.
- Encourage the child to learn through the relationships they have with people, places and things.
- Make sure that if you are taking learning outdoors that you do a risk assessment.
- Only use tools that might cause harm that are appropriate to the age group that you are teaching.
- Tell learners not to be afraid of making mistakes and that learning from mistakes is an essential part of growing up.

PART 4
PLANNING, DELIVERING AND ASSESSING LEARNING

INTRODUCTION TO PART 4

So far, the emphasis has very much been on how learners think and learn, and the personal qualities that teachers need to have in order to do what is right for their learners. Teachers also have a responsibility to their organisations to make sure that learning is delivered in a professional manner that doesn't compromise the integrity of the organisation or the teaching profession. In this respect, they must ensure that:

- The curriculum is planned in such a manner that it meets the need of the individual and the organisation.
- Lessons are planned and delivered in a way that ensures learning intentions are always achieved.
- Assessment methods are valid and reliable.
- Assessment is carried out with integrity throughout the learning journey.
- Feedback is given in a constructive manner as soon as possible after the assessment.
- Evaluation of teaching is done to ensure the standards required by the profession are being met.
- Quality is assured throughout the organisation.

The extent of the teacher's involvement in the planning and evaluation phases will depend on the organisational policies. Some teachers will be given pre-set curricula and lesson plans and have little scope for variation from these. Others will literally be given a blank sheet of paper and total freedom in planning lessons. Similar restrictions or freedom to act may be applied to assessment and evaluation.

In the sections that follow, there are nine models relating to curriculum design. The first six view the curriculum as being driven by the end product (the learner destination) or the process (the learner journey). The other three look at adapted forms of curriculum design. The next three sections cover key aspects of planning, delivering and assessing learning and include entries from a more contemporary selection of writers on the subject. The final section covers models on reflective practices and evaluation of quality.

SECTION 4.1: CURRICULUM PLANNING

Although the idea of curriculum is not new, the way we conceptualise it has altered considerably over the years. Terms such as 'learning programme', 'course syllabus' and 'training provision' have been, and continue to be, synonymous with curriculum.

For the purpose of this section I am using curriculum to refer to 'all the learning experiences which are planned and delivered', in other words:

- What is taught?
- Who is taught?
- How is it taught?
- Where is it taught?
- When is it taught?

Curriculum design is a systematic process with many complexities. That is the reason why it is important to know a variety of models of curriculum design. This section is divided into three sub-sections: curriculum as a product model, curriculum as a process model and specialist forms of curriculum.

The product models focus on the hard outcomes of the learning process: tangible achievements such as awards or qualifications. Teaching is very much teacher-led and curriculum planning is structured and systematic. The three models represent a development in curriculum design that goes from a very systematic, linear approach to a more interactive, cyclical approach. The 'how to use it' entries are similar but reflect this development.

The process models focus more on softer outcomes: learner development, both personal and professional. Teaching is more learner-centred and curriculum planning is interactive and involves greater appreciation of the needs of the learner. The three models represent a development from a relatively narrow perspective of learner involvement through to a *catch all* level of involvement. The 'how to use it' entries are less systematic and call for more reflection and value judgements.

The transition through the three product models and into the process models reflects the development in teaching methods from the *behaviourist* approach to the *cognitivist* and *humanist* approaches (see Part 1). It is important to stress that there isn't one single blueprint for curriculum design that fits all situations. The aspects that influence curriculum design include the characteristics of the learners, the subject matter and the context in which learning takes place.

In this section I have also added three variations on the theme of curriculum which offer different perspectives about curriculum design.

Tyler proposed a model of curriculum development that was simple and systematic. Central to Tyler's model was the formation of behavioural objectives that provided a clear and unambiguous notion of what learning outcomes were required. From these objectives, Tyler maintained that content and teaching methods would be straight-forward and results easier to evaluate.

The Rational Objective Model can be depicted as:

Tyler suggests that key questions to be asked at each stage of the model include:

* What is the purpose of the teaching?
* What experiences will attain these purposes?
* How can these experiences be organised effectively?
* How can we determine when the purposes are met?

Supporters of Tyler's model consider it to be a well-ordered structured approach to curriculum planning. Critics of the model argue that the approach is too mechanistic and obsessed with measurability.

How to use it

Use this approach when you know what outcome you want from the learning. It is a model based on the behaviourist approach to teaching. It's therefore the most teacher-centred of the curriculum models, so take control by:

* *Formulating objectives* – establishing the purpose of the learning requires you to make decisions about who are the decision-makers. These may be the organisation's governors, the academic staff, government, industry or learners. Quite probably it may be a mixture of all of these. Let's be honest, formulating a set of objectives that meets all demands isn't going to be easy and you may have to prioritise between the various factions.
* *Selecting content* – this may be pre-determined by an awarding body or exam board. You may have some scope for your own spin on this but make sure you read what's required and don't do as my geography teacher did and instead of teaching us about population in Australia, taught us about population in Austria. Both are great countries but with completely different demographics and climates.

- *Selecting teaching methods* - now this is where you can be original. My advice here would be to look at the three learning domains (see Theories 106-108) and work out what approaches are best to meet the knowledge, skills or emotional demands of your learners. You may also want to look at the different learning styles of your learners (see Theories 45-51) to help you gauge what their learning preferences are.
- *Delivering teaching* - this is the easy bit. Just turn up and strut your stuff.
- *Measuring outcomes* - reflecting on what you did during the session is one of the most important aspects of this and any of the curriculum models. Being an expert reflective practitioner is important so read Theories 125-127 to help you here.

There's a lot of reading for you here but I promise you it will be worthwhile in the long run.

In the classroom

Use this if you want a model that:

- is simple and systematic
- has an unambiguous notion of what learning outcomes are desired
- is easy to evaluate.

Critical Perspective

What do you think about critics of Tyler's model that the approach is too mechanistic and too obsessed with measurability?

For more on the rational objective model, read:

Print, M. (1993) *Curriculum Development and Design*. Crow's Nest, NSW: Allen & Unwin.

Tyler, R.W. (1949) *Basic Principles of Curriculum and Instruction*. Chicago: University of Chicago Press.

Taba proposed a model of curriculum development that was based on Tyler's objective model (see Theory 97) but built in an interactive or instructional approach in which the learning experience provided the basis for curriculum design.

The model is based on five mutually interactive elements and can be represented as follows:

Taba stressed a number of internal aspects that were critical within the process. These were:

- the importance of having specific criteria related to objectives and content
- the selection and organisation of learning experiences related to the criteria
- the choice of teaching strategies for optimum learning experiences
- having appropriate evaluation measures in place.

This model is sometimes referred to as a 'grassroots' model because it requires the curriculum to be developed by teachers. Supporters of this model claim that it encourages teachers to develop an ability to *think-in-action* (see Theory 125). Critics argue that it relies too heavily on the infallibility of teachers.

How to use it

The importance of this model is that you must work closely with colleagues and managers to ensure that content, learning objectives, teaching strategies and evaluation measures are compatible with the learning needs of the learner.

Do this by:

- meeting with your learners to find out what learning outcomes they want from the programme
- using the consensus view to formulate the course objectives. Make sure that these are specific to your learners' needs, and can be measured and delivered to an acceptable standard within an acceptable timeframe
- starting to pull together the materials that will be used and the methods that you will use to deliver them
- evaluating progress at each learning interlude.

I have been involved in too many programmes in the past where assessment and evaluation was a summative process (at the end of the programme). In this model, these processes are formative (continuous throughout the programme).

In the classroom

Use this if you want a model that:

- is interactive
- involves meeting learners' needs
- encourages you to think-in-action.

Critical Perspective

What do you think about critics of Taba's model who say that it relies too heavily on the infallibility of teachers?

For more on the grassroots model, read:

Print, M. (1993) *Curriculum Development and Design*. Crow's Nest, NSW: Allen & Unwin.
Taba, H. (1962) *Curriculum Development: Theory and Practice*. New York: Macmillan.

Stenhouse developed his interactive model in response to what he perceived as the gap between what the organisation intends to do and what it actually does. He proposed that the curriculum could be improved through inquiry into the internal working of the organisation and the broader political, economic, social and technological trends (what is referred to as a *situational analysis*) and how these impact on curriculum design and delivery.

This is represented as:

He saw curriculum development as composed of three broad elements. These are that a curriculum should:

- attempt to communicate the essential principles and features of a learning programme
- be capable of effectively translating these principles into practice
- be open to critical scrutiny.

Supporters claim that this model is not just a package of materials or content directed towards examinations, and that the emphasis is on translating educational ideas into workable practices that develop teachers as well as learners. Critics argue that the model doesn't fit into the educational agenda for accountability.

How to use it

I like Stenhouse's use of curriculum development as being like a *recipe for a dish*.

In the metaphor, he claims that the curriculum can be assessed from both a nutritional or gastronomic viewpoint, in other words does it do you good as well as looking or tasting good? He also suggests that curriculum development can be assessed in terms of practicality in which getting the ingredients for something as exotic as *Lingue Licorne et Alouettes* (which include things not readily available such as lark's tongues and unicorn's horns) may make delivery of the dish impossible. In Stenhouse's view, the curriculum, like a creative dish, has to be imagined as a possibility, subjected to experimentation (adding a bit of this and a bit of that) and grounded in practice before it can be offered for public consumption.

In terms of using the model, the main difference in approach between the Stenhouse and Wheeler models is that Stenhouse pays more attention to an initial *situational analysis*. If you choose this model then use the following as the basis for your situational analysis:

- SWOT (Strengths, Weaknesses, Opportunities and Threats) analysis to determine those factors internal to the organisation.
- PEST (Political, Economic, Social and Technological) analysis to examine trends external to the organisation.

If your thoughts about a good meal is to open up a jar, add a few ingredients and serve it up as a feast fit for a king, then shame on you! Or is it just because you are too busy to devote time to finding out the best way of meeting your learner's needs? It may be the rhetoric of Stenhouse's model is too detached from the reality. You decide!

In the classroom

Use this if you want a model that:

- needs to have a wider appreciation of society's needs
- is more about learning than passing exams
- is robust and open to critical scrutiny.

Critical Perspective

What do you think about critics of Stenhouse's model that it doesn't fit into the educational agenda for accountability?

For more on the interactive model, read:

Print, M. (1993) *Curriculum Development and Design*. Crow's Nest, NSW: Allen & Unwin.
Stenhouse, L. (1975) *An Introduction to Curriculum Research and Development*. London: Heinemann Educational.

Wheeler's model has many similarities with Tyler's rational objective model (see Theory 97) in that it is still very much teacher-centred. The main difference is that whereas the objective model suggests that evaluation serves purely to ascertain the extent to which objectives have been achieved, Wheeler argues that evaluation need not be a terminal stage in the process and that it should be a cyclical process.

Most representations of Wheeler's model ignore the important stage in the process of expressing learning outcomes in terms of expected changes in behaviour. Adding this stage, I have represented Wheeler's model as:

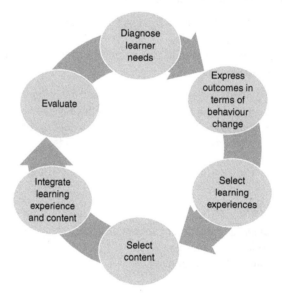

The characteristic of each of these elements can be summarised as:

- Diagnose the needs of your learners.
- Express learning outcomes in terms of expected behavioural changes.
- Design learning experiences to take account of expected changes in behaviour.
- Design content to take account of expected changes in behaviour.
- Learning experiences and content should be interrelated.
- Evaluation should be used to inform diagnosis of learner needs.

Supporters of this model claim that it puts the needs of learners first. Critics argue that it doesn't go far enough and is still too product-oriented.

How to use it

Our team were once asked to help put together a training programme for managers of General Practitioner (GPs) surgeries. We delivered this programme to a number of groups over a four-year period. The curriculum was determined by the course team working in tandem with the body that financed and controlled GP provision in the region. We had good attendance and a good pass rate (both in excess of 90%). So good was all of this that I concentrated my PhD research on evaluating the impact of the programme on GP practice managers. My conclusions in the PhD were that, far from being a success, we had failed practice managers by not talking to them in advance about the content. We had a prescription for learning based on what the Health Authority felt was necessary (focused on surgery rules and regulations). What practice managers really wanted was to be able to deal with the daily messes that they encountered in the practice.

Don't make the same mistake that we did. If you are developing a curriculum based on the rational cyclical model:

- Place the interests of your learners first by diagnosing their needs.
- Always express your outcomes in terms of what change in behaviours you expect from your learners as a result of the learning experience.
- Have feedback mechanisms in place that provide you with ways to measure your learners' progress.
- Use the feedback to make any necessary changes to future programmes.

I have always believed in the principles that: learners should be active participants in the learning programme; the learning experience should be meaningful to the learner; and learning should have a reflective and critical focus. In this instance, we found out about the inadequacies of the GP Practice Manager's Programme three years after learners had graduated and when it was too late to do anything about it.

In the classroom

Use this if you want a model that:

- focuses on diagnosing the needs of the learner
- expresses learning in terms of expected behavioural change
- uses evaluation in a cyclical process rather than as an end measure.

Critical Perspective

What do you think about critics of Wheeler's model who argue that although it does try to cater for the needs of learners, it doesn't go far enough and is too product-oriented?

For more on the rational cyclical model, read:

Print, M. (1993) *Curriculum Development and Design*. Crow's Nest, NSW: Allen & Unwin.
Wheeler, D.K. (1967) *Curriculum Process*. London: University of London Press.

Walker presented a descriptive model, referred to as the naturalistic model. It can be represented as a three level model:

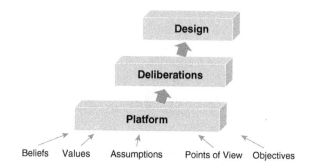

The characteristics of each level are:

- The base level - the **platform** - provides the foundations on which the curriculum can be constructed. Within the platform are the values, beliefs, aims and objectives of the organisation.
- The centre level - **deliberations** - are the discussions, debates, arguments and negotiations that need to take place with the various key stakeholders.
- The top level - **curriculum design** - can only be completed once all of the deliberations have taken place and there is consensus on what the curriculum should look like.

Supporters of this model claim that through this approach a number of different stakeholders would have the opportunity to contribute to the development of the curriculum. Critics argue that the deliberation process can be time-consuming and laborious.

How to use it

Writing this entry the day after Nelson Mandela died compelled me to reflect on the parallels between what Mandela achieved and Walker's model.

When he was elected President in 1994, Mandela allowed everyone to present their views and opinions about the problems in South Africa, while striving for consensus. He realised that deliberation, not force, was the way forward and encouraged all parties involved in the peace process to generate possible solutions. The results of the deliberation phase were then transformed into a draft for a united South Africa.

Drafting a curriculum model pales in comparison to tackling the evils of apartheid but never the less if done wrongly will have a negative impact on learners and teachers alike. Make sure that:

- You have a good understanding of the beliefs, values and points of view of all concerned. This will give you a platform from which you can start the deliberation process.

- If conflict arises in the deliberation process then this has to be resolved. Once you have consensus then you can start to make decisions about the various components of the curriculum.
- Elements that influence various components of the curriculum include: *internal* – the aspects of the organisation operations that you can control, such as staff, structure and systems; and *external* – the political, economic, social and technical influences over which you have little or no control.

A word of warning! Developing a curriculum that involves deliberation can take time: the new South Africa, like Rome, wasn't built in a day. If you are serious about giving all parties involved ample opportunity to contribute then make sure you have a realistic timescale to work to.

In the classroom

Use this if you want a model that:

- is built on the beliefs and values of the organisation
- involves all stakeholders in the design
- meets the needs of all stakeholders.

Critical Perspective

What do you think about critics of Walker's model who argue that the deliberation process is complicated and too time-consuming for teachers to contemplate using?

For more on the naturalistic model, read:

Walker, D. (1971) A naturalistic model for curriculum development. *The School Review 80*(1), 51–65.
Walker, D. (2003) *Fundamentals of Curriculum: Passions and Professionalism*. Mahwah, NJ: Lawrence Erlbaum Associates.

Grundy, influenced by the work of Paulo Freire (see Theory 9), suggested that curriculum development should be based on social analysis in the critical science tradition. In other words, we do things because of a strong commitment to the action in question. She suggested five elements make up this process.

Grundy described the principles that underpin these elements as a form of praxis in which:

- The main constituents are action and reflection.
- Action takes place in the real world, not the hypothetical world.
- Learning operates in the world of interaction; social and cultural.
- Commitment assumes a process of meaning-making, which recognises meaning as a social construction.

Grundy emphasised that the teacher and learner negotiate the content and together confront the real problems of their existence and relationships.

Supporters of this model argue that it focuses on freedom of action and is committed to the development of both teacher and learner. Critics feel that it lacks some of the rigour associated with other models.

How to use it

J.K. Rowling's *Harry Potter* series is based on a school for young wizards and witches. Imagine such a school established hundreds of years ago when there was tension between wizards/witches and mortals and the need to keep both factions apart. Over the years, society has become more enlightened and the two factions have learned to live peacefully together, even marry. Despite this, traditionalists in the school still feel that the school needs to be more selective, only admitting students from pure-blood magical families. As a result of this divide and pressure from the government's Department for Magic, the head of the school has decided to call a meeting between the school's curriculum leaders to discuss how they can best respond to the government's call to be more inclusive and to open its doors to wizards and witches not of pure-blood families.

Imagine a rather unusual curriculum development meeting. The panelled oak walls are hung with moving portraits of venerable witches and wizards, happily chatting away to each other, while the four curriculum leaders are gathered in the Head's office. All are intrigued by one of the more liberal professor's suggestion that part of the school should be converted into a Department for Half-Blood Learner Development. We join the group as they explore the purpose of the education they plan to offer.

After listening to one of the professors discussing the importance of practical subjects such as Wand Artistry and Mixing Potions and another arguing for more academic subjects such as Fortune-Telling and Astrology, the head remarks, 'I should like to think that we could help build a better world through education: A world where no mortal ever suffered at the hands of a hateful Wizard, and where everyone could live together productively and peacefully without fear'. Even the portraits fall silent at the enormity of the task.

Emulate the sentiments of the head by:

- looking at the principles, beliefs and desired outcomes of the learning experience
- discussing with all stakeholders what learning goals they can expect to achieve from the experience
- building a learning programme that fulfils all expectations.

Although this is an imaginary school, the issues it faces of inclusivity and exclusivity are very much at the centre of the curriculum debate. It's worthwhile examining your own feelings on this issue.

In the classroom

Use this if you want a model that:

- is based on the wider needs of society
- relies on social and cultural interaction
- involves negotiation between all stakeholders on course content.

Critical Perspective

What do you think about critics of Grundy's model who argue that it's not as rigorous as some of the other models?

For more on Grundy's ideas, read:

Grundy, S. (1987) *Curriculum: Product or Praxis?* London: Routledge.

Bruner extended his ideas on *discovery learning* (see Theory 23) to incorporate curriculum design. He argued that teachers waste time trying to match the complexity of information to the learner's cognitive stage of development and claimed that any subject can be taught effectively in some form to learners at any stage of their development.

Bruner explained that this was possible through structuring information in such a way so that complex ideas can be introduced at a simplified level first, and then revisited at more complex levels at later stages in the curriculum as learners are encouraged to link the learning to their experiences and existing knowledge of the subject. He referred to this concept as the spiral curriculum. This is often represented as:

Increase the intensity of learning

Focus on problem resolution

Focus on the relevant

Support learners to find their niche

Engage learners in curriculum design

Bruner suggested that the principles that underpin this model are:

- The information is reinforced and solidified each time the student revisits the subject.
- It allows a logical progression from simplistic ideas to complicated ideas.
- Learners are encouraged to apply the early knowledge to later course objectives.

Supporters of Bruner's model argue that through this knowledge, meaningful learning can be achieved. Critics argue there is no clear empirical evidence of the overall effects of the spiral curriculum on improvements in student learning.

How to use it

When I first read Bruner's statement that any curriculum subject can be taught effectively in some intellectually honest form to any learner regardless of their interest in the subject and their stage of development, I treated this with a pinch of salt. I realised however that he wasn't suggesting that my 5-year-old grandson would be able to master quantum mechanics by the age of 7, but that he could learn about aspects of quantum mechanics such as force, mass and momentum by playing with my precious *Scalectrix* cars (as if I'd let him do such a thing). It was through building on the knowledge gained by playing in this way that he would be better equipped to make the connections with more complex learning in later life. Here are a few tips towards helping aspiring teachers (and granddads) support their wards' development:

- Encourage them to be intuitive thinkers. Do this by setting yourself up as a role model and showing them that making mistakes isn't necessarily bad, providing you learn from the experience (of course, you don't have to tell them every mistake you've ever made).
- Don't be overly critical when they forget facts. There are some interesting theories in Section 1.5 in this book on neurolism [sic] about how we retain information. What is important is that you encourage them to make connections between the new knowledge and their existing understanding which will help them to be better at working problems out for themselves.
- Start with a few simple-to-achieve tasks and then build up to more challenging but still do-able tasks. This will encourage them to develop their skills as problem solvers and encourage them not to be afraid of making mistakes.
- Always try to get them to contextualise what they have learned in terms of what they already knew about the subject and what they want to learn more about.

Supporting people to be good learners requires you to help build their self-confidence. Some of your learners will be lacking this in abundance. Try not to be the sort of teacher who gives your learners the answers to all of the problems, this will decrease, not increase, their self-confidence. Remember, they are your answers to your perception of the problem.

In the classroom

Use this if you want a model that:

- establishes desired outcomes
- introduces subject matter at a basic level
- builds on the complexity of the subject.

Critical Perspective

What do you think about Bruner's assertion that starting with a few simple-to-achieve tasks and then building up to more challenging but still do-able tasks will encourage learners to develop their skills as problem solvers and encourage them not to be afraid of making mistakes?

For more on the spiral curriculum, read:

Bruner, J.S. (1966) *Towards a Theory of Instruction*. New York: W.W. Norton.
Kelly, A.V. (2009) *The Curriculum: Theory and Practice* (6th edn). London: SAGE.

Jackson used the term *hidden curriculum* to describe aspects of the curriculum that are not made obvious to the learner. He felt that these aspects were underpinned by the 3Rs that learners had to learn in order to survive in the classroom; *rules, routines* and *regulations.*

He argued that these aspects needed to be hidden from some learners because of a possible reluctance on their part to accept them as part of the learning process. A summary of the principles that underpin his ideas on this are:

- Some knowledge is beyond the capabilities of some learners.
- Recall is the highest form of intellectual achievement.
- Authority must be trusted at all times.
- Independent judgement and creativity are inconsequential.
- Emotion and feelings are irrelevant in education.
- There is never more than one answer to any question.
- Passive acceptance is a more desirable response than active criticism.

Supporters of this approach claim that learning is affected by the classroom and the organisational culture and that the hidden curriculum is a valid method of developing autonomy and responsibility. Critics argue that the curriculum should be transparent to all concerned.

How to use it

There was a whole raft of theory relating to the hidden curriculum that came out in the late 1970s. Most of this seemed to be an anathema to the cognitivist (see Theories 17–23) and humanist (see Theories 24–27) movements that were active during the time. I want to look at the 'how to use it' by reflecting on two very different experiences that I had as a teacher that highlight the different aspects of the *hidden curriculum.*

I have worked in offender learning environments in both prisons and probation run premises where the emphasis is very much on abidance with rules, routines and regulations. I felt that in these environments, learning was being used as a palliative, rather than an educational, tool. This is sometimes considered part of the *rehabilitative agenda.*

I have also worked with teachers and management at a centre that works with learners who have severe physical disabilities. The centre offers a raft of educational programmes which are underpinned by the wider social and personal development of the learner: building up self-esteem, supporting them to be independent and more confident in social situations. This is sometimes referred to as the *readiness agenda.*

That's all I want to say on the use of the *hidden curriculum.* I do however want you to work out for yourself how you can apply the theory in your own teaching. Make a list of aspects of your curriculum which you need to happen but which are not part of the planned curriculum. Describe the positive and negative effects of each aspect. Consider whether one outweighs the other and how comfortable you are with this.

HIDDEN CURRICULUM

In the classroom

Use this if you want a model that:

- includes learning other than in the planned syllabus
- recognises that some learners may be reluctant to accept parts of the planned curriculum
- gives an opportunity for extended learning.

Critical Perspective

Do you think that having hidden aspects of the curriculum is a useful tool to use in your own teaching?

For more on the hidden curriculum, read:

Jackson, P. (1991) *Life in the Classroom*. New York: Teachers College Press.
Tummons, J. (2009) *Curriculum Studies in the Lifelong Learning Sector*. Exeter: Learning Matters.

Dewey extended his ideas on *experiential learning* (see Theory 7) to incorporate curriculum design. He argued that the aim of education is to promote growth and suggested that it was only through this growth that learners would be able to adopt a wider range of purpose and means of achieving these purposes. This in turn would promote further growth. In order to achieve this Dewey proposed that the purpose and contextual features of education should be determined by learners and not by teachers. He referred to this as the *flexible curriculum*.

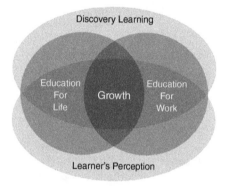

The principle features of this model are that the curriculum should:

- be based on the learner's own perception of their interests
- enable learners to engage fully in the design of the curriculum
- support learners to find their niche in life
- be focused on practical activity centred around projects that the learner found relevant
- emphasise the importance of learning from the perspective of facing difficulties and problem resolution
- ban rote learning and encourage discovery learning.

Supporters of this model argue that the role of teachers should not detract from the learner's capacity for learning autonomy. Critics claim that it is too learner-centred and diminishes the role of the teacher.

How to use it

I think that Dewey remains, well after his death, one of the most influential figures in the progressive movement because his ideas are built around learners being allowed to explore issues of their own desire or interest. As a learner, I find that to be a compelling and fundamental principle of learning.

Peggy was 87 when I first met her in 2009. She was a resident in a home for the elderly. At this time I was doing some work for a community college which took learning out to the community. Peggy was one of eight women at the home who were nicknamed the *women who learn*. They were all over 75 and had enrolled on a *Computers for the Terrified* course. Her motivation for doing the course was that she 'didn't want to be left out when her grand-children were talking about computers'. By the end of the 12-week course, Peggy could access and send emails, apply for online offers and even designed and printed the invitation cards for the home's Christmas party. In 2012, Peggy was nominated for a lifelong learning award in recognition of her efforts as a learner.

I saw an advert the other day for people to come to an over-60s club and 'have a cup of tea, a chat and a game of bingo'. Don't get me wrong, there's nothing wrong with any of these activities, it's just that, I feel that we owe the Peggys of this world something more than just pigeonholing them because of age, gender or circumstances. I would have liked to have seen this club offer courses in creative writing or digital photography or, better still, ask the learners what they wanted to learn.

This is the whole point in Dewey's theory, that the purpose of education should be determined by learners and not by teachers. I'm not saying that teachers should play no role in the process, as some learner demands may not be practical. I am, however, advocating that learners should be allowed wherever possible to have a say in curriculum design that has some meaning to them.

In the classroom

Use this if you want a model that:

- allows learners to have a say in what and how they are taught
- encourages the process of learning to learn
- focuses on practical activities centred around projects that the learner will find relevant.

Critical Perspective

What do you think of Dewey's claim that the purpose of education should be determined by learners and not by teachers? Do you agree with his critics that this diminishes the role of the teacher?

For more on Dewey's ideas, read:

Dewey, J. (1958) *Experience and Nature*. New York: Dover.
Dewey, J. (1963) *Experience and Education*. New York: Collier Books.

SECTION 4.2: LESSON PLANNING

Two famous slogans come to mind here: *To fail to plan is to plan to fail*; and the 4Ps, *Poor Planning = Poor Performance* (an ex-army colleague suggests there are 6 Ps – don't email me if you know the missing Ps).

Most people employed as observers of teaching and learning, including Ofsted inspectors, will be briefed that if the teacher doesn't have a lesson plan, they should refuse to continue with the observation. I suggest that this raises the question of what constitutes a lesson plan? Does it have to be written? Does it have to comply with any specific format? Does it need to cover specific points? Over the years, I've seen some dreadful lessons based on 10-page lesson plans and some inspirational lessons written on the back of a fag packet (well, maybe a bit more than that).

Lesson plans are important because they:

- provide a structure for the session
- set out important logistical issues such as who, what, where, when and how
- establish the link between lesson objectives and assessment methods
- gives anyone having to cover a session important information to work on
- provides anyone observing the lesson with information about the session that they may not be able to witness as part of the observation.

It is important to remember that lesson plans are there as an aid for the teacher and shouldn't be a millstone that restricts flexibility on the part of the teacher to deviate if necessary to enhance learning.

The entries in this section cover some contemporary thinking on lesson planning as well as some of the more classical ideas built around the work of Bloom and his colleagues in the 1950s and 1960s on setting lesson objectives.

An important theme throughout all of the entries is that a good lesson plan doesn't automatically mean it will be a good lesson, but it is a very important part of the process.

Although Bloom made contributions to the development of taxonomies in all three learning domains, it was his work in the mid-1950s on learning in the cognitive domain that provided the basis for ideas for preparing learning objectives which have been developed and used by practitioners throughout the world.

Bloom's taxonomy is based on a six-level structure which can be represented as:

Each level can be summarised as:

- Level 1: **Knowledge** – recalling or recognising information.
- Level 2: **Comprehension** – understanding the meaning of the information.
- Level 3: **Application** – putting ideas emerging from the information into practice.
- Level 4: **Analysis** – interpreting and assessing practice.
- Level 5: **Synthesis** – developing new approaches to practice.
- Level 6: **Evaluation** – assessing how well the new approaches are working.

Bloom argued that understanding and being able to apply knowledge was essential before higher levels of intellectual development such as analysis, synthesis and evaluation could be reached. He suggested that this model was useful in designing learning objectives that would match the level of the learners' abilities and desired learning outcomes.

How to use it

Read the following extract from Robert Burns' *Ode to a mouse* and then answer the questions. Google simple.wikipedia.org/wiki/To_a_mouse for a translation.

Wee sleekit, cow'rin, tim'rous beastie,   *I'm truly sorry man's dominion*

O, what a panic's in thy breastie!   *Has broken nature's social union,*

Thou need na start awa sae hastie,   *An' justifies that ill opinion*

Wi' bickering brattle!   *Which makes thee startle!*

I wad be laith to rin an' chase thee,   *At me, thy poor, earth born companion,*

Wi' murdering pattie!   *An' fellow mortal!*

Now answer the following:

1. What do you know about the size of the mouse?
2. Why do you think the mouse is cowering?
3. Why doesn't the poet want to kill the mouse?
4. What does this tell you about the nature of the poet?
5. How can the poet's principles be applied in other contexts?
6. What lessons can you learn from this poem?

Here's how to understand Bloom's taxonomy in the answers to the question and suggestions for verbs to use when writing lesson objectives at each level:

- The answer to question 1 just requires you to recognise that the mouse is small (*wee*). Key verbs to use are: State, recall or list.
- Question 2 needs you to understand that the mouse is cowering because it's small and fearful. Key verbs to use are: explain, illustrate or describe the reasons for.
- Question 3 requires you to think about what's going on and appreciate the poet's compassion. Key verbs to use are: apply or solve.
- Question 4 needs you to interpret the extent of the poet's remorse that men should feel the need to kill mice. Key verbs to use are: compare and contrast, or break down.
- Question 5 will need you to explore this compassion and remorse in other contexts. Key verbs to use are: generalise or explain.
- Question 6 needs you to evaluate the impact that man's presence has on the world in general. Key verbs to use are: judge or reconcile.

Each of the questions relates to a level within the taxonomy going from basic knowledge through to evaluation. Setting lesson objectives on this basis will be easy if you use the verbs listed above – well, providing you take note of verse 7 in the poem which cautions *The best-laid schemes o' mice and men; Gang aft agley* (go often astray).

In the classroom

When planning a lesson:

- appreciate the level at which you are teaching
- align the learning objective to the assessment methods
- don't try to reach analysis and evaluation until understanding and application has been mastered.

Critical Perspective

Look at a lesson that you are planning and, by using the verbs listed in the answers to questions 1-6, write a lesson objective for each of the levels in Bloom's taxonomy. Can you see how the verb used dictates the level of the learning objective?

For more on teaching in the cognitive domain, read:

Bloom, B. and Kratwohl, D. (1956) *Taxonomy of Educational Objectives*. London: Longman.

Of a number of taxonomies developed for the psychomotive domain, Dave's version in the late 1960s is the most prominent related to adult learning and the one that is most commonly referred to.

Dave's taxonomy is based on a five-level structure which can be represented as:

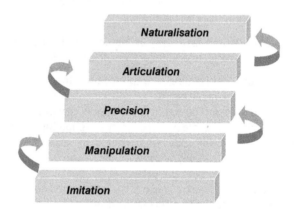

Each level can be summarised as:

- Level 1: **Imitation** – observing and replicating the actions of others.
- Level 2: **Manipulation** – reproducing the action from memory.
- Level 3: **Precision** – executing the action accurately without help.
- Level 4: **Articulation** – integrating a range of skills.
- Level 5: **Naturalisation** – automatic mastery of skills.

Dave argued that the ability to first observe and imitate skills, and then to replicate skills from memory, had to be mastered before higher levels of artistry could be achieved.

There are two other theories worth looking at in this category: Elizabeth Simpson who writes about physical movement, coordination and the use of motor skills; and Ann Harrow who writes about reflex, basic and complex movement and the importance of physical fitness.

How to use it

Cover the bits below the poem then read the following and see if you can make sense of it:

Bunny ears, bunny ears, playing by a tree:

Criss-crossed the tree, trying to catch me.

Bunny ears, bunny ears, jumped into the hole:

Popped out the other side, beautiful and bold.

Did I tie you up in knots on this one? This is a verse that parents and teachers use to teach children how to tie their shoelaces. The ears represent the loops to be made with the laces and crossing and popping through, the technique for tying them.

Here's how to understand Dave's taxonomy using the verse and some suggestions for verbs to use when writing lesson objectives at each level:

- Use the verse whilst demonstrating the process. Get the learner to imitate everything you do, step-by-step. Key verbs to use are: copy, mimic or replicate.
- Get the learner to say the verse out loud whilst doing the procedure on their own. Key verbs to use are: act, execute or perform.
- Get the learner to do the procedure without having to say the verse. Key verbs to use are: master, calibrate or demonstrate.
- Show the learner pictures of more complicated knots and ask them to tie the knots. Key verbs to use are: adapt, create or construct.
- See if the learner can come up with their own knot design. Key verbs to use are: design, develop or perfect.

I use this exercise with trainee teachers in one of two ways. I ask some members of the group to put together a script for tying shoelaces, without diagrams, that a child could follow. I then ask other members of the group to pair off and, without saying what the end product should look like, sitting back-to-back, to describe the process. Try these exercises, they're fun and demonstrate the importance of the *tell-show-do* technique in teaching skills.

In the classroom

When planning a lesson:

- Be prepared to **tell** the learner what they will be able to do by the end of the lesson.
- Think about the best way to **show** them how to do it (demonstration, video, etc.).
- Plan to get them to **do** it.

Critical Perspective

As well as Dave's taxonomy, I recommend that you look at Simpson's and Harrow's taxonomies. Do that and see which theory of levels in the psychomotive domain works best for you.

For more on teaching in the psychomotive domain, read:

Dave, R.H. (1970) Psychomotor levels. In R.J. Armstrong (ed.), *Developing and Writing Behavioural Objectives* (pp. 20-21). Tucson, AZ: Educational Innovators Press.

Harrow, A. (1972) *A Taxonomy of Psychomotor Domain*. New York: David McKay.

Simpson, E.J. (1972) *The Classification of Educational Objectives in the Psychomotor Domain*. Washington, DC: Gryphon House.

Krathwohl and Bloom suggested a structure for developing attitudes and feelings. They produced a five-level model, which can be represented as:

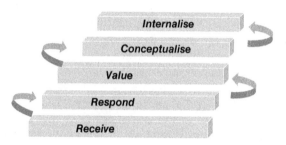

Each level can be summarised as:

- Level 1: **Receive** - showing a willingness to be open to a change in values.
- Level 2: **Respond** - participate in exercises that may challenge existing values.
- Level 3: **Value** - examine how the new values conflict with those already held.
- Level 4: **Conceptualise** - reconcile internal conflicts with existing values.
- Level 5: **Internalise** - adopt a belief system based on the new values.

Krathwohl and Bloom argued that a willingness to be receptive to challenging feelings and emotions, and a genuine desire to want to change, were essential elements of this model.

This is probably the most difficult of the three domains for the majority of teachers to feel really comfortable in. It is more complex than the other two taxonomies with differences in levels more subtle, especially between levels 3, 4 and 5.

How to use it

Here are two examples of teachers who I have observed over the years:

- Alan teaches Political History to 16-18-year-olds. I observed him teaching his class about the suffragette movement. In the session he talked about the fight for women to have the vote and some of the atrocities they had to endure. He impressed on his students how precious it was to have the right to vote and to do so when they had the opportunity.
- Bernie teaches Environmental Studies to 14-16-year-olds. In the session I observed, she showed them video clips of environmental disasters and reports predicting even greater disasters. She impressed on her students the need to act in a responsible manner and to recycle and re-use materials.

Here's how to understand Krathwohl and Bloom's taxonomy by looking at how each of the above teachers engaged with their learners and some suggestions for verbs to use when writing lesson objectives at each level:

- You need to make sure that your learners are willing to listen to what you have to say on the subject so hit 'em with some eye-catching stats or case studies. Key verbs to use are: follow, identify or locate.
- Once you've got their attention, get them involved in group discussion where they can express their views on the subject. Key verbs to use are: discuss, select, tell.
- Don't be alarmed if they oppose your thoughts on the value of subject. Key verbs to use are: differentiate, justify, share.
- Get them to reconcile what values they currently hold and how compatible these are in a civilised society. Key verbs to use are: defend, modify or relate.
- If they are willing to change their beliefs, get them to internalise this and behave in a manner consistent with their new beliefs. Key verbs to use are: discriminate, question or qualify.

A word of caution here: it may not be within your domain as their teacher to try to influence your learners' political or cultural beliefs.

In the classroom

When planning a lesson:

- Have material that will attract your learners' attention with some eye-catching statistics or stories about the subject.
- Plan to get the group to share their understandings or feelings about the subject.
- Have a strategy for getting each learner to reflect on their beliefs about the subject and question any inner conflicts they may have about what is right or wrong.

Critical Perspective

What do you do if you notice that one of your learners is displaying extreme political or religious views?

For more on teaching in the affective domain, read:

Bloom, B. and Krathwohl, D. (1956) *Taxonomy of Educational Objectives*. London: Longman.
Reece, I. and Walker, S. (2007) *Teaching, Training and Learning* (6th edn). Sunderland: Business Education Publishers.

SOLO stands for Structure of Observed Learning Outcomes. It is a model developed in 1982 by Biggs and Collis to describe the levels of increasing complexity in learners' understanding of subjects. There are five levels in the model which can be divided into surface and deep learning. These can be represented as:

Each level can be summarised as:

1. **Pre-structural**: learners acquire items of unconnected information. They have very little organisation in their learning and little sense of achievement.
2. **Uni-structural**: learners make simple and obvious connections between information. They fail to see the significance of any of the connections.
3. **Multi-structural**: learners make more and some less obvious connections between information. They fail to see the significance in some of the connections.
4. **Relational**: learners see the relationship between the connections. They see the significance of the relationships.
5. **Extended abstract**: learners make connections with information beyond the immediate subject area. They have the ability to generalise from the specific to the abstract.

Biggs and Collis argue that the SOLO model can also be used as an assessment tool and in making learners think about the strengths and weaknesses in their own learning.

How to use it

I'm writing this entry at Christmas 2014. My 9-year-old grandson Charlie has just told me that he wants *Minecraft* figures for his presents this year. I ask him what's *Minecraft*?

Charlie, immediately recognising that I'm in the **pre-structural** of learning, explains how you have to find blocks and start constructing shelters to keep you safe.

OK, I start thinking, that doesn't sound as if it would tax the mind of someone with a PhD in Education, and ask Charlie to tell me what to do. He shows me a set of drawings of the various blocks. I'm now in the **uni-structural** stage and can see how the blocks fit but still haven't grasped the concept of the game.

I'm impressed by how calm Charlie stays as he starts to explain the dangers that lurk in the form of zombies and creepers and spiders. Unless I build a structure that protects me from these dangers, the game is over for me. He tells me that, until I'm in the **multi-structural** stage where I can develop a structure that has walls, windows and stairs, I'll never keep creatures out or be able to escape if they get in.

Now I'm beginning to understand the complexities of this game and, as I enter the **relational** stage, I start to appreciate how several aspects of the game relate to each other, such as: survival, creativity, observing and decision-making.

Thinking I have mastered the game and built an impregnable fortress, Charlie reminds me that I need to move to a higher level of thinking, what he refers to as **extended abstract**, and think about defences to prevent the creatures from reaching the fortress in the first place. When I asked him if fences or moats might work, he smiled and asked me if I wanted Santa to bring me some *Minecraft* figures.

This isn't *exactly* what happened but why spoil a good story with the truth?

In the classroom

When planning a lesson:

- Appreciate what stage in their level of understanding of the subject each learner is at.
- Plan learning objectives that will take learners to the next stage.
- Make sure that they have tasks that demonstrate complete mastery of the stage before they are allowed to progress to the next level.

Critical Perspective

OK, so I may have exaggerated the *Minecraft* story to make a point. Can you think of an example where as a learner you progressed through the *pre-structural* to extended abstract levels?

For more on the SOLO model, read:

Biggs, J.B. and Collis, K. (1982) *Evaluating the Quality of Learning: The SOLO Taxonomy.* New York: Academic Press.

Biggs, J. and Tang, C. (2011) *Teaching for Quality Learning at University* (4th edn). Buckingham: Open University Press.

Pritchard is a lecturer in education. He is acknowledged as writing in a very practical, pragmatic manner and has devised a checklist for planning lessons which covers the following:

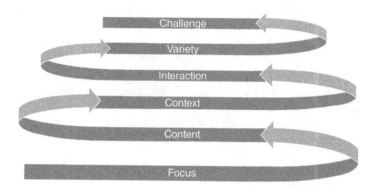

Each point on the checklist can be summarised as:

- Is there a clear focus, with explicit learning objectives?
- Is the content based on the learners' existing knowledge?
- Is the lesson set in an appropriate context?
- Is there scope for social interaction and for activity?
- Is there variety and choice involved in approaches and responses to work?
- Are suitable 'brain-friendly' conditions in place?

Finally, by following the list, make sure that the lesson is planned in such a way that it aims to move the learners' learning forward. Pritchard warns that although not all lessons will tick all of the boxes – for example some lessons may have little opportunity for interactive work – teachers should make an effort to work towards meeting the conditions suggested in the list.

How to use it

Over the years, I've seen a vast array of lesson plans. The best one I've seen was by an IT tutor, Lindsay who mind-mapped her lesson plan. She covered all of the key points in Pritchard's checklist on one, easy-to-access page but, by use of colour in the mind map, in a way that elements within the plan stood out.

Whichever format you prefer, here are some key points to check:

- Make sure that each learning objective is SMART (see Theory 111) and expressed in terms of what the learners will know or be able to do by the end of the session, not what you intend to do.

THE LESSON CHECKLIST

- Test prior knowledge. Finding out what your learners already know, or can do, will allow you to pitch the lesson and may enable you to identify some experienced learners who you can use to support others.
- Make sure your learners can see the relevance of the subject to their own desired learning outcomes.
- Remember the adage that: 'I hear – I forget; I see – I remember; I do – I understand' and never miss an opportunity for organising group activities.
- Don't be afraid to vary your teaching approaches; doing the same thing in the same way is a recipe for boredom and mental fatigue for you as well as your learners.
- Challenge but don't overtax your learners with a mass of brain curdling information.
- Plan lessons in such a way that they aim to move the learners' learning forward.

Although Pritchard's checklist is a useful tool, you need to heed his warning that there is no ideal lesson plan that will achieve any given set of objectives. In this respect, lesson planning can be described as an art, not a science.

In the classroom

When planning a lesson:

- Write SMART lesson objectives and share these with your learners.
- Make sure the content of the lesson is relevant to your learners.
- Don't be afraid to take risks and vary your teaching approaches.

Critical Perspective

Look at a lesson that you are planning or have already planned. How many boxes in Pritchard's checklist can you tick with confidence?

For more on lesson planning, read:

Pritchard, A. (2005) *Ways of Learning*. London: David Fulton Publishers.
Reece, I and Walker, S. (2007) *Teaching, Training and Learning* (6th edn). Sunderland: Business Education Publishers.

t's difficult to attribute this particular tool to any one individual, but a number of sources refer to an article by Doran in the November 1970 issue of *Management Review* as where the term first appeared as a management tool. SMART is an acronym that covers five key attributes that any set of objectives should have. Related to lesson planning, these are:

- **Specific**: the lesson objective should be clear and unambiguous.
- **Measurable**: there should be some way of tracking progress.
- **Acceptable**: there should be consensus within the class on what's to be done.
- **Realistic**: learners should be able to achieve what's being asked of them.
- **Timebound**: there should be a time scale within which the objectives will be achieved.

Some SMART users use the term *achievable* instead of *acceptable* but many prefer the notion that learning objectives should have an element of learner contribution, thus the use of *acceptable*. I would also add:

- **Exciting**: each lesson should have a challenging objective.
- **Rewarding**: there should be appropriate acknowledgement of achievement.

Thus, making the objective even *SMARTER*.

How to use it

Don't underestimate the effort it takes to write a good learning objective, but also never lose sight of the fact that they are the stepping stones which will determine how well you can engage with your learners.

Kath was a librarian at a university where I taught. She was frequently being asked to show students how to use the library facilities so she enrolled on a basic level teaching course. One of the assessments for this course was that she do a 30 minute teach-in with her peers on the course. She started the session by explaining that she was going to talk about a subject that was particularly dear to her own heart and held up a book titled *How to Have an Orgasm*. After a period of stunned silence, she said, 'yes, by the end of this session you will be able to trace a book in the library in less than two minutes using the Dewey Decimal Classification system'. Wow, that was a smart way to start a lesson!

Here are some tips as to how to set SMART objectives:

- Make sure you can describe, in a clear and unambiguous manner, what learners will be able to do by the end of the session and how this fits in with their long-term learning intentions.
- Tell the learners how their progress will be monitored. Think about having a set of milestones against which they can track their own progress.
- Make sure that everyone in the class accepts the planned objectives. If there is general disagreement over this, don't be afraid to revise the objectives.

SMART OBJECTIVES

- Although you will want to set objectives that stretch and challenge your learners, they should still be achievable. Setting objectives that are too difficult will demoralise or demotivate your learners.
- Attach a deadline for completion of each milestone. Recognise that learners will learn at different rates and therefore think about individual deadlines rather than a group one.

I'm not sure how often Kath used this approach with new students using the library for the first time but it would certainly have grabbed their attention as well as enhancing her own reputation in the university.

In the classroom

When planning a lesson:

- Make your lesson objectives specific to your learners' needs and seek agreement on their acceptability.
- Have some system in place for monitoring progress.
- Don't make the level of challenge too difficult to make learners despondent or too easy to make learners complacent.

Critical Perspective

Look at a lesson that you are planning or have already planned. Can you say with confidence that you have set SMART(ER) learning objectives that describe in a clear and unambiguous manner what learners will be able to do by the end of the lesson?

For more on SMART objectives, read:

Doran, G. (1970) There's a SMART way to write management goals and objectives. *Management Review, 70*(11), 35-36.

Clarke et al. describe the *learning intentions* of any lesson as being what the outcome of the learning looks like. They claim that it needs to be a combination of surface, deep or conceptual ideas, depending on how the lesson fits in with the wider syllabus. They argue that good *learning intentions* are those that make it clear to the learner what's expected of them so that they know exactly where and when to invest effort, strategies and thinking. Their thinking on *learning intentions* can be summarised in the following six key points:

- Teachers should share the learning intentions with their learners to give them a good picture of what success looks like.
- Learning intentions should be inclusive as not all learners will be working at the same rate or starting from the same place.
- Because of the complexities of curriculum design, learning doesn't happen in neat, linear sequences.
- One activity can contribute to more than one learning intention. Conversely one learning intention may require more than one activity.
- Learners may learn things not intended (positive or negative). Teachers need to be aware of unintended consequences that may result from this.
- Teachers should end each lesson by reviewing what stage learners have reached on their intended learning journey.

Clarke et al. argue that transparent learning intentions can lead to greater trust between the learner and the teacher which they claim will make both parties engaged in the learning process and more committed to achieving the learning outcomes. They offer a formula for the learning equation, which can be represented as:

$$LI = 3C + HE + CU$$

Where: LI stands for **learning intentions**; the 3Cs for **challenge** (this is relative to what the learning outcome is and to the learner's current level of performance and understanding), **commitment** (this refers to the learner's determination to reach their learning goal) and **confidence** (this can be something that the learner has a natural abundance of, or something that can be nurtured by positive feedback from the teacher or their peers); HE stands for **high expectations**; and CU for **conceptual understanding**.

How to use it

With any good intentions, the criterion for success is to know when we've got there. I feel that I'm starting to get somewhere with new teachers when they don't start the lesson by saying 'I'm going to teach you...' and use the phrase 'by the end of the session, you will be able to...'. I know that they've got the idea when they start to be more specific about what the learning outcome will be.

LEARNING INTENTIONS

I'm going to use the equation listed on the previous page to explain how to use learning intentions to achieve learning outcomes:

- Don't make the challenge too difficult that the learner sees it as unattainable and becomes despondent. Conversely, don't make it too easy that the learner becomes complacent.
- Gauge the level of commitment the learner has. If this is likely to be insufficient to achieve the goal, get them to reflect on whether they need to raise the level of commitment or reduce the extent of the goal.
- I read somewhere that a useful yardstick you can use to assess someone's level of confidence is when they progress from saying 'I think I can' to 'I know I can' and then from 'I thought I could' to 'I knew I could'. Your role is to use the phrases 'I know you can' and 'I knew you could'.
- Learner expectations are usually realistic; often erring on the side of caution. You might want to be aware of this and aim one notch higher for them than they do for themselves. Be aware however that there may be occasions when one notch lower may be more appropriate.
- There are at least three levels of understanding – surface, deep and conceptual – that may be taking place in a lesson. Conceptual understanding is the combination of surface and deep understanding (see Theory 109 for more on this).

In the classroom

When planning a lesson:

- Plan to challenge your learners but don't make the level of challenge too difficult or too easy.
- Encourage your learners to have high expectations and the confidence to achieve these.
- Gauge individual learner's commitment to achieve their goals.

Critical Perspective

Do you agree with Clarke et al.'s claim that transparent learning intentions can lead to both the teacher and the learner being more engaged in the learning process?

For more on learning intentions, read:

Clarke, S., Timperley, H. and Hattie, J. (2003) *Unlocking Formative Assessment*. Auckland: Hodder Moa Beckett.

Clarke, S. (2011) *Active Learning Through Formative Assessment*. London: Hodder.

SECTION 4.3: DELIVERING LEARNING

The question of whether teaching is an art or a science is the subject of debate amongst many experienced as well as trainee teachers. Some argue that teachers need to be methodical in their planning and delivery, relying on research and well-structured approaches. Others claim that teachers are performers who respond to their audience's reaction, relying on instincts and creativity. There is a third body who look on teaching as a hybrid of the two - a performance with a scientific base or a science with artistic license for intuition and creativity.

The entries in this section make no attempt to classify teaching as either an art or a science but do lay down a structure with some scope for interpretation based on the principles of learning covered in Part 1:

- Teaching is about directing learners (behaviourists).
- Teaching is about transferring knowledge to learners (cognitivists).
- Teaching is about supporting learners to be able to process information (neurolists).
- Teaching is about guiding learners (humanists).

Whichever approach you adopt, certain conditions must exist in order for effective teaching to take place. These conditions include:

- Having the freedom to be risk takers.
- Being willing to try new ideas.
- Not being bound by having to cover particular content.
- Experimenting with various teaching styles.
- Having time to reflect on your teaching.
- Constructing a model of teaching that works for each of them in their specific setting and with various groups of students.

Who knows what you are capable of achieving in your delivery with these conditions in place?

Hattie's concept of *visible learning* is based on two key principles:

a. When teaching is visible, the learner knows what to do and how to do it.

b. When learning is visible, the teacher knows whether learning is happening or not.

He argues that the interaction between these principles is the basis for the achievement of learning outcomes. He also asserts that the ideal learning state is when learners become their own teachers and teachers become learners of their own teaching.

Hattie claims that in order to change the focus in education towards learning and impact, teachers need to develop different ways of thinking. He outlines eight **mind frames** which he feels teachers need to adopt in order to fully embrace the principles of visible learning. Hattie's eight mind frames are that teachers should:

- Accept that their fundamental task is to evaluate the effect of their teaching on learners.
- Recognise that success or failure in learner achievements are about what they as teachers did or did not do.
- Talk more about the learning than the teaching.
- See assessment as feedback about their impact.
- Engage in dialogue, not just monologue.
- Enjoy the challenge and never settle for just doing their best.
- Believe that it is their role to develop positive relationships in the classroom and staffroom.
- Inform all about the language of learning.

Hattie claims that embracing the eight frames are the essential ingredients for creating an impact on all learning and achievement, and that teachers becoming evaluators of their own impact is the basis for the greatest single advance in education practice.

How to use it

Here are some tips on how to apply the principles of visible learning:

- Always seek feedback on how your teaching is going. You can get this from your learners, your peers or through more formal observation of your teaching. Don't wait until the end of a teaching session before seeking feedback. This may be too late to change or enhance your teaching methods.
- Appreciate that your role is as a change agent. You may have read elsewhere in this book that your role is as a *facilitator* or *mediator* and are beginning to feel a bit of role conflict coming on. Whatever role you assume, remember the fundamental principle of teaching is to create a change in behaviour in your teaching.

- Don't get too preoccupied with the latest fads and trends in teaching approaches. Discussions that just focus on teaching practice and totally ignore learning are meaningless. You need to have an appreciation of both to be an effective teacher.
- Recognise that, although assessment of learner progress is primarily about the learner's performance, it will also tell you a lot about your performance. In this respect you need to move away from the notion of 'assessment of' and towards 'assessment for'.
- Accept that, although there is a place and time for formal teaching, the emphasis should be on listening to your learners; their ideas, their problems, the barriers they are facing, their successes, their failures and their views on your teaching.
- If you are at the stage when teaching is no longer a challenge and you don't get the *buzz* when learners achieve, then maybe it's the time to reflect on whether or not teaching is the career for you. If you think this is unfair, just think about a time when you sat in on a session when the teacher/trainer was just going through the motions. How did you feel?

In the classroom

- Always seek feedback on your performance from reliable sources.
- Use assessment of your learners' performance as an indicator of your performance.
- Create a learning climate where errors are welcomed.

Critical Perspective

Do you agree with Hattie's claim that his *eight frames* are essential ingredients for effective learning and achievement?

For more on visible learning, read:

Hattie, J. (2009) *Visible Learning: A Synthesis of 800+ Meta-analyses on Achievement*. London: Routledge.
Hattie, J. (2012) *Visible Learning for Teachers*. London: Routledge.

It's difficult to determine whether it was Bloom or Carroll who first came up with the notion of *mastery learning*. Both were clearly influenced by the work of Washburn and Morrison in the 1920s. Carroll's basic premise was that nearly all learners reach a predetermined level before moving on to the next stage and that the focus of attention should therefore be on allowing the learner sufficient time to master each level. His model is often represented by the equation:

Degree of learning = *f* (time spent/time needed)

In this equation, Carroll explains that time spent is the result of opportunity and perseverance, in which the opportunity is created by the teacher and perseverance is something the learner has to do.

Bloom concurred with Carroll's thinking, adding that over 90% of learners can master what they are taught and that it is the teacher's role to find the means to enable them to do this. He set down four key stages for teachers in his model for *mastery learning*, which can be summarised as:

- Organise the subject matter to be taught into manageable learning units.
- Develop specific learning objectives for each unit.
- Introduce appropriate formative and summative assessment measures.
- Allow sufficient time for learners to address errors and reach the desired level of mastery.

Both Carroll and Bloom believed that the effective planning and implementation of teaching strategies which allowed sufficient time for assessment and feedback was the cornerstone of mastery learning.

How to use it

On 13 November 2014, Ayan Quereshi from Birmingham became the youngest ever Microsoft-acknowledged computer specialist. At the age of 5 years and 11 months he passed the Computer Specialist course at Birmingham City University. On the same day, Peggy Gwilt, aged 87, of Walsall used excel for the first time to produce a spreadsheet outlining the activities available at her day centre. Peggy had been a learner on the Walsall Adult & Community College based *Computing for the Terrified* course. Apart from both living in the West Midlands, Ayan and Peggy had one other thing in common; to master what they had achieved took considerable time and effort. Both became frustrated when they made mistakes but the expertise and support given by teaching staff at both organisations gave them the impetus they needed to succeed.

Here are some tips on how to support your learner to master a subject:

- Break down the subject matter into a series of bite-sizable chunks. The chunks should be organised into a logical sequence of lessons that follow on from each other (see Theory 29).

MASTERY LEARNING

- Tell learners what they will be able to do once they have mastered the subject matter in each lesson.
- Allow them sufficient time to master the content of the lesson.
- Conduct frequent assessments to ensure they have mastered it. These can consist of simple questions and answers, quizzes or written tests.
- Don't move on to the next level till they have demonstrated mastery of the present level.
- Encourage the learners not to be fazed if they fail an assessment but to learn from their mistakes and put things right.

If you are faced with having to teach a group of learners with a wide range of mixed abilities, rather than have one lesson plan covering the whole group, have individualised learning plans defining the level of mastery that each individual can be expected to achieve. This may mean more work but the results will be worth it.

In the classroom

- Have individual learning plans for each member of the group.
- Break each plan down into a series of learning milestones.
- Don't let the learner move on unless they master the learning in each milestone.

Critical Perspective

Mastery learning is based on the notion of managing learning rather than managing learners. Critics of the concept however assert that mastery approaches to instruction are rigid, mechanistic, involve teaching strategies that can only give students the simple skills required to survive in a closed society, and that they do not appreciate the complexities of school learning. Are you for or against it?

For more on mastery learning, read:

Bloom, B.S. (1971) *Mastery Learning*. New York: Holt, Rinehart & Winston.
Carroll, J.B. (1971) Problems of measurement related to the concept of learning for mastery. In J.H. Block (ed.), *Mastery Learning*. New York: Holt, Rinehart & Winston.

Books by Reece and Walker have probably been read by more trainee teachers than any other books of their kind. They provide a very practical guide, often drawn from the experience of teachers, which covers the full range of issues related to teaching and learning. Here is a list of motivational techniques that they claim are effective and easy to use:

- **Verbal praise**: giving praise for effort or achievement. Doing this in front of others can have a very positive effect on the learner.
- **Feedback on assignments**: giving regular and timely feedback on assignments is important to show learners what progress they are making.
- **Arousal**: arousing the curiosity of learners with baffling and sometimes perplexing problems will pander to their instincts for exploration and suspense.
- **Unexpected**: mixing teaching approaches will reduce the risk of learners becoming bored with the same old routine and will keep learners stimulated.
- **Using material the learner is familiar with**: keeping abreast of the latest fads and trends will make sure the learner is familiar with the lesson content.
- **Unusual contexts**: encouraging learners to use newly acquired knowledge in different contexts will broaden their appreciation of the subject.
- **Games and simulations**: using games and simulations will increase learners' interest and level of participation in the learning.

Reece and Walker point out that there are many factors that will dampen a learner's enthusiasm to want to learn. Some of these may be factors outside of the teacher's sphere of influence but everything that goes on in the classroom is within their ability to control. They argue that teachers should try to minimise the adverse effects of poor teaching techniques by: not being dull or uninteresting; teaching at the right level and pace; having the right heating, lighting and seating arrangements; not letting learners sit in the same position for too long; not making the topic too difficult or too easy; and giving constructive feedback as soon as possible after the task or assignment has been completed.

How to use it

I've chosen to demonstrate how to use their ideas by referring to teaching sessions that I've observed where teachers used the suggested technique either particularly well or very badly:

- Glynis was always quick to praise her learners' efforts as well as their achievements. It was good to see how pleased learners were by a simple nod of approval or thumbs up when they did something good.
- Bill was generally acknowledged by his colleagues and learners as being an outstanding teacher. Bill's problem was that, although he put heart and soul into his teaching, he considered marking assignments and giving feedback to be a chore. He missed the point that feedback on assignment was important to his learners so that they could see what progress they were making.

- Christine loved to confuse and baffle her learners by introducing topics that appeared to bear no relevance whatsoever to the subject matter. It was fascinating to watch the reactions on her learners' faces as one-by-one the penny dropped. What was initially perplexing and annoying for some was completely turned on its head as they made the connections.
- Dave hated being predictable. In the handful of times that I observed him teach, I can't remember one occasion when the room layout was the same. He used conference style, theatre and cabaret style, and horseshoe design. He mixed formal teaching with group work, even sitting back on one occasion and getting the learners to teach him the subject and test his understanding.
- Karen taught literacy and numeracy to learners who were profoundly deaf. She mixed using material that the learners were familiar with such as signing cards with a number of games such as *Hangman* and *Kengo*. It was good to see the look of anticipation on her learners' faces as she got the board games out and their enjoyment in playing them. Karen would always end her lesson by reinforcing the key points in the lesson.

Remember, there are many ways of stimulating your learners' interest in a subject but don't go overboard and be too lavish in your praise, unpredictable or baffling to the stage of being chaotic or overuse game playing.

In the classroom

- Praise effort as well as achievement.
- Look for novelty in your teaching.
- Give feedback on performance as soon as possible.

Critical Perspective

Reece and Walker argue that an external stimulus is required for learning to occur. The learner is required to respond to the stimuli and takes a more passive role with the teacher determining learning goals, appropriate stimuli to achieve and an appropriate sequence for delivery. In what circumstances do you think this argument is valid?

For more on teaching techniques to enhance motivation, read:

Petty, G. (2014) *Teaching Today: A Practical Guide* (5th edn). Oxford: Oxford University Press.

Reece, I and Walker, S. (2007) *Teaching, Training and Learning* (6th edn). Sunderland: Business Education Publishers.

Shayer and Adey developed the concept of *cognitive acceleration* in the 1980s. Their work builds on ideas by Piaget (see Theory 20) and Vygotsky (see Theory 19) and is based on the principle that the teacher acts as a mediator; setting up the learning context and only intervening to guide the learners towards the planned learning goal. Shayer and Adey argue that:

- If learners are given a challenge without preparation, they will fail the task.
- If teachers give the answers, learners may remember the facts.
- If learners develop the answers themselves, they will understand.
- If learners are then encouraged to discuss how they could apply the thinking process they have undertaken to other areas then they 'become cleverer'.

The stages in a cognitive accelerated lesson can be represented as:

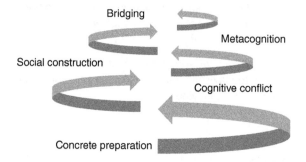

Each stage can be summarised as:

- **Concrete preparation**: the linkage between what's already known and what is to be learned is established.
- **Cognitive conflict**: what's to be learned is presented to the learners in the form of a problem where the solution is not immediately obvious.
- **Social construction**: learners are encouraged to work together to solve the problem, free from any teacher intervention.
- **Metacognition**: learners are asked to explain their thinking process in how they solved the problem.
- **Bridging**: learners are then asked to reflect on how the new learning links to existing experience and the new learning can be used in everyday life.

In tests conducted in schools in the 1980s, Shayer and Adey were able to show that the grades of pupils being taught science and maths through cognitive acceleration improved significantly.

How to use it

Here's how to use concrete acceleration:

- Assume the role of mediator where your task is to set up a good learning context and intervene only if your learners need guidance towards their learning goal.

- Set the scene by explaining what your role is. Agree any ground rules that may be important and what timescale the group will be working to.
- Describe the task. This could be a problem or a challenge. Tell the group that you will clarify any issues related to the task but not on the process they need to adopt to solve the problem.
- Leave the group to get on with solving the task. If your organisation's policies allow it, consider leaving the room. At the very least, sit as far away from the group as you can. Tell the group to give you a call when they have the answer.
- If you are concerned that groups are struggling then casually drop in and give them a few clues that might set them off in the right direction. Make sure that you don't make the clues so obvious that you are virtually giving them the answer. This will defeat the object.
- If you have divided the main group into sub-groups then get the sub-groups to discuss the relative merits of the other groups' solutions. Get them to explain how they reached their solutions. If there are sub-groups, see if you can get consensus on which solution works best.
- Get the group to discuss how they can adapt and adopt the process to deal with other problems.

Be aware that not all learners will react positively to this approach. Be ready to deal with any learners who refuse to participate. There may be some tips elsewhere in this book to help you out if this does happen.

In the classroom

- Assume the role of mediator.
- Set the group a challenge that is not too difficult to cause them to be despondent but not too easy to make them complacent.
- Ask the group to describe the process they undertook to solve the problem and how they could apply this to other problems.

Critical Perspective

The premise behind Shayer and Adey's model of cognitive acceleration is that the organisation will sanction teachers to set up the learning context and then take a back seat and allow the group to get on with solving the task. Do you work for such an organisation and are you capable of playing such a passive role in lessons?

For more on Shayer and Adey's ideas, read:

Adey, P. and Shayer, M. (1994) *Really Raising Standards*. London: Routledge.
Shayer, M. and Adey, P.S. (2002) *Learning Intelligence: Cognitive Acceleration Across the Curriculum from 5 to 15 Years*. Milton Keynes: Open University Press.

Alexander has written extensively over the past decade about how effective dialogue in the classroom can have a significant impact on learner involvement and learning. He has coined the phrase that 'talking to learn is almost as important as learning to talk'. He described the essential principles of dialogic teaching as being:

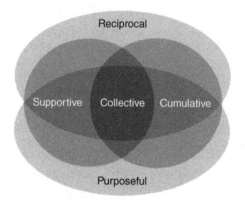

Each of these principles can be summarised as:

- **Collective**: teachers and learners working as a group or class to address learning tasks together.
- **Reciprocal**: teachers and learners listening to each other, sharing ideas and considering alternative viewpoints.
- **Supportive**: learners being encouraged to articulate their ideas freely without fear of embarrassment or negative feedback.
- **Cumulative**: teachers and learners building on their own and each other's ideas to form a coherent line of thinking.
- **Purposeful**: teachers plan with clear learning intentions and specific educational goals in mind.

Alexander argues that classroom dialogue is an essential tool for learning where learner involvement is what happens throughout the lesson, and that talking to learn should replace the ineffective talking for teaching that happens in most classrooms.

How to use it

I'm usually sceptical about slogans like *talking to learn* and have been around long enough to see fads and trends in education come and go. When I was at school, and even to an extent doing a degree at university in the 1960s and early 1970s, I guess the adage was that students should be seen and not heard.

Here are some tips if you want a dialogic classroom:

- Don't think that good teaching is merely a case of technique; there are so many other aspects that need to be considered, including personal qualities such as patience, tolerance, understanding and a willingness to listen to others.
- Encourage your learners to express their ideas, take risks and not to be afraid of making mistakes. Creating a classroom atmosphere where learners can do this without fear of being embarrassed is important and will promote this freedom of expression.
- Plan each lesson with a clear focus on your learners' desired outcomes. Link assessment of learning to the planned outcome. For example if the planned outcome is that they can make a paper airplane that will fly 6m across the room don't set them a test on the history of aviation.
- Take up every opportunity to share your ideas with your learners, to learn from them and to build on each other's ideas until their desired outcomes are achieved.

I guess as this is the only entry where I've used slogans, I may as well be 'in it for a penny rather than a pound' and if 'everything comes in threes' drop in that 'you have two ears and only one mouth – so use them in that proportion'. Sorry for that!

In the classroom

- Deliver each lesson with a clear focus on what your learners' desired outcomes are.
- Encourage your learners to express their ideas without fear of negative comments.
- Don't be averse to taking sensible risks in lesson planning and delivery.

Critical Perspective

Alexander claims that dialogic teaching promotes activity, deepens thinking and enriches understanding. His critics argue that once pupils start to spontaneously engage in communication, the level of noise in the classroom rises and the teacher finds it difficult to decide which pupil to pay attention to. Are you for or against this type of approach to teaching?

For more on Alexander's ideas, read:

Alexander, R. (2001) *Culture and Pedagogy*. Oxford: Blackwell.
Alexander, R. (2005) *Towards Dialogic Teaching*. York: Dialogos.

Tomlinson argues that *differentiation* shouldn't be defined in terms of teaching methodologies or instructional strategies but should be viewed as a way of thinking about teaching and learning, based on the following set of beliefs:

- Any group of learners will differ in their motivation to learn, their knowledge of the subject and their preferred styles of learning.
- These differences will have an impact on individual learner's desired outcomes and the support they need to achieve these.
- Learners respond best when they are pushed slightly beyond the level where they as individuals can work without assistance.
- Learners need to see the connection between what's being taught and their own interests.
- Each learner should have the opportunity to explore the subject in terms of what they want to get out of the subject.
- Learners learn better in a classroom environment where they feel significant and respected.

Tomlinson suggests that the prime focus of any organisation should be to maximise the capacity of each learner to reach their desired learning outcomes. She claims that this cannot be achieved unless: lesson planning and delivery satisfies the needs of every learner; learners have choices about what and how to learn; learners are allowed to play an active part in setting learning goals; the learner can see the relevance of the subject matter.

How to use it

One of the most contentious aspects facing teachers in adult education is how to handle a spread of capabilities in any one class that may cover four or five different levels from pre-entry through to level 2 or 3. Although there will also be a capability spread in schools and higher education, this may not be so pronounced due to streaming or standardised entry qualifications. Whatever organisation you teach in, here are some tips if you want a differentiated classroom:

- Get to know where each learner is on their learning journey, what their strengths and weaknesses are, where they want to get to and what support is necessary to help them along the way.
- Be flexible in how you group learners so that they can work independently, in small groups or as a whole class, in such a way that you can make the most of the opportunities created by their differences or similarities.
- Have additional material or extension tasks ready for learners who complete tasks before others in the class.
- Get more experienced learners to pair up with and support weaker learners.
- Keep a watchful eye on all group working to monitor what learning is actually taking place.

DIFFERENTIATION

- Remember that equality is not about treating everyone the same. It may be necessary to spend extra time with one individual, providing this is within reason and doesn't compromise the learning of other members of the group.

I often use the analogy of a manufacturing process to describe teaching. In this process we take half metre metal lumps of 30 x 20 cm, run them through a lathe and we get a candleholder that is worth more than the original raw material. Isn't that what we do with learners? Well, in that they go through a learning process that gives them added value, I suppose there are some similarities. Where there are differences of course is that not every learner is a homogenous lump of 30 x 20, not every learner goes through the process at the same pace and there is no standardisation of end result. This is what differentiation is all about.

In the classroom

- Get to know what level each learner is at and what they want to achieve, and plan your teaching to help them achieve it.
- Get stronger learners to buddy-up with weaker learners to support them.
- Have extension tasks ready for learners who complete tasks early.

Critical Perspective

Tomlinson argues that differentiation will maximise the capacity of each learner to reach their desired learning outcomes. What do you think of my analogy of the manufacturing process to describe the learning process?

For more on differentiation, read:

Tomlinson, C.A. (1995) *How to Differentiate Instruction in Mixed-Ability Classrooms.* Alexandria, VA: ASCD.
Tomlinson, C.A. (2005) *Differentiation in Practice.* Alexandria, VA: ASCD.

SECTION 4.4: ASSESSMENT AND FEEDBACK

Assessment and feedback are critical to the process of teaching and learning. Assessment serves the purpose of accountability; it justifies certification of an award or recognition of competence on the part of the learner. Feedback is the means by which the teacher informs learners of their progress.

Assessment and feedback however are something that shouldn't take place at the end of a teaching session. Both are activities that should happen at a number of stages in the learners' (and I would include here, teachers') journeys. The different forms of assessment can be summarised as:

- **Inductive**: at the very beginning of the journey to establish whether the learner is right for the course and that the course is right for the learner.
- **Formative**: on-going throughout the lesson to establish that the learner is following what's being taught.
- **Summative**: at the end of every lesson to determine that learning objectives have been achieved.
- **Deductive**: at the end of a course of learning to gauge whether the course has been taught properly and learners have gained their desired outcomes.

This section explores some contemporary views on the value of assessment as measures of both the teachers' and the learners' performance and progress. I've also included a more traditional measure (Johari Windows) of how good we are at giving and receiving feedback on performance.

Black and Wiliam have become two of the most influential thinkers on the subject of formative assessment and Wiliam's groundbreaking lectures on the subject have influenced changes in policy and practice. In 1998, they collaborated on *Inside the Black Box* which suggested that assessment for learning is based on five key principles:

- Learners are actively involved in the learning process.
- Effective feedback is essential and must be based on clear learning intentions.
- Teaching methodologies are flexible and adapted in response to assessment results.
- Learners are willing and able to self-assess and assess the efforts of their peers.
- The impact of assessment on learners' motivation and confidence is accepted.

Black and Wiliam maintain that where formative assessment is used effectively, the standards of achievement are raised across the board whilst raising the benchmark for everyone. They also claim that learners learn more effectively when they are encouraged to take on more responsibility for their own learning and assessment.

They argue that for formative assessment to be effective:

- Teachers need to get inside their learners' heads and to connect with their thinking and feelings.
- Learners need to know what they are supposed to be learning and how to recognise when they have achieved this.

According to Black and Wiliam, assessment for learning is not just about helping teachers to teach and assess more effectively, but about encouraging and enabling learners to take more responsibility for the process.

How to use it

I like Black and Wiliam's use of the analogy of travelling on a journey to describe the strategy for formative assessment. The three things any traveller needs to know are: 'Where am I going to?', 'How am I getting there?' and 'Where do I go to next?'

There's a classic scene in Lewis Carroll's *Alice in Wonderland* where Alice asks the Cat 'which way to go from here?' The Cat replies, 'That depends a good deal on where you want to get to'. Alice replies 'I don't much care where'. To which the Cat answers 'Then it doesn't matter which way you go'.

Here are some tips in how to use formative assessment to improve learner performance and point them in the right direction:

- Clarify with your learners what the planned learning outcomes are and what the criteria for success are. You must make this transparent to all of your learners so that they are in no doubt as to what needs to be done.
- Don't wait till the end of the session (or worse still, the complete course) to tell learners how they have done. Agree a set of milestones with your learners that they feel comfortable working towards and give them frequent feedback as to how they are doing.

- Get learners into the habit of assessing their own work and that of their peers (see Theory 121).
- Act as a class facilitator, not controller (see Theory 25).

When you use formative assessment, accept that it will take more time, may be relative to individual learners and possibly more subjective than other forms of assessment.

In the classroom

- Always clarify what the learning intentions are and how they will be measured.
- Give your learners frequent assessments of their progress throughout the session.
- Encourage a culture of self-assessment and peer-assessment in the class.

Critical Perspective

Critics of Black and Wiliam's ideas argue that although ensuring that learners are clear with what it means to be successful may be important, success doesn't always fit neatly into a checklist of learning expectations. Moreover, they suggest, some lessons can easily take a complete change in direction and that this isn't necessarily a bad thing. What do you think about these criticisms?

For more on formative assessment, read:

Black, P.J. and Wiliam, D. (1998) *Inside the Black Box*. London: NFER.
Black, P.J. and Wiliam, D. (2009) Developing the theory of formative assessment. *Educational Assessment, Evaluation and Accountability*, 21(1), 5-31.

Brown et al.'s *Ten-Point Assessment Manifesto* is part of a contribution they make that consists of 500 tips on assessment. The manifesto is based on the principle that learners need to be able to understand what is expected of them, can relate it to their desired learning outcomes and are confident that the assessment tools being used are valid and reliable.

A summary of the ten points is that assessment should:

- be based on an understanding of how learners learn
- play a positive role in their learning experience
- be clearly explained
- be valid by measuring what they are intended to measure
- be reliable and consistent and wherever possible be free from subjectivity
- allow for learners to be given feedback on their performance
- encourage teachers and learners to reflect on their performance
- be an integral component of course design and not something that is bolted on as an afterthought
- have the appropriate amount of assessment
- be understandable, explicit and open to public scrutiny.

Brown et al. argue that effective assessment enhances learning, influences what a learner perceives as the important learning goals in a lesson and engages learners with different learning styles.

How to use it

Albert Einstein once wrote that, 'Not everything that counts is countable, and not everything that is countable counts'. Because that which is countable is easier to assess, both teachers and learners have a tendency to rely on this as the basis for assessment. Because of this, a number of writers argue that the assessment tail can be accused of wagging the dog.

Here is a checklist to go through when devising your assessment strategy:

- Don't rely on one single form of assessment. You should look to use a diverse range of assessment tools so as to cater for the needs of the individual learners and make a positive contribution to their learning.
- Make sure that the purpose of the assessment is made clear to the learner and is understood by the learner and everyone who has a stake in the learning process.
- Make sure the assessment tool is actually assessing the things you want it to assess.
- Make sure the assessment tool will obtain comparable and consistent results if it was used at a different time, in a different place or with different learners.
- Use assessment methodologies from which meaningful feedback can be given and both you, and your learners, can reflect on performance.

THE TEN-POINT ASSESSMENT MANIFESTO FOR SUMMATIVE ASSESSMENT

- Design teaching and learning elements of your programme which take account of the sort of assessments learners will encounter.
- Don't compromise the quality of teaching by overloading your learners, or over burdening yourself, with unnecessary amounts of assessment.

Remember that the assignments you design constitute the means by which learning can be assessed. In this respect, they should always align with course goals and lesson objectives. If the purpose of the lesson is to learn how to make an omelette then don't engage learners in a debate about what came first, the chicken or the egg.

In the classroom

- Don't make assessment tests too difficult for your learners to understand.
- Make sure that you are consistent in your assessment of learners.
- Make sure that assessments are an integral component of your lesson plan.

Critical Perspective

What do you think that Einstein meant when he wrote that, 'not everything that counts is countable, and that not everything that is countable counts'? Do you have any experiences of this either as a learner or a teacher?

For more on summative assessment, read:

Brown, S., Race, P. and Smith, B. (1996) *500 Tips on Assessment*. London: Kogan Page.
Rowntree, D. (1987) *Assessing Students: How Shall We Know Them?* London: Kogan Page.

Clarke is an ex-primary school teacher and researcher at the University of London's Institute of Education. Her work on assessment methodologies, and in particular peer assessment, is well-respected and often cited in educational literature. She describes the different forms of peer assessment as including: checking against success criteria, discussing and comparing quality, using open learning objectives to identify success and using a variety of tools for assessment.

Implicit in Clarke's work is the notion that having a good peer assessment programme requires time and effort. In this respect there are three stages that need to be followed:

- *Develop*: the teacher sets down the strategies for peer assessment and the process for undertaking the assessment. The criteria for success is made clear to all involved so that there can be no misunderstanding over assessments.
- *Establish*: the teacher provides learners with an outline of the criteria for success. Learners are allowed to agree on what process they want to undertake when conducting the assessment.
- *Enhance*: the teacher and the learners work together to identify what criteria for success is appropriate for the planned learning outcomes and what process for undertaking the assessment will work best.

Clarke argues that if the only person assessing performance and giving feedback is the teacher, the learners become powerless with little stake in their learning. She claims that, with appropriate training, learners are able to use their own language and figures of speech to give feedback to their peers in a way that sometimes teachers may find difficult to do.

How to use it

I want to look at the application of peer assessment from two perspectives: teacher to teacher and learner to learner. The expectation is that being judged by a peer should lead to a more objective viewpoint as there will be less of a vested interest in the actual assessment. Well, that's the expectation.

Peer assessments have become an important part of performance evaluation in industry and commerce. I first encountered this process when I worked as a trainer in a major UK car company. It basically involves performance evaluators seeking the views of an individual's performance from the individual's peers as well as line-managers. I asked one of the trainees how their review had gone. His words were 'One of them stuck the knife in me. I know who did it and I'll get the b*****d back when it's his turn'.

For Clarke's ideas to flourish there needs to be:

- Transparency over what the peer assessment is to be used for. This should be agreed by participants before the assessment takes place.
- Agreement as to the specific nature of the assessment. This could relate to some aspect of the teacher/learner's performance that they want the peer to comment on.

- A willingness to reflect on feedback given by the peer. This doesn't mean that the person being assessed has to agree with the peer's comments but a stark refusal to even consider what's being said makes the whole exercise worthless.
- A willingness to share thoughts on the assessment with the peer. This is a great learning opportunity for both parties to look at the process they have gone through and determine what improvements they could make in future peer assessments.

Peer assessment will work if the climate within the organisation/classroom is right for this. This may not be appropriate where the set-up is governed by a blame culture or where peer assessment comments can influence achievement of qualifications, pay or promotion.

In the classroom

- Ask your peer to comment on a specific aspect of your performance.
- Agree how the assessment will be used.
- Act on the comments. This doesn't mean that you have to make any changes if you don't think the comments were appropriate.

Critical Perspective

What do you think of the critics of peer assessment who argue that the process has a degree of risk with respect to reliability of grades as peer pressure to apply elevated grades or friendships may influence the assessment or, at the other extreme, that students may be discriminated against if students 'gang up' against one group member?

For more on peer assessment, read:

Clarke, S. (2011) *Active Learning Through Formative Assessment*. London: Hodder.

Luft and Ingham claimed that the more open we are and the more receptive we are with others, the better we will be able to communicate with them. They developed the Johari (taken from their first names) Window as a means of depicting this. In the window frame there are four panes categorised by what we know about ourselves and what others know about us.

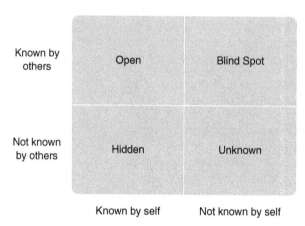

Credit: With kind permission from Rachel Luft

The panes are described as:

1. **The Open**: these are things known by self and by others.
2. **The Blind Spot**: these are things not known by self but known by others.
3. **The Hidden**: these are things known by self but not known by others.
4. **The Unknown**: these are things not known by self or by others.

Luft and Ingham devised a characteristic test to help people gauge the degree of what they know about themselves and how this correlates with what others know about them (this can be accessed by googling Johari Test). They suggest that the responses can be mapped onto a grid that produces a window frame that will have unequal sized panes. The ideal frame for effective communication is where the *Open* pane is the largest one.

How to use it

As a teacher, merely sharing information about yourself with your learners or colleagues may not be sufficient to enlarge the *Open* pane; you should also be receptive to what the learners or colleagues feel about you.

Here are some tips to help you, as a teacher, to have a more open communication pane:

*   Don't be afraid to ask for feedback. Make sure your learners and peers know that you want this and care about what they have to say. Don't come over as a know-it-all; act

on what they have to say. You may not always agree with what they have to say as long as you understand and respect what they are saying.

- Be willing to share things about yourself. Let the people you are teaching and working with know what you are thinking. Making them aware of what you are thinking will help them to understand what you are trying to achieve with them.
- Be receptive to finding out more about yourself. The process of self-discovery is often ignored by teachers who look on the exercise as a one-way process. This process becomes shared discovery when you work on things together with the person or people you are teaching.
- Realise that you cannot change others or yourself when there is a lack of awareness about what needs changing. The processes of self-discovery and shared discovery will help you to deal with this.

My favourite poet Robert Burns once wrote: *O wad some power the giftie gie us/ To see oursels as others see us!* Although I love the verse, I wonder whether some things others see in us shouldn't be kept from us. When it comes to our teaching delivery however we need to know how we are doing from a range of different sources.

In the classroom

- Don't be afraid of eliciting feedback on your performance as a teacher.
- Ask colleagues to do some peer observations of aspects of your teaching that you may be uncertain on (e.g. use of ICT or behaviour management).
- Consider carefully what others say about your performance. You may not always agree with what they had to say but at least show that you have given it thought.

Critical Perspective

In this entry, I suggest that some people might not want to know what other people think about them. For example, I never ask for feedback from the many failed job interviews that I've had, even though I know that the feedback should benefit me. What do you think; am I being over-sensitive?

For more on Johari's Windows, read:

Luft, J. and Ingham, H. (1955) *The Johari Window: A Graphic Model for Interpersonal Relations.* Los Angeles: University of California Western Training Lab.

Gould and Roffey-Barentsen argue that their six stage model provides a systematic and consistent approach to giving feedback. This is a progressive model and can be represented as:

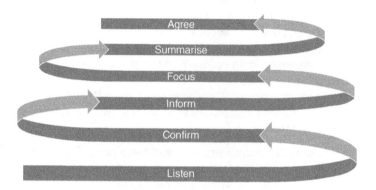

The elements can be summarised as:

- Listen to what the learner has to say about their performance.
- Confirm that you have listened to and understood what the learner had to say.
- Inform the learner of the thinking behind your assessment of their performance.
- Focus on specific points in the performance.
- Summarise the points that have been discussed.
- Agree what action the learner needs to take to improve performance.

Gould and Roffey-Barentsen stress that giving constructive and helpful feedback is at the heart of successful assessment and that learners will be more motivated to improve when they are given clear and honest feedback about strengths and areas for development.

How to use it

Gould and Roffey-Barentsen are experienced and well-respected writers on issues related to teacher training, particularly in adult and further education. I would however add an additional stage to the beginning of their process; that of explaining the purpose of the assessment. Here is my modified version of how to apply their theory:

- Start by explaining the purpose of the assessment. This should be done before the assessment but you'll lose nothing by recapping on it before you give them feedback.
- Ask the learner what they felt about their performance. Listen carefully to their response. You will get a lot of so-so responses: 'it was okay', 'I did all right'. Get them to be a bit more specific by asking 'what did you feel you did well?' and 'what do you feel you could improve on?' From this, you will be able to gauge the level of their self-awareness and how to pitch the feedback.

- Show the learner that you have listened to what they had to say and understood their position by summarising the key points they made.
- Avoid giving out any grades or performance markings until you have discussed specific points arising from the assessment. A good way to start this is to agree or disagree with points that the learner makes about their performance. I try to start off with some positives, have some key areas for development and finish up with some more positives. Whatever approach you adopt remember to focus on the specifics of what took place during the session and not on the person. Statements like 'you always do this' or 'this is typical of you' should be avoided at all costs.
- Make sure you summarise and record any points that are raised and agree what further action is necessary. Build in some form of measurement and timeframe for improvements (see Theory 111).

In the classroom

- Always listen to what the learner had to say about their performance or the assessment process.
- Focus on giving feedback on specific incidents that took place during the assessment.
- Agree and record what needs to be done to improve and when it must be done by.

Critical Perspective

What do you think about starting the feedback session by asking the learner what they thought about their performance?

For more on feedback, read:

Gould, J. and Roffey-Barentsen, J. (2018) *Achieving Your Diploma in Education and Training* (2nd edn). London: SAGE.

Petty, G. (2009) *Teaching Today: A Practical Guide* (4th edn). Cheltenham: Nelson Thornes.

Shute uses the analogy of feedback as being likened to a good murder, in that a learner needs *motive* (a desire for it), *opportunity* (can do something with it) and *means* (the ability to use it effectively). She argues however that, even with motive, opportunity and means there is still a massive difference in the effect that feedback has on performance.

Shute suggests a nine-point set of guidelines for using feedback to enhance learning. These can be summarised as:

* Focus feedback on the task not the learner.
* Provide elaborated feedback to enhance learning.
* Present elaborated feedback in manageable units.
* Be specific and clear with feedback.
* Keep feedback as simple and straightforward as possible.
* Differentiate between performance and goals.
* Be unbiased and objective when giving feedback.
* Promote a learning goal orientation through feedback.
* Provide feedback immediately after a learner has attempted a task.

Shute also differentiates between using feedback to enhance learning for high-achieving learners (which she claims could be delayed and facilitative) and low-achieving learners (which she claims should be immediate and directive).

How to use it

Although Shute is one of the lesser-known writers on education theory, her work is often cited by other writers. Her article on using feedback to enhance learning is worth reading in its entirety. I particularly like her use of a line from the *Matrix* that goes 'I'm trying to free your mind, Neo. But I can only show you the door: You're the one that must walk through it'. This to me sums up what feedback is all about.

Here are some ideas of how to apply her theory:

* Always focus your feedback so that it addresses specific features of what the learner has done and what they need to do to improve performance, and not on aspects of the learner's personality or characteristics.
* Don't overwhelm your learner with a mass of feedback in any one go. Give feedback in bite-sizable chunks and allow the learner to reflect or act on each piece before moving on to the next bit of feedback.
* Be specific and clear in giving feedback and remember the KISS mnemonic and keep it (feedback) simple and straightforward.
* Make the distinction between short-term outputs and long-term outcomes by explaining the differences between how well a learner is performing on a particular task and what needs to be done to achieve their learning goals.
* Don't give learners the answer to a problem before they have attempted to solve it.

I'm not sure I fully understood what the *Matrix* was about but, once it was explained to me, like Shute's ideas, I found it to be compelling.

In the classroom

- Focus on what the learner has done, not who they are.
- Be specific and clear when you give feedback.
- Don't overwhelm your learner with a mass of feedback all in one go.

Critical Perspective

What do you think of Shute's assertion that the purpose and timing of feedback should be different for high-achieving learners than it is for low-achieving learners?

For more on feedback to enhance learning, read:

Rowntree, D. (1987) *Assessing Students: How Shall We Know Them?* London: Kogan Page.
Shute, V.J. (2008) Focus on formative feedback. *Review of Educational Research*, 78(1), 153-189.

Section 4.5: Evaluating Teaching and Learning

Ask a group of people to give you the name of a quality watch or car and the likelihood is that products such as Rolex and Rolls Royce will feature high on the list. This is because there is a tendency to measure quality in terms of price and prestige. The implications of this are that most people, unable to afford such luxuries, will be deprived of quality. It is important therefore that we measure the quality of teaching not in the above terms but relative to fitness for purpose: Will the teaching do what the learners want it to do? Is it accessible in terms of price and availability? Is it delivered with integrity? In this section, the focus on achieving quality in teaching is very much with reflection and evaluation.

The professional standards for many teachers, coaches and mentors emphasise the need for everyone working in the education and training sector to have reflection and evaluation of their own practice as part of their continuing personal and professional development. Choosing to be a reflective practitioner because it is a requirement of the profession is not however sufficient reason to do it. Becoming, and continuing to be, an effective teacher is impossible without a strong commitment to reflective practice.

The terms reflection and critical reflection are becoming more popular in working practices, with many arguing that reflection is an essential aspect of personal and professional development. What isn't clear from the literature is exactly what reflection entails. At one end of the spectrum, the emphasis is on reflection as a systematic, scientific approach (e.g. Aristotle and Dewey). At the other end reflection deals with the implicit and the intuitive (Schön, Brookfield and Bolton). Both ends of the spectrum provoke questions relating to the scope, objectivity and quality of reflection.

In this section the focus in the first three entries is on the implicit and intuitive reflective models that have more depth to them than the systematic and scientific approaches. These include:

- Schön's model because he distinguishes between reflecting during as well as after the event;
- Brookfield's model because he suggests reflecting from different perspectives and;

- Bolton's model because she advocates a much deeper and often unsettling method of reflection.

The emphasis switches in the next series of entries away from reflection towards evaluation and quality assurance. Each of these entries can be viewed at an organisational management or individual teaching level. The section is completed with two entries that view learning from an organisational perspective.

Schön suggested ways in which practitioners could become aware of their implicit knowledge and learn from their experiences both in and out of the classroom. Schön believed that reflection begins in working practices, particularly where the practitioner is confronted with unique and conflicting experiences; what Schön refers to as 'the swampy lowland messes'. He argues that it is from these experiences that practitioners develop their own connections between the theory and practice which works for them.

Schön proposed two types of reflection:

- **Reflection-on-action**: this is after-the-event-thinking whereby the practitioner reviews, describes, analyses and evaluates past practice with a view to gaining insight to improve future practice.
- **Reflection-in-action**: this is thinking-while-doing whereby the practitioner examines their experiences and responses as they happen. This is about them thinking on their feet and making snap decisions about what to do next.

Although Schön argued that *reflecting-on-action* was important for practitioners to gain insight to improve future practice, it was *reflecting-in-action* that he claimed was at the core of *professional artistry* where practitioners develop the talent to *think-on-their-feet* and improvise. In both types of reflection, Schön suggested that practitioners seek to build new understandings that will shape their actions.

How to use it

Let's be clear here, we all participate in both reflecting in and on practice. It's the thing that distinguishes us from a machine. On that subject, have you ever read Isaac Asimov's short story *Runaround* and his three laws of robotics? I wondered whether I could apply the laws to something like teaching. How does this look?

1. A teacher may not injure a learner (physically or psychologically) or, through inaction, allow a learner to come to harm.
2. A teacher must obey the orders given to them by their line manager, except where such orders would conflict with the first law.
3. A teacher must protect their own existence as long as such protection does not conflict with the first and second laws.

I'm not sure whether, like the Robot, your head will explode if you have a conflict with any of the laws but I think the metaphor does explore some of the dilemmas facing teachers in the classroom and the need for them to think on their feet. Here's an incident that I observed happen to a teacher that demonstrated her ability to do just that.

Sarah was a Spanish teacher who was asked to teach Spanish to a group of residents in a Probation Service Bail Hostel where there was zero tolerance towards inappropriate behaviour. This was an experiment, and a variation from the traditional literacy and numeracy classes that were being delivered in offender institutions. It looked doomed to failure when Jim, an offender resident at the centre, refused to participate. Sarah told him '*Allí está la puerta. Úsala!'* When Jim asked what that meant, Sarah told him, 'There's the door, now use it!' Jim knew that Sarah meant business and that exclusion from the class might lead to him being returned to prison. Sarah also knew that if this happened, she might have to face repercussions from the other members of the group. Jim stayed and, by the third session, was helping some of the less-able learners with Spanish phrases.

Sarah's ability to assess the situation and think on her feet helped to avoid a potentially damaging situation for all concerned. Having the composure and confidence to handle a situation like this is something that takes time and effort to develop.

In the classroom

- Accept that bad things happen in the classroom.
- Stay calm when they do happen.
- Act in a composed but assertive manner when dealing with them.

Critical Perspective

What do you think about Schön's claim that teachers are often faced with dealing with the 'swampy lowland messes' that happen in the classroom? Would you have done what Sarah did when confronted with a disruptive element in her Spanish class?

For more on Schön's ideas, read:

Schön, D. (1983) *The Reflective Practitioner.* New York: Basic Books.
Schön, D. (1987) *Educating the Reflective Practitioner.* San Francisco: Jossey-Bass.

Brookfield argues that outstanding practitioners undergo a process of self-critical reflection whereby they constantly appraise their assumptions about their practice by seeing practice through four complementary lenses. It is through these lenses that the practitioner is able to access multiple, and distinctly different, vantage points from which to review practice.

Brookfield's critical lenses are the:

- **Autobiographical** lens - this is where the teacher relates their experiences as a learner to reflect on what they are doing as a teacher.
- **Learner's** lens - this is where the teacher looks at themselves through their learner's eyes to reflect on whether they are interpreting their actions in the way they are intended.
- **Colleague's** lens - this is where the teacher uses their peers to help them reflect on hidden assumptions they may have about their practice.
- **Theoretical literature** lens - this is where the teacher undertakes research to make sense of, or question, their assumptions.

Brookfield argues that in order to become critically reflective, using the lenses will produce a completely different picture of who we are and what we do. He is however cautious about the value of teachers sharing reflections with colleagues, claiming that public exposure of reflections that might indicate poor judgement can be damaging. He suggests that some teachers have a tendency to be self-effacing and feel unworthy of being part of the profession - what he refers to as the *imposter syndrome*.

How to use it

A danger point in any profession, let alone teaching, is when we begin to realise that our old ways of thinking and acting are no longer relevant, but that new ones have not yet formed to take their place. Reflecting through different lenses is a good way of dealing with this:

- The **autobiographical** lens is where you reflect on how much your experiences as a learner influence your actions as a teacher. For example does having a history as being a *bad learner* make you a *bad teacher* or have you reflected on what you saw through this lens to make you a *good teacher*? If it's the former, get out of teaching as soon as possible as you have ingrained bad habits. If it's the latter, good! You are engaging in critical reflection.
- The **learner** lens is not just about getting your learners to fill in evaluation forms; it is about 'getting into their heads'. You know that every person is different and there are likely to be varying interpretations on what you say or do. Find out by talking to them about their learning experiences, listening to what they say and understanding their needs and abilities.
- If something that you do doesn't have the desired effect, then work out why not. Use the **colleague's** lens to help you understand more about why things went wrong in

the session. It might be that there are circumstances, other than how you performed during the session, that dictated whether you met the individual's needs or not.

- If you need to rationalise why something happened in the way that it did and there is no-one who you can discuss it with, undertaking research and finding **theoretical models** to help you reflect is a good way of doing this.

Simply failing to get the right end result in a lesson may not mean that the whole teaching process was flawed. Be critical in your analysis of why you didn't get the right result but don't throw the baby out with the bathwater. Look for good things that happened during the lesson.

In the classroom

- Accept that good things as well as bad things happen in the classroom.
- Don't be afraid to involve others to help you analyse what went right or wrong.
- Adapt your teaching to take account of your analysis.

Critical Perspective

Brookfield suggests we can look at a situation from our own viewpoint, from our colleagues' viewpoints, from those of students, and also from perspectives derived from theoretical literature. Choose a recent situation you have encountered in your classroom and think about how it may be looked at through these four critical lenses.

For more on Brookfield's ideas, read:

Brookfield, S. (1990) *The Skilful Teacher*. San Francisco: Jossey-Bass.
Brookfield, S. (1995) *Becoming a Critically Reflective Teacher*. San Francisco: Jossey-Bass.

Bolton argues that the working lives of teachers are stimulating, full of dilemmas, uncertainties and satisfactions. She talks about the futility of using mere reflection as an analytical tool and suggests that reflective practitioners need to adopt a *looking-through-the-mirror* approach which allows them to explore the wider, and rather perplexing, other side of the reflection.

Bolton suggests that anyone journeying through the mirror will experience three paradoxes which are at the heart of reflection. These are:

- In order to acquire confidence, you have to let go of certainty.
- You get nowhere by looking for something when you don't know what it is.
- You achieve nothing by beginning to act when you don't know how you should act.

Bolton proposes that the results of facing up to these paradoxes are essential prerequisites for reflective practitioners and will encourage teachers to have respect and faith in themselves, trust in the reflective process and recognise that uncertainty is vital for learning and change to take place.

How to use it

I just love reading Bolton's work. She uses the metaphor of Lewis Carroll's Alice going through the looking glass to introduce you to ways of making the familiar strange and, in doing so, envisaging ways in which the familiar can be changed. In the metaphor, Alice finds herself in a world where everything was as different as possible to her expectations and where the only certainty is uncertainty. She survives by being able to respond flexibly and creatively to a number of unforeseeable events and forces.

Chances are that there are pieces of yourself hidden in Alice's journey: characters that you have encountered, characteristics in some of these characters that you identify in yourself, and paradoxes that you have had to deal with. You can look on Alice's adventures as either a children's story or a poignant reflection of the inner journey, a process of self-discovery.

Wow, I bet you never thought a book about a young girl's trip down into the underworld could have so much hidden depth. If you ever get tempted to dive head first into a rabbit hole, here are some tips from Bolton in how to survive:

- Don't be the type of teacher who thinks they know all of the right answers. Be the type who is able to respond flexibly and creatively to a range of influences, needs and wants of the learners that you are working with, and to the unexpected events that occur during your sessions with them.
- Approach situations with an open mind. The interesting thing about the *looking-through-the-mirror* approach is that we have no idea what to expect or where the process will lead us. Trust in the process, and your ability to deal with the uncertainties that occur will improve.

- Don't be impulsive. Although you need to think on your feet, and have belief in your ability to do the right things, not pausing for even the slightest moment to reflect in action may reduce your effectiveness as a teacher.

Although I have to confess that *Alice in Wonderland* is not my favourite story, it is a fantastic metaphor to describe the learning-through-reflection process.

In the classroom

- Don't come over as being someone who knows all the answers.
- Approach situations in the class with an open mind.
- Think before you act.

Critical Perspective

In this entry, I describe the use of *Alice in Wonderland* as a 'fantastic metaphor' to describe Bolton's approach. In the first chapter of Lewis Carroll's *Through the Looking Glass*, Alice expresses her concern that, 'if I don't make haste, I shall have to go back through the looking-glass before I've seen what the rest of the house is like'. What do you think she meant by this in terms of reflection?

For more on Bolton's ideas, read:

Bolton, G. (2018) *Reflective Practice: Writing and Personal Development* (5th edn). London: SAGE.

Tummons is a major contributor to the education debate, both in his written work and through programmes for schools broadcast on the TV. In his work, he sets down a list of pragmatic principles for effective evaluation of curriculum delivery which can be summarised as:

- **What should be evaluated?** Things that have an impact on performance such as: material resources, successes and failures, employer feedback, distance travelled, moderation and verification, learners, audit and inspection, and tutors.
- **How should we evaluate?** Using techniques to gather data on the performance such as: questionnaires, inspections, observations of teaching, staff-student committees, self-assessment reports and audit reports.
- **Where and when should evaluation happen?** This can take place both within and across the organisation. It can be formal and at the end of a programme, or informal and on-going throughout the programme.
- **Who should be involved in the process?** Stakeholders in the evaluation process include: teachers and trainers, learners, management, employers, parents, examining and awarding bodies, funding agencies, local and central government.

Tummons argues that the role of evaluation has become less about a meaningful exploration of courses and curricula and more about surveillance and interference with the working lives of teachers. He suggests that the focus on paperwork and procedures obscures the real reason for evaluation - to improve the quality of learning. He claims that in the evaluation of learning, everything counts in creating an environment that supports individuals to reach their potential.

How to use it

In any educational establishment, everything is interconnected. The old saying that a chain is only as strong as its weakest link was never truer than in this instance. This applies to the learner's very first point of contact through to celebrating effort and achievement.

In the early part of the twentieth century, if disabled children survived infancy, the majority were destined to spend their lives in long-term institutions, hospitals, workhouses and even asylums. The Disability Resource Centre (DRC) in Birmingham was established in 1992 to provide people with disabilities the opportunity to train for employment and independent living. During a study tour of adult education in Turkey, I was privileged to spend a week in the company of two of the trainers at the DRC. I was impressed by the enthusiasm and passion they both had for their work and the pride they had in what the DRC had achieved in training over 2000 disabled learners. When I returned from the study tour, I visited the DRC and could understand why they were so proud. Everything I saw from the excellent facilities, the attitude of the staff and the thought given to delivering programmes that met the needs of their learners typified the points that Tummons makes in his ideas.

Here are some tips on how to emulate the work of the DRC:

- Having a great building that's easily accessible for parking is one thing but with thought and a bit of imagination, even the most dilapidated premises can be made welcoming. Bright colours and eye-catching wall designs will create a good feeling as people walk in.
- Make sure learners have a sufficient amount of the most appropriate teaching materials.
- Be sensitive to what all stakeholders have to say about your organisation and, if appropriate, act on their comments. In this respect, don't sit back and wait for their comments - get off your backside and ask them what they think.
- Get out and about and look at what similar organisations are doing and what you can adapt and adopt to suit your own organisation.
- Ask yourself if you are an active participant in the evaluation process. If not, do something about it.

In the classroom

- Make sure the session meets the needs of your learners, both in terms of content and delivery.
- Have a learning environment that is attractive and welcoming.
- Listen to what people have to say about your classroom and look for exemplar classrooms that you can learn from.

Critical Perspective

What do you think about Tummons' argument that evaluation has become less to do with improving the learning experience and more about lumbering teachers with meaningless observations and paperwork?

For more on evaluation, read:

Tummons, J. (2007) *Becoming a Professional Tutor in the Lifelong Learning Sector*. Exeter: Learning Matters.

Tummons, J. (2009) *Curriculum Studies in the Lifelong Learning Sector*. Exeter: Learning Matters.

Argyris and Schön claim that individual and organisational learning can be characterised in terms of a three-level evolutionary model consisting of single-, double- and triple-loop learning.

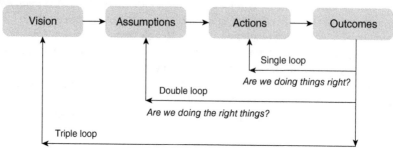

Credit: Adapted from Argyris 1990 and Nielsen 1993

The characteristics of single-, double- and triple-loop learning are:

- **Single-loop** learning is the basic level of performance measurement. It focuses on actions and asks the question, 'are we doing things right?'
- **Double-loop** learning is more geared to quality assurance. It focuses on error prevention and asks the question, 'are we doing the right things?'
- **Triple-loop** learning represents the highest form of self-examination. It focuses on the vision the organisation has of what it wants to be and asks the question, 'how can we be sure what's right is right?'

Argyris and Schön argue that transformation doesn't have to be based on a single dramatic event; it may be more about addressing a few small things that need changing.

How to use it

Someone in an underperforming college once asked me about another college which had been graded 'Outstanding' in their latest Ofsted inspection. They asked me 'what can we do to catch up with them?' I told them, 'I wasn't aware they were waiting for you'.

Too often the emphasis on performance evaluation is built on the old quality control processes of *inspection-detection-rectification-retribution*: let's look at what our people are doing, let's catch them out doing something wrong, let's get them to put it right and let's find out who's to blame. If this is what your organisation is doing they have stalled in single-loop learning. Here's how to progress to double- and triple-loop learning from both an organisational or individual perspective:

- Don't get engrossed in the blame culture. It's inevitable that your organisation, you and your learners make mistakes: the essence of double-loop learning is to learn from these mistakes.

- By enthusiastic application of double-loop learning you may have assured the quality of your teaching but how does this measure up with what others are doing?
- Don't sit back and wait for things to happen. If this is the culture in your organisation, then do something about it and get out there and look for areas for improvement. Go and have a look at other teachers in your organisation or in other organisations and see what you can learn from them.
- Ask yourself if your vision of the organisation matches that of the organisation's leaders and managers. If not, ask yourself, what can you do about this?

You may be in a position to influence change in the organisation or your views may fall on deaf ears. The question to ask yourself is, 'can I live with myself if I don't try to do something?'

In the classroom

- Don't get involved in the blame culture. Accept that you and your learners make mistakes. It's how you learn from this that will define you as a teacher.
- Never get complacent about your teaching; you may be good but good isn't good enough.
- Look at what other teachers are doing and see what you can adapt and adopt in your own teaching.

Critical Perspective

Do you think that I am being fair when I criticise educational establishments for their obsession with the quality control process of *inspection-detection-rectification-retribution*?

For more on organisational learning, read:

Argyris, C. and Schön, D. (1974) *Theory in Practice*. San Francisco: Jossey-Bass.

Pedler M., Burgoyne, J. and Boydell, T. (1997) *The Learning Company*. Maidenhead, UK: McGraw-Hill.

Argyris, C. (1990) *Overcoming Organizational Defenses*. Boston, MA: Allyn and Bacon.

Nielsen, R.P. (1993) Woolman's 'I am We' triple-loop action-learning: Origin and application in organization ethics. *Journal of Applied Behavioral Science* 29(1): 117-138.

Bush and Middlewood argue that education provides a unique leadership and management challenge because it is geared to the development of human potential. They base this argument on the belief that if the development of learners is at the heart of the organisation's business, this can only be done effectively if leaders and managers value the staff who deliver this service. They suggest that if leaders and managers want to support staff to flourish they should:

- **Be good role models**: leaders and managers need to demonstrate a commitment to their own learning, and personal and professional development.
- **Support all staff as learners**: leaders and managers need to recognise that all members of staff are different and have different aspirations both personally and professionally.
- **Encourage the sharing of learning**: leaders and managers should have a network of people who they share knowledge and processes with and act as mentors and mentees with them.
- **Build an emphasis on learning into all management processes**: leaders and managers should not be caught up in the trap of doing things how they've always been done if these are not proving effective.
- **Develop a culture of enquiry and reflection**: critical reflection shouldn't be done in isolation so leaders and managers should develop communities of reflective practice where enquiry and reflection becomes a shared activity.
- **Assess the effectiveness of staff learning**: leaders and managers need to have an appreciation of whether or not staff learning policies and practices are proving effective.

Bush and Middlewood claim that valuing and developing staff provides the best prospect of enhanced and sustainable performance by the organisation but that progress in this direction is likely to be uneven and possibly turbulent. They argue that dealing with this is the ultimate task of leaders and managers.

How to use it

Although I have emphasised the important role that leaders and managers play in supporting their staff to flourish, I could easily have used this model to look at the role of teachers in respect of their learners. Here are some key questions to ask, whether you are a leader/manager supporting staff or a teacher supporting learners:

- Am I being a good role model and showing the people I am supporting that I practise what I preach and view my own learning and personal and professional development as being of paramount importance?
- Do I recognise that the people I am supporting are different and have different needs and aspirations, both personal and professional?
- Do I demonstrate a willingness to learn from a wide network of people including managers, colleagues, staff and learners?

- Am I receptive to new ways of doing things?
- Do I reflect on my practice as a manager/teacher and am I willing to share my reflections with others?

If you were able to answer 'yes' to most of these questions, you have reacted well to the challenge issued by Bush and Middlewood. If you have answered 'yes' to all of the questions, you sound a bit too good to be true to me.

In the classroom

- Be a good role model to your learners.
- Be prepared to listen to what your learners have to say and be willing to learn from them.
- Reflect on how each session has gone and look for ways of improving what you do.

Critical Perspective

Bush and Middlewood argue that valuing and developing staff provides the best prospect of enhancing and sustaining performance in an organisation. Do you feel valued by your organisation and do they give you plenty of development opportunities?

For more on the role of leaders and managers, read:

Bates, B. and McGrath, J. (2013) *The Little Book of Big Management Theories*. London: Pearson.
Bush, T. and Middlewood, D. (2013) *Leading and Managing People in Education* (3rd edn). London: SAGE.

131

Barber was Chief Adviser to the Secretary of State for Education in the UK from 1997–2001 and founder of the US Education Delivery Institute. Working alongside Moffit and Kihn at the consultancy group, McKinsey, he developed a model for organisational leaders to ensure educational organisations have a more positive impact on the delivery of learning. They referred to the model as *deliverology*, which they defined as 'a systematic process for driving progress and delivering results in government and the public sector'.

The model is based on five principles which can be summarised as:

- *Develop a foundation for delivery*: the key stages here are to define an aspiration, to review the current state of delivery, to build the new delivery unit and to establish a guiding coalition that can remove barriers to change, influence and support the unit's work at crucial moments and provide counselling and advice.
- *Understand the delivery challenge*: in this stage it's important to evaluate past and present performance and understand the drivers of performance and relevant systems activities.
- *Plan for delivery*: this is where the reform strategy must be determined, targets and trajectories set and delivery plans produced.
- *Drive delivery forward*: this is done by establishing the routines to drive and monitor performance, solving problems early and rigorously, and sustaining and building momentum.
- *Create an irreversible delivery culture*: the final stage involves building the system's capacity and communicating the delivery message.

Barber et al. argue that at the core of *deliverology* is the need for effective relationship-building; what the authors describe as 'unleashing the alchemy of relationships'.

How to use it

Although I have included *deliverology* in this section as a macro-model dealing with quality assurance within the organisation, I could easily have taken a micro perspective of the model and used it in the section dealing with teaching delivery. Rather than just repeat the model in Section 4.3, I have chosen to show how to use the model from both a macro and micro level. Here are some key questions to ask:

- What is it the organisation/learner wants to achieve? Where do they currently perceive themselves to be? What do they need to do to get to where they want to be? Once these questions have been answered, set about getting a commitment to action to achieve the aspiration.
- What do we know about how the organisation/learner has performed in the past? Is the evidence we have on past performance reliable, relevant and valid? Do we understand what's causing under-achievement? Are we capable of dealing with this? Once these questions have been answered, identify the people who can make a change.

- What are the barriers that the organisation/learner have put up to resist change? Accept that change may take time. You may need to identify the factors that are influencing the organisation/learner to be resistant to change. Organisational and individual planning is vital and will need constant reflection, revision, reworking and realistic support.
- How much time and energy can we devote to support the organisation/learner to change? Accept that the barriers and problems affecting change are real for the organisation/learner and you need to have an appreciation of the severity of the problem and how important the organisation/learner considers the solution to be. If both of these factors are significant, then persist in addressing them.
- Once you have the organisation/learner thinking positively about change, don't allow the momentum to stall. Make sure you let everyone know about what's been achieved and the efforts made to get there.

Change should be considered a process rather than a product or, if you prefer, a journey rather than a destination. It's important that organisational leaders, managers, teachers and learners pause to reflect and consider where they are on the journey. In this respect, the cornerstone of change is all stakeholders thinking about their role, their impact, their successes, their failures and their efforts.

In the classroom

- Determine what your learners want to achieve.
- Find out what barriers individual learners are facing.
- Support learners to think positively about their learning potential.

Critical Perspective

What do you think Barber, Moffit and Kihn mean by the phrase 'unleashing the alchemy of relationships'?

For more on deliverology, read:

Barber, M., Moffit, A. and Kihn, P. (2010) *Deliverology 101*. London: Corwin/SAGE.
Hattie, J. (2012) *Visible Learning for Teachers*. London: Routledge.

132

I n *Quality is Free*, published in 1980, Crosby discussed the costs to organisations of providing goods or services that are not quality in terms of warranty claims and poor public relations. His belief was that an organisation that established a quality programme will see savings that more than compensate for the cost of implementing the quality programme.

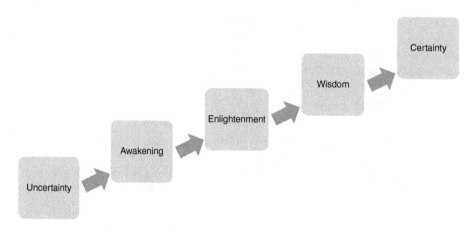

Underpinning Crosby's belief was the principle of *doing it right the first time, every time*, which he felt you only achieve once you reach a level of operational maturity which, from a teaching perspective, involves going through the following stages:

- **Uncertainty**: not knowing why you have a problem with the quality of your teaching, thus creating a tendency to want to blame others.
- **Awakening**: questioning if it's absolutely necessary to always have problems with the quality of your teaching, but not yet willing to devote resources to addressing problems.
- **Enlightenment**: this is demonstrated by your commitment to start identifying and devoting sufficient resources to start resolving problems with your teaching.
- **Wisdom**: believing in the value of error prevention as a routine part of all lesson planning and delivery operations.
- **Certainty**: knowing why you don't have a problem with the quality of your teaching.

Crosby argues that it is a 'long, long way from Uncertainty to Certainty. But travelling that road is what the fun of management (teaching) is all about'.

How to use it

Crosby used the analogy of quality having much in common with sex to describe its complexity:

> *Everyone is for it (under certain conditions of course); everyone feels they understand it (even though they wouldn't want to explain it); everyone thinks execution is only a matter of*

following natural inclinations (wouldn't it be wonderful if it was); and of course, most people feel that all problems in these areas are caused by other people.

Here's how to use Crosby's model in your own teaching:

- Start the journey from uncertainty to certainty by taking stock of where you are at this moment in time. Get as many people as possible in the organisation to give you feedback on your teaching. Ask them to be honest in their answers.
- Don't be afraid if the general opinion is that you are in the early stages of maturity. Moving from doing things wrong and being oblivious (unconscious incompetence) to still doing things wrong but knowing you are doing it wrong (conscious incompetence) are the first steps you need to take (see Theory 39 for more on this).
- Attacking the cause of the problem needs to be a precise and accurate measure of the right things in terms of the learners' requirements. Don't run the risk of paralysis by analysis but do get a complete picture of the problem and then make sure you devote adequate resources to addressing it (Enlightenment).
- Of course, the proof of effectiveness (Wisdom) is in the prevention of problems, not just in your capacity to fix them. Define your learner's requirements, agree performance standards before you start teaching and then make absolutely sure nothing will happen to compromise this.

Remember the cost of quality is the expense of doing things wrong. Not knowing that you have a problem with your teaching and inadvertently passing this on to your learners is a recipe for disaster; not just for them but for you also.

In the classroom

- Don't be in a state of unconscious incompetence.
- Look for feedback on your performance.
- Act on the feedback.

Critical Perspective

What exactly did Crosby mean when he asserts quality as being free? How does this apply to how you evaluate teaching and learning in your organisation?

For more on quality management, read:

Crosby, P. (1980) *Quality is Free*. London: Penguin.
Deming, W.E. (2000) *Out of Crisis*. Cambridge, MA: MIT.

133

When Pedler et al. published their influential work on the *Learning Company* in 1988, they spawned a generation of public and private sector bodies wanting to be recognised as *learning organisations*. The principles underpinning the notion of a learning organisation were founded on the belief that such an organisation needed constantly to change to meet the needs of its staff and learners. The five key areas that a learning organisation needs to address are:

- **Strategy**: this is where organisational policy and strategy formation, together with implementation and evaluation, should be consciously structured as a learning process that involves all members of the organisation.
- **Intra-company learning**: this involves promoting the notion that all departments see themselves as customers and suppliers to each other. In this respect they engage in constructive dialogue, negotiate and deliver excellent services to each other.
- **Organisational structures**: the aim here is to create structures within the organisation that not only cater for existing needs but can cope with future changes.
- **Inter-company learning**: this involves keeping a close look on what competitors and other organisations are doing and learning how their processes can be adapted and adopted to suit the organisation.
- **Learning climate**: this is about encouraging people to share their knowledge and experiences with others and constantly look for professional and personal developmental opportunities of their own.

When the authors published the second edition of the book in 1998, they admitted that one of their basic principles was essentially flawed and that the idea that change needed to be done constantly was a potential recipe for chaos and disaster within an organisation. They suggested that the word *constantly* in their definition should be replaced with *consciously*, implying that, in order to be effective, the organisation needed to have an awareness of where it was and a willingness or desire to want the change. They also suggested that change needed to be incremental with periods of consolidation – a series of steps rather than a continuous curve.

How to use it

Pedler et al. claim that this theory will help you to support the organisation to formulate a transformation plan together with a process for implementation, evaluation and improvement. It is not a gung-ho approach but one that allows the organisation to develop, formulate and revise as they progress. Here are some steps to follow:

- Get staff to define what the vision for their school is. A good method here is to get them to describe this in terms of a metaphor. Use the same methods to describe where they are now and compare the two images and discuss how they can get from the present image to the vision.

- Get them to come out of the metaphor and into the real world by looking at the strengths and weaknesses within the organisation. Focus particularly on internal relationships, systems and structures. Ask whether these help or hinder them to achieve the vision.
- Get them to look at what other schools are doing. Establish benchmarks for performance on issues that they may be doing well that they should try to emulate or exceed.
- Then get them to look at what other organisations, not just their competitors, who have similar processes to you (e.g. Reception, Finances and Human Resource Management), are doing and to establish benchmarks for processes that they may be doing that they should try to emulate or exceed.
- Get them to encourage a learning climate within their school by setting themselves up as a role model and making resources and facilities for self-development available to all staff members.
- Finally, suggest that the school finds a way of expressing their vision in a simple statement or what's referred to as a *mission statement*. Something simple like 'Good enough is not good enough for our staff and children; we always need to strive to do even better' will do.

If you don't like using metaphors in the exercises, then just skip that part of the process and focus on the real world.

In the classroom

- Have I got the staff to clearly define what the vision for the school is?
- Have I encouraged them to develop a learning climate within the school?
- What can I do to help them to benchmark what other schools are doing?

Critical Perspective

What do you think about the authors changing the word *constantly* in their definition of a learning organisation to *consciously*?

For more on the learning company, read:

Pedler, M., Burgoyne, J. and Boydell, T. (1998) *The Learning Company: A Strategy for Sustainable Development* 2nd edition. London: McGraw-Hill Education.

Pedler, M., Burgoyne, J. and Boydell, T. (2000) *The Learning Company Toolkit*. Maidenhead: Peter Honey Publications.

Senge was influential in analysing what different organisations do to build learning capacity and why some organisations use learning better than others. He suggested five components, or disciplines, that must be followed to enhance the potential to create a successful environment for the organisation to learn. This is what Senge describes as *expanding its capacity to create its future*. The disciplines are depicted as:

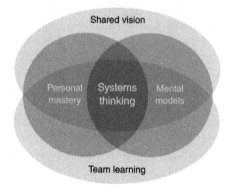

The characteristics of the disciplines when applied to teaching and learning are:

* **Shared vision** - this includes the shared and collective goals, values and mission that characterise the learning organisation.
* **Mental models** - these are the beliefs, values and assumptions that form the basis of the personal vision.
* **Team learning** - this is based on the belief that the intelligence of the team exceeds the intelligence of the individuals within the team.
* **Personal mastery** - this should be intrinsic and stem from a personal vision of effective teaching.
* **Systems thinking** - this discipline (the fifth one) is the conceptual framework for systems within the organisation that binds all of the other disciplines. It is the process of understanding how systems behave and interact with other systems.

Senge argued that it is important that all five disciplines are followed or else the depth of learning will be compromised.

How to use it

If you want the staff in your school to be serious about creating a better operational future for their organisation and their learners, start by asking them what is it they want to create, and what is their vision of an outstanding organisation. Taking time early on to discuss this is crucial to build common beliefs, unleash people's aspirations and hopes, and unearth reservations and resistances. Once you have established this, here are some tips about how to progress:

- Make sure all members of staff are in tune with what's influencing beliefs, aspirations and resistances to change. Address all of these. Don't be afraid of challenging people about these beliefs.
- Ask people how much they actually know about themselves and the impact that their behaviour has on others. Don't be afraid to encourage them to have this behaviour challenged and to consider how they can enhance the quality of their interaction and relationships both inside and outside of their organisation.
- Encourage all members of the organisation to go through the same practices as above and reflect on how much they know about themselves and other members of the organisation. Make sure that they organise more robust and honest discussions within the organisation on the organisation's beliefs, values and mission.
- Tell them not to be fooled into thinking that the people who count are the usual suspects who turn up for monthly meetings. If that's how they think and have followed everything so far, tell them that they'll have great individuals or teams working in a rubbish organisation.
- Impress on them that no department in an organisation operates in a silo. Each department is interdependent on each other. An organisation will only be great if everyone involved wants to make it great.

In the school

- Impress on staff the need to define clearly what is it they want to create.
- Don't be afraid of challenging people about the beliefs and assumptions they have about the organisation.
- Question if they see the importance of learning as a collective body rather than as an individual undertaking.

Critical Perspective

Senge has *systems thinking* as the discipline that binds all of the other disciplines. Do you agree with him that this deserves pride of place?

For more on Senge's ideas, read:

Senge, P.M, Cambron-McCabe, N., Lucas, T., Smith, B. and Dutton, J. (2012) *Schools That Learn: A Fifth Discipline Fieldbook for Educators, Parents, and Everyone Who Cares about Education*. New York: Doubleday.

SUMMARY OF PART 4

Part 4 has been about planning, delivering, assessing and evaluating the curriculum.

There are nine models demonstrating the range of factors that need to be taken account of when determining what shape the curriculum should take. Organisations that put the emphasis on learners achieving qualifications may lean more towards a product-based curriculum, whereas organisations that consider softer outcomes to be more important will be more interested in a process-based curriculum.

The focus then switched from the macro-level of curriculum planning to the micro-level of lesson delivery and assessment. There has been a mixture of theories and models, ranging from the earlier learning taxonomies of the 1960s to more contemporary concepts such as the SOLO model, learning intentions and cognitive acceleration.

The final section looked at evaluation. The section started off with three models of reflection, varying by scope and scale. The last three entries in this section relate to evaluation and can be read either from an organisational or individual teaching perspective.

Part 4 could be viewed as a toolbox for teachers, trainers, coaches or mentors to use when working with learners. No effort has been made to suggest that any one tool should be used to the exclusion of others. Which tool you decide to use will depend on the learner, the subject matter and the context in which you are working with them.

The key points to emerge from this part of the book are:

- Product-based curriculum design may be best suited for organisations whose future funding depends on learners gaining accredited qualifications.
- Process-based curriculum design may be more appropriate for organisations that focus on their learners' personal development.
- The hidden curriculum can be used for good intentions rather than furtively.
- Curriculum design and delivery should take account of the differences in the needs and abilities of the learners.
- Lesson objectives should be specific, measurable, acceptable, realistic and timebound.
- Teaching and learning intentions should be open and transparent to all concerned.
- Any subject matter can be mastered if the learner is given sufficient time and support to allow them to do this.
- Talking to learn is as important as learning to talk.

- Learning from playing can be just as important for adults as it is for children.
- Assessment of learning should be valid, reliable and appropriate.
- Assessment of learning should be a frequent occurrence throughout the lesson.
- Feedback should be given as soon as possible after assessment.
- Teachers should seek feedback on their teaching from a variety of appropriate sources, including learners and colleagues.
- Reflection should be an important part of the teaching and learning process.
- Quality is about fitness for purpose.
- Impress on staff the need to define clearly what is it they want to create as a learning organisation.
- Don't be afraid of challenging people about the beliefs and assumptions they have about the organisation.
- Question if they see the importance of learning as a collective body rather than as an individual undertaking.

A FINAL WORD ON TEACHING

Here are some general tips to emerge from the various sections to help you along the way:

- **T**hink outside of the box. Great ideas or learning experiences rarely happen as a result of people doing the same thing over and over again. Teaching your learners to be competent is okay but supporting them to be independent thinkers or creative is where the real value lies.
- **E**ncourage your learners to be positive and have high aspirations for themselves. Telling learners they are a failure will induce them to have further thoughts of failure and the inevitable will happen. Remember just because someone fails at something, it doesn't mean they are a failure.
- **A**ct naturally. Don't try to be something that conflicts with who you really are. If your natural disposition is to be humorous and friendly then, providing you behave ethically and don't step over the boundaries of what's right and wrong, these are characteristics that you can apply in your teaching. If by nature you are morose and distant then putting on a clown's outfit and trying to entertain your class won't work.
- **C**hallenge your learners to think for themselves. Spoon feeding them the answers will not help their understanding of the subject. Remember the adage: I hear – I forget; I see – I remember; I do – I understand.
- **H**ave the courage not to be afraid of making mistakes. Remember there is a thin dividing line between success and failure. Getting things right all the time doesn't necessarily mean that you are a good teacher. The important thing is to learn from your mistakes.
- **I**nvolve your learners in the design and delivery of the learning programme. Make sure the learning goals are *SMART* (specific, measurable, acceptable, realistic and time bound).
- **N**ever think that you are on your own. Whether it's planning a new programme or preparing a lesson, there are other people that you can turn to for help. The level of support that you get from them may be based on what support you've given them in the past. Remember, what goes around comes around.
- **G**et to know your learners. This doesn't mean socialising with them but making the effort to find out what interests or hobbies they have. I always use an ice-breaker

with a new group where they have to tell me or the other members of the group three things about themselves: two are true and one is made up. I, or the group, have to guess which the false one is. This is great fun and gives all of those concerned insight into whom they will be working with.

I hope that you have enjoyed reading this book as much as I've enjoyed writing this. Please share with me any thoughts that you have by visiting my website or emailing me.

INDEX

empiricism 3, 5, 14-15, 93-4
empowerment 244-5
engagement 228-9
Engelmann, S. 40-1
enlightenment 340-1
equilibrium 198-9
equipment 214-15
Erikson, E. 190-1
ethical sense 199
ethnic identity 202-3
evaluation 255, 323-347
evaluation and creativity 102-3
existence 134-5
existence, relatedness and
    growth (ERG) model 134-5
existential intelligence 84-5
existentialism 22-3
exosystem 194-5
expectancy 38-9
expectancy theory 136-7
expectation 136-7
experience of life 68-9
experiential learning 20-1, 276-7
extraneous cognitive load 76-7
extrinsic motivation 300-1

F
facilitation 64-5
failure, learning from 8, 9
family and community 244-5
fears and dreams 199
feedback. see also
    assessment and feedback
Festinger, L. 80-1
the fifth discipline 344-5
fine motor skills 208-9
fixed mindsets 144-5
Flatau, E. 246-7
Fleming, N. 120-1
flexible curriculum 276-7
Fonagy, P. 230-1
Forest Routes 246-7
Forest Schools 246-7
formal operational stage 50-1
formative assessment
    309, 310-11
forming 174-5
formulation 228-9
fourteen points for
    motivation 142-3
free child state 224-5
freedom to learn 17, 238-9
Freire, P. 24-5, 270
Freud, S. 185
Froebel, F. 208-9

G
Gagne, R. 38-9
Gardner, H. 84-5
generalisation 38-9
germane cognitive load 76-7
Gesell, A. 198-9
Gestalt movement 46-7
gifts and occupations 208-9
global approaches. *see* different
    school approaches
globalism and global competency 202-3
Goldschmeid, E. 214-15
Goleman, D. 86-7
Gould, J. 318-19
government styles (learning) 130-1
grassroots model 262-3
Gregorc, A. 126-7
Gregorc's Style Delinator (GSD) 126-7
Grinder, J. 226-7
group accountability 150-1
group alerting 150-1
group development model 174-5
Group Development Observation System
    (GDOS) 176-7
group focus 150-1
group maturity model 176-7
the GROW model 164-5
growth mindsets 144-5
Grundy, S. 270-1

H
Hare, R. 158-9
Hattie, J. 152-3, 292-3, 296-7
Hebb, D. 72-3
Hermann Brain Dominance Instrument (HBDI)
    118-19
Herrmann, N. 118-19
heuristic learning 214-15
hidden curriculum 274-5
Hierarchy of Needs (Maslow) 66-7
high expectations 292-3
higher order needs 66-7
holistic development 244-5
Honey, P. 124-5
humanism 3, 59-69, 295
humanitarians 118-19
The Hundred Languages of Children 240-1

I
ICEDIP model 102-3
identity 197
identity vs role confusion 190-1
imagens (non-verbal code) 78-9
imitation 282-3
important knowledge 8

mental models 344-5
mental self-government model 130-1
Mentalisation-Based Treatment (MBT) 230-1
mentor scale 168-9
mentoring. see coaching and mentoring
Merton, R.K. 12
mesosystem 194-5
metacognition 302-3
Mezirow, J. 68-9
microsystem 194-5
Middlewood, D. 336-7
Miller, G.A. 74-5, 76
mind frames 296-7
mind styles 126-7
mindful breathing 222-3
mindful eating 223
mindful listening 222-3
mindful tasks 223
mindful time 223
mindfulness 222-3
mindsets 144-5
mistakes 22
    learning from 8, 9
Moffit, A. 338-9
momentum 150-1
Montessori, M. 236-7, 240
moral life of children 200-1
moral reasoning 204-5
morality 197-205
Most Knowledgeable Others (MKOs) 48-9
motivation 133-145
motivational techniques 300-1
motor characteristics 199
movement management 150-1
multi-structural level 286-7
multiculturalism and reflective
    nationalism 202-3
multiple intelligences 84-5
Mumford, A. 124-5
musical intelligence 84-5
Myers-Briggs Type Indicator (MBTI) 128-9
Myers, I.B. 128-9

N
nativists 3
naturalisation 282-3
naturalistic intelligence 84-5
naturalistic model 268-9
nature vs nurture debate 3, 5, 10-11, 14-15, 88-9,
    194-5, 198-201
needs 66-7
needs theory 140-1
negative reinforcement 34-5
Neill, A.S. 238-9

neo-behaviourism 38-9
nerve cells 72-3
Neuro-linguistic Programming (NLP) 226-7
neurodiversity 220-1
neurolism 71-91, 295
neurological disorders 219, 220-1
neuroplasticity 88-9
neuroscience 3, 72
Nietzsche, F.W. 18-19
nine levels of learning 38-9
non-verbal code (imagens) 78-9
norming 174-5
nurturing parent state 224-5

O
open-mindedness 44-5
openness 168-9
operant conditioning 34-5
orchestrate the immersion 90-1
organisational structures 342-3
organisers 118-19
overlapping 150-1
overloading learners 154-5

P
Paivio, A. 78-9
Pavlov, I. 32-3, 34
peak experience 66
Pedler, M. 342-3
peer assessment 314-15
performance 38-9
performing 174-5
personal mastery 344-5
personality types: Myers-Briggs Type Indicator
    (MBTI) 128-9
perspectivism 18-19
PEST (Political Economic, Social and
    Technological) analysis 265
Petty, G. 102-3
philosophical outlook 199
philosophy, educational.
        see educational philosophy
phonics 212-13
Piaget, J. 50-1, 187, 242, 302
Plato 3, 5, 10-11, 14
Play 208
play and pastime 199
positive reinforcement 34-5
post-conventional level 204-5
potential 144-5
power (N-Pow) 140-1
pragmatism 20-1
pragmatists 124-5
praxis model 270-1